Science in the Service
of Human Rights

Pennsylvania Studies in Human Rights

Bert B. Lockwood, Jr., Series Editor

A complete list of books in the series is available from the publisher.

Science in the Service of Human Rights

Richard Pierre Claude

PENN

Philadelphia

University of Pennsylvania Press

Published by
University of Pennsylvania Press
Philadelphia, Pennsylvania 19104-4011

Library of Congress Cataloging-in-Publication Data
Claude, Richard Pierre, 1934–
    Science in the service of human rights /
Richard Pierre Claude.
        p. cm. (Pennsylvania studies in human rights)
    ISBN 0-8122-3679-3 (acid-free paper)
    Includes bibliographical references and index.
1. Science—Moral and ethical aspects.   2. Human rights.
I. Title.   II. Series
Q175.35 .C53   2002
174′.95—dc21   2002020400

For Gregor Pierre Claude
cherished debating partner

Contents

Introit

As science and technology make ever more rapid advances, we seem to have more to worry about. Cyberspace threats to personal privacy are no longer matters of science fiction as corporate and government intelligence are equipped to monitor electronic mail. Incautious steps toward human cloning raise fears about the revival of the pseudoscience of eugenics, presuming to tell us who is fit to live. Daily news reports present serious ethical questions. Did China violate the human rights of prison inmates in 2001 by harvesting their kidneys and other human organs without their informed consent, in turn selling them to overseas buyers?[1] Do the victims of HIV/AIDS in sub-Saharan Africa have a human right to benefit from pharmaceutical treatments proved effective but beyond the financial means of most of those otherwise facing certain death?[2] Did the United States violate the human rights of American mathematicians by restricting them from traveling to a conference of the International Mathematical Union in Havana based on Washington's ban on travel to Fidel Castro's Cuba?[3] These questions cannot be answered simply, but more significantly, they cannot be answered fully, and perhaps not at all, without some understanding of internationally defined human rights.

I believe that taking human rights into account can supply guidance in arguments over alleged misuses of science and technology. Of course, debates about Chinese organ harvesting, about subsidized medicine for African AIDS victims, and about the face-off between national security and human rights affecting Americans traveling to Cuba can readily become emotion-laden and intense. Indeed, notions about rights typically challenge deeply held assumptions about fairness in the workings of economic, social, and political structures. Raising these flags is no cause for fear of analysis turning into a nihilistic romp; rather, ideas about rights should be welcomed as providing a framework for debate.

This book concerns ideas about rights and offers a framework for debate about their applicability to issues in the applied sciences and technology. The public concerned with such topics needs access to these ideas insomuch as freedom and responsibility are at the moral core of the scientific pursuit of truth, and therefore people interested in science policy are at a disadvantage for making critical judgments when they are not familiar with human rights. That scientists are sometimes not rights-literate should be no surprise because the fragmentation of knowledge in our modern society is such that few scientists, engineers, technicians, or health professionals know about the existence and content of international human rights declarations and covenants. They seldom know that the norms formulated, recommended, and declared in 1948 have slowly matured to the status of binding international law. Today, the Universal Declaration of Human Rights is the moral backbone of international human rights law involving diverse international agreements and even provisions of some codes of professional ethics. Since 1948, important legal developments have shaped and extended our understanding of human rights, including human rights standards specifically drafted with science, technology, and health professionals in mind.

These standards take on moral stature from their historical origins. They are components of our human heritage owing to the abhorrence of most people at the conditions of World War II, when engineers were directed by the Nazis to design efficient human extermination machines, physicians were ordered to conduct ghoulish experiments on minority groups categorized as "useless eaters," and physicists were called on by politicians irreversibly to open the genie's bottle of nuclear energy, roasting and irradiating hundreds of thousands of people. With these political misuses of science and barbarous experiences in mind, the founders of the United Nations sought to introduce human rights into the international commitments of member states on the untested theory that governments that respect people's rights and liberties are less likely to terrorize and make war on one another. The optimists among them hoped that by restraining the mailed fist they would foil the warrior's inhumane misuse of science and technology that had lately wrought such human misery. Committed to that peace-through-human-rights blueprint, the architects of the United Nations and the framers of the Universal Declaration of Human Rights were confronted with the monumental question of how to structure new world arrangements whereby those in power who control the weapons of war and who command their technological designers can be bridled both by an attentive public and by rational principles favoring international peace.

The central two-part thesis of this book explores and proposes some answers. First, empower people at the grass roots level with a full arsenal and awareness of human rights; second, connect scientists by a link of responsibility to the public and its right to share in the benefits and applications of their work. As important, fortify respect for the human rights of those who conduct the work of science. Scientists, like everyone else, need an environment of fundamental rights and liberties so that they are no mere puppets of political authorities, while at the same time they should be aware that the public has the right to share in scientific advancement and its benefits. Of importance both to scientists and to the public at large are such human rights as free speech, assembly, and participation in public affairs as well as rights to information about public policy, travel, and protection of intellectual property. These safeguards are central to the scientific enterprise, but also basic to the public's prospects for enjoying and sharing the applications of science.

Having proposed that the ties between science and human rights values and between scientists and human rights safeguards are crucial to the survival and welfare of humanity, I use two methods to sharpen the meaning of the key science-linked human rights found in international standards. To shed light on certain rights, I rely on the framers' debates, recognizing that they supply an inconclusive but appropriate place to start figuring out the scope and meaning of scientists' rights and people's rights to enjoy the benefits of science. Second, I adopt the "violations approach" advanced by Audrey Chapman, director of the Science and Human Rights Program of the American Association for the Advancement of Science.[4] This involves identifying the "core minimum" requirements of each right and clarifying its meaning in the light of modern-day violations.

Finally, I argue that scientists' rights and everyone's rights to enjoy the benefits of science, potentially at odds with one another, find balance in a "binary theory of science-linked rights." It is a harmonizing theory that is potentially helpful in guiding policies of human rights protection, for example, in the contentious field of intellectual property rights, ever more problematic in patents disputes over human tissue and biotechnology. This line of analysis leads to the important issue of who, if anyone, is involved in oversight and implementation procedures to ensure the safeguarding of fundamental human rights. At least within the United Nations, the answer is that the structures for accountability are weak, but, as discussed at several points here, there are signs of improvement.

Structural weakness at the international level is probably a long-term feature of our global political system. This is so because international law is not a mature system of law with fully developed institutions for legislation, adjudication, policy implementation, and enforcement. As such, it is a field in which the role of politics is especially obvious. For example, human rights advocacy groups are becoming ever more vocal in their demands for accountability for rights violations, and they provide much of the driving force in the global human rights movement. Because human rights nongovernmental organizations (NGOs) are often led by lawyers, I am eager to showcase the significant contributions by others in recent years, drawing on the expertise of professionals in the applied sciences, statistics, and the health professions. In fact, some NGOs, such as Doctors Without Borders and Physicians for Human Rights, are specifically mandated to apply their expertise to human rights problems, and increasingly, professional associations, North and South, are setting up science and human rights programs. From the British to the Brazilian Association for the Advancement of Science, such groups, too seldom publicly noticed, put scientists in a constructive and praiseworthy role behind the public's right to enjoy and share the benefits of the applications of science.

I would like this volume to serve as a tribute to those many scientists, statisticians, engineers, health professionals, forensic specialists, and others in technical fields who have demonstrated admirable qualities of global citizenship offering their expertise in the service of human rights. They manifest Andre Sakharov's axiom, so apt for the twenty-first century: "It is now both morally and technologically true that we can no longer ignore the way people are treated in their human rights from one country to another." Indeed, I have attempted to illustrate the potential and vitality of Sakharov's maxim with many examples; his prescription providing a thematic thread through every chapter of this book.

As important actors in global affairs who are concerned with the interplay of science and human rights, various public interest advocacy groups and professional associations with human rights committees have typically undergone several stages of development and growth, moving from passive response to active outreach. In their initial stage of activism, professional societies and associations typically faced human rights abuses visited on their members by reacting cautiously, hanging their hopes on polite letter-writing that shows a collegial, nonpolitical, and formalistic response in solidarity with overseas counterparts facing persecution— Soviet refusniks in the 1970s and at the same time Argentine scientists driven from their labs and posts by the military junta's anti-Semitism. Responding to such outrages was an act of consciousness-raising for science academies and NGOs, leading them to more proactive strategies, until they finally developed mature programs that mobilized their professional expertise to alleviate the suffering of humanity everywhere. In this advanced phase, societies of scientists, engineers, and health professionals reach their deepest commitment to humanitarian assistance and human rights consistent with standards of scientific freedom and responsibility.

In many ways and with many illustrations including the protests by nuclear scientists about the misuse of their work, I try to show that more and more science professionals have joined the international human rights movement, offering their expertise in the service of human rights. Examples range widely, whether in forensic pathology that supplies courts with evidence from criminal investigations regarding those responsible for human rights violations; undertaking DNA research affirming the identities of loved ones separated from families by war conditions; applying statistical methods to enhance the analysis of data collected by human rights monitors; designing encryption codes to protect the privacy of communications of human rights advocacy groups; and offering psychiatric treatment for torture survivors. I also note that countless creative examples of grassroots activities drawing on science and technology do not fly under the banner of human rights, but in fact involve professional activities whereby scientists, concerned citizens, and policy-makers cooperate for mutually beneficial objectives serving people's human rights. To the people in Haiti who benefit, it may not matter if volunteers working for Partners in Health explicitly recognize the human rights dimensions of their work as they design nutrition programs for the poor and sick.

The last section of the book emphasizes politics, defined in terms of cooperative activities directed toward promoting the common good, including interventions specifically beneficial for the cause of human rights. I conclude by showing that at the turn of our new century, the politics of human rights has actually passed up the conventional structure of rules made by states and governments. Now we are rapidly moving toward a new world of multilayered relations among various forms of authority (government, courts, citizens, and markets) and assorted kinds of rules and principles (laws, conventions, and social norms) working together in pursuit of common objectives and new modes of governance and working out new accommodations to conflicting interests.

Governance depends on respect for principles and the voluntary adherence to guiding norms, rules, and decision-making procedures. As globalization takes on a bad name but inexorably proceeds, new fields of governance are hesitantly but progressively moving to reduce worldwide harm. The adoption of corporate compacts, newly defined human and environmental rights, and newly revised human-rights-rich codes of professional ethics testify to the acceptance of related principles among multinational organizations, including science associations and societies.

Optimally, acceptance of such principles should not be imposed by coercive regulation but best comes to fruition through internalized acceptance by ever more people, both within the science community and the general public. Justice C. G. Weeramantry formerly of the International Court of Justice[5] has written extensively on this topic. A distinguished Sri Lankan scholar and jurist, he is appropriately wary of regulation affecting the scientific enterprise, pointing out the importance of honoring the requirements of peer review and self-regulation within the science community. He argues that "as one travels up the scale from internally induced self-awareness to externally imposed rules of conduct, there is a progressive erosion of the autonomy of the profession." "Ideally," he concluded, "all regulation should come from within." I take this proposition seriously, and argue at several points that human rights standards linked to science should become—as they are not today—the subject of widespread education.

On December 10, 1994, the United Nations proclaimed 1995–2004 as the Decade of Human Rights Education. Curriculum development, bibliographies, and training programs designed to integrate human rights standards into the humanities, law, and the social sciences are taking place worldwide, and funding agencies are supporting the objectives of the Decade, seen in this period as a democracy-building strategy for a rapidly changing world. What is generally missing in human rights education, however, is attention to the many intersection points between human rights and science. College courses on environmental policy are rapidly proliferating, but largely without perspectives drawn from the often allied field of human rights. I seek to remedy this omission while taking into account disparate reading publics: some concerned with science and society on a technological fast track occasionally begetting Frankenstinian misapplications of technology; some beset with the pressures weighing on people's human rights because of economic and political globalization; others troubled by questions about technological advances outstripping moral progress in public affairs; and others alarmed by human rights violations to members of the science community. Such people may fall in many categories—scientists and students of science, human rights activists, scholars, policy-makers, and the general public. They are the intended audiences for this book.

For the sake of convenience, the term "science" used in this volume encompasses the physical, psychological, and social sciences and technology, including engineering and the health professions. In 1974 the United Nations Educational, Scientific and Cultural Organization defined science as an enterprise whereby humankind, "acting individually or in small or large groups, makes an organized attempt, by means of the objective study of observed phenomena, to discover and master the chain of causalities; brings together in a coordinated form the resultant sub-systems of knowledge by means of systematic reflection and conceptualization, often largely expressed in the symbols of mathematics; and thereby furnishes itself with the opportunity of using, to its own advantage, understanding of the processes and phenomena occurring in nature and society."[6] I have always thought this definition was complete as far as it goes, but it obviously leaves out consideration of the scientist as a human being. This book concentrates not so much on science as a discipline as on scientists as carriers of human rights and responsibilities, as people capable of bringing science into the service of human rights, and as the custodians and trustees of everyone's right to enjoy and share the benefits of science and its applications.

I
International Standards

Science is now capable of rewriting the genes in our crops without public consultation; identifying human gene cells, which are patented for financial gain without benefiting the contributors; and providing the know-how for busybody officials to monitor people's electronic mail. The *Bulletin of the Atomic Scientists* carries strong warnings about questionable policies for nuclear waste disposal. Albert Einstein put us all on notice in the middle of the last century: "The splitting of the atom has changed everything save the way men think, and thus we drift toward unparalleled catastrophe." One of the signs of drift is the pretense occasionally emerging from diverse quarters that science lacks any moral chart or compass. But standards do apply, and at many levels, national and even local legislative standards, university research guidelines, and codes of professional ethics. Least understood are human rights standards worked out at the international level to which I address Part I of this book.

In Chapter 1, "Links Between Science and Human Rights," I try to frame the broad controversy about the applicability of human rights to science by introducing two historical considerations. First, by reporting some of the views of surviving scientists invited by the United Nations to reflect on the technology-driven catastrophes of World War II, I elicit their own outlook on the appropriateness of global standards of human rights, including some bearing on scientific freedom and responsibility. In recounting their views, so obviously anchored in the mid-1940s, I am nevertheless able to explore the critical case against claims on behalf of "scientific neutrality" said to wall off science from the reach of moral norms including human rights. Second, I introduce the menu of human rights standards announced by the United Nations in 1948, underscoring those provisions of the Universal Declaration of Human Rights that take a two-pronged approach, first saying that the applications of science should be directed toward people's common benefit and, second, seeking to safeguard the freedom of scientists to travel, associate, and communicate freely.

In Chapter 2, "Science in the Universal Declaration of Human Rights," I report on a famous argument between prominent delegates to the first UN meetings, Eleanor Roosevelt and Alexie Pavlov. Their showcase dispute sheds light on the views of those who drafted a radical and important proposition in the Universal Declaration of Human Rights. Article 27 states that "Everyone has the right . . . to share in scientific advancement and its benefits." To infuse meaning into this standard and to reclaim this debate for contemporary renewal in the twenty-first century, I try to lay out the United Nations drafting history of human rights standards related to science and argue for their relevance to contemporary issues recounting concrete modern examples connected to the uses of science and technology.

UN responsibility for standard setting in the field of human rights involves more than the process of drafting model legislation. Since 1945, the United Nations has taken three interrelated steps toward the advancement of human rights: (a) their formulation; (b) promotion through information, education, and training; and (c) implementation through the design and creation of appropriate institutions and procedures. These developments are thematic throughout Part I of this book focusing on "Standards," primarily those in UN instruments.

Formulating Human Rights Linked to Science

When the first winds of the Cold War began to blow in 1948, drafters of the Universal Declaration of Human Rights (UDHR) wisely rejected attempts to link science to standards external to the scientific enterprise, for example, gratuitous political and ideological objectives. Involved were hard-fought battles described in Chapter 2 between the Soviets and their allies who wanted science confined to politically defined objectives serving international peace and economic development, and Westerners who discounted this Eastern "ragbag of ideological limitations" on the scientific enterprise. Emerging from such spirited deliberations are the provisions of the UDHR on the rights of professionals to scientific freedom and intellectual property, as well as everyone's rights to share in scientific advancements and its benefits. These notions, first declared in 1948, were eventually formalized in 1976 in the treaty language of Article 15 of the International Covenant on Economic, Social and Cultural Rights. The resulting legally binding standards of human rights related to scientists' and other people's rights are the subject of Chapter 3, where the "core minimum requirements" for science-linked rights are delineated, and Chapter 4, where "steps to be taken" by compliant governments are described, illustrated, and clarified by reference to contemporary examples, including examples of violations.

Setting universal standards applicable to human rights and science necessarily requires continuous critical review and exploration since we are all affected by changing circumstances and since the advancement of science continues at a rapid pace. The problem of formulating human rights is an on-going UN activity, as illustrated by the Declaration on the Use of Scientific Progress (1975), discussed in Chapter 3. The drafting process for that instrument shows the inevitable influence of international politics. For example, the 1975 Declaration was entirely put together by the Soviet Union and their allies without any support of the Western countries, all of which abstained from voting on it in the General Assembly. According to Sadako Ogata, the telltale sign of Soviet clout is evident by the Declaration nowhere referring to individual rights and everywhere enumerating the obligations imposed on states.[1] More recently, the drafting of the UN Principles on Human Rights and the Environment (1994) and the Universal Declaration on the Human Genome and Human Rights (1999) were unsullied by Cold War politics but controversial nevertheless. They are daily taking on more significance, and these instruments are discussed in Part III of this book.

Promoting Science-Linked Rights

A second UN task is the promotion of human rights, by which is meant campaigns to "market" human rights to increase knowledge about the public support for international human rights instruments such as the International Covenant on Economic, Social and Cultural Rights. UN efforts to promote human rights include information exchanges and educational courses. Where technical issues are involved, training is essential. For example, the High Commissioner for Human Rights encourages the development of training programs in the forensic sciences, which draw on anthropology and medical pathology, and that have effectively brought technology into the service of human rights and on behalf of victims of human rights violations, "particularly in countries without sufficient expertise in forensic science."[2] These matters come up for review in Part II of this book. In addition to education and training, sometimes the United Nations promotes human rights by initiating essential research, undertaking special studies on human rights issues. For example, in 1998 the Human Rights Commission received the results of a Special Rapporteur's study focusing on threats to life and health in Africa. As a result, the commission affirmed "that the illicit movement and dumping of toxic and dangerous substances and wastes constitute a serious threat to the human rights to life and health of individuals, particularly in developing countries that do not have the technologies to process them."[3] Moreover, it called on the Chemical Division of the UN Environment Program to offer technical assistance in developing countries, such as making recommendations on adequate measures to control, reduce, and eradicate toxic wastes.

Implementing Article 15 Rights

In principle, international human rights conventions leave the task of directly enforcing their standards to treaty signing states, which are expected to enact the necessary legislation and other measures. But UN organs typically play a supervisory role in such implementation. To the bedrock principles of the UDHR, the framers of the Covenant on Social, Economic and Cultural Rights added implementation principles and procedures that hold states accountable for treaty violations. Thus governments are obliged to report to the UN on their treaty compliance, but as discussed in Chapter 4, the related procedures for UN oversight have heretofore been widely criticized as weak. Foreshadowing discussion of international politics in later parts of this book, Chapter 4 notes the important role nongovernmental organizations can play in strengthening the UN committee charged with overseeing science-linked rights. Without independent sources of information, they cannot knowledgeably and effectively hold governments accountable for falling short in implementing the promises they have made.

Among these promises are some involving state duties to take the steps necessary for "the conservation, the development and the diffusion of science." While these strategic objectives sound like a trio of abstract terms, they take on life with examples in Chapter 4. Moreover, it may seem strange, even to students of human rights, to find strategies for the preservation of science embedded in a solemn human rights covenant. But the rationale involved is important. The reason that the conservation, development, and diffusion of science link it to human rights is that science is a human construct operating in a social milieu, and the work of scientists is central to the welfare of all humankind.

Chapter 1
Links Between Science and Human Rights

> There is a built-in moral component right in the core of the
> scientific activity itself. The desire to find the truth is itself a moral
> impulse, or at least contains a moral impulse.
>
> —C. P. Snow

In this chapter I undertake two tasks. First, I focus on the nature of science. Because it is a discipline given to objective fact-finding addressed to hypotheses and using inductive methodologies, it appears by its reliance on empiricism to exclude all consideration of value-laden issues. Whether this view stands up to scrutiny or not, it remains obvious that science is a discipline pursued by human beings. Scientists are people who unquestionably depend on standards of human rights to protect a value most important to them, their scientific freedom. Therein lies the first link between science and human rights. If you find this notion agreeable, you should press on to the second link-building part of the chapter where I introduce the modern field of internationally defined human rights. Here I emphasize the scientist's question: what's in it for me?—as well as the larger public's question: do I have a right to benefit from the advancements of science?

Historical Background

History gives plenty of evidence as to why scientists must prepare themselves for a role as politically well informed global citizens. Sooner or later, most scientists come to understand the importance of freedom values because civil liberties standards such as free speech and freedom of association, to travel, and share information tie in with components of the scientific enterprise. The independent thinking expected of scientists can potentially attract repression because some of the qualities of modern science that are its strengths also put it at loggerheads with political authority. For example, science is characterized by

- a reverence for truth that leads its practitioners to robust query and dissent;
- avoidance of surmise based on ideological presuppositions in favor of reliance on empirically verifiable facts and measurable data;
- a process of verification that requires open dissemination, communication, and the need for replication;
- a universality of discourse and goals whose common language and pursuits go beyond national borders.

All or any of these characteristics may be seen as threatening by ideologically rigid political regimes. Thus scientists today can readily speak of science and human rights as interdependent, without at the same time promoting the contamination of science by politics.

Such contamination was all too prevalent when Nazi Party functionaries dominated the setting of scientific research agendas in Germany and the hiring and firing of personnel. For example, in Nazi Germany where biology was misdirected to support theories of racism, one in ten senior research biologists and professors lost their jobs and were forced to emigrate, while those who were leftists or Jewish perished in concentration camps. Such horrors as well as a diaspora of talented technicians reinforced the view that totalitarian rule has profoundly negative implications for scientists in their personal lives and for their professional work.[1] In the aftermath of World War II, some scientists became sensitive to human rights on the basis of their experience as citizens and victims of tyranny and abuse. With scientists' consciousness raised about the damage done by the absence of rights and liberties, it is not surprising that some inveighed against repressive political regimes.

They also had good reason to speak out as scientists concerned with values of scientific freedom and responsibility and mindful of the roles they played during the war years. It was physicians who participated in the Nazi's nefarious acts of human experimentation. For example, the World War II death camps for Jews, Gypsies, homosexuals, war prisoners, and dissidents were the sites of barbarous acts under the guise of science. Pseudoscientific activities included high altitude experiments—subjecting victims to rapid and excruciatingly painful high-pressure and then sudden low-pressure chamber changes; freezing experiments—submerging victims in ice water to test survival rates; inoculation of victims with such pathogens as malaria, small pox, yellow fever, and typhus; the use of poison bullets; and diverse sterilization experiments, including exposing prisoners to massive x-ray exposure.[2] A comparable if less widely publicized record was set by Japan. In occupied Manchuria (Northern China), the notorious "Unit 731" conducted bacteriological experiments and vivisections on prisoners called "maruta," the Japanese word for logs. That experimental station and others were closed just hours before the office of the emperor announced his country's surrender on 1945 August 15. Laboratories were ordered to destroy "all evidence on special research," especially that showing that scientists were working on a biological warfare plan to attack the United States by sending balloon bombs carrying infectious bacteria on the jet stream.[3]

It was scientists and engineers who developed the atomic bomb, and some of the greatest of them led the discussion on the need to control nuclear energy. Arthur H. Compton, Albert Einstein, J. Robert Oppenheimer, and Leo Szilard spoke out against secrecy and for international control of nuclear energy in the best-selling book of 1946, *One World or None: A Report to the Public on the Full Meaning of the Atomic Bomb.*[4]

Of course, some scientists disagreed with the *One World* report, and even with the notion of participating in debate over the policy implications of their work, clinging to the view: we just build the tools of war, which most of you regard as bad. But as scientists, that is no concern of ours. It is the user who is evil. As Joseph Turner said, characterizing this position in *Science* magazine in 1960, "being a good scientist no more gives one special privileges in determining national policy than being a good information clerk at an airport entitles one to select destinations for travelers." He said the analogy supports the conclusion that the "special competence of scientists lies in the discovery of technical facts: decisions of public policy rest with elected or appointed public officials."[5]

If scientists were robots, this argument might make sense, but withered under the scrutiny of C. P. Snow, a British literary figure and philosopher of science. He took on the issue of the scientist's citizenship role, observing broadly that while scientists seek truth using empirical and not normative methodologies, that does not absolve them from their fundamental responsibilities as human beings. Snow condemned the attitude of supposed scientific neutrality as moral "contracting out."[6] Science is not morally neutral, he argued, giving as his reason that scientists have the power to pass judgment on whether the fruits of their labors are good for humankind. As scientists, he asserted, we must not "contract out"our moral judgment for that would scuttle the self-correcting capacity of science and of scientists to alert humanity to danger, including self-inflicted harm.

UNESCO Survey

With the end of World War II came a need for reconstruction and a yearning for peace. In the wake of the slaughter of millions of civilians in the war, the wasting of vast areas of Asia and Europe, and the development of the atomic bomb, international efforts to take moral account of the technology that made such mayhem possible were organized all over the world. To cite an example, in 1945 the Inter-American Conference on the Problems of War and Peace reacted to wartime conditions with an awkwardly phrased resolution saying states should protect citizens against the use of scientific discoveries that "create fear and unrest."[7] Fortunately, international normative development to protect people did not stop with this Mexico City resolution, as the year 1945 also marked the founding of the United Nations in San Francisco. The 46 states that had declared war on one or more of the Axis powers convened to design a new international organization. They set it up "to save succeeding generations from the scourge of war," which the UN Charter said "brought untold sorrow to mankind," not once, but "twice in our lifetime."[8]

After World War II, a vigorous argument ensued among diplomats over whether states joining the new United Nations should be bound by a common set of human rights standards. In the mid-1940s, public discussion was rife with ideas favoring a postwar global "bill of rights." Like serious people from all walks of life, scientists entered the fray because many felt they had an interest in the debate.

A group of savants including scientists were invited to enter the debate by one of the component units of the nascent United Nations. The UN Educational, Scientific and Cultural Organization (UNESCO) was designated to promote education, science and culture in the service of world peace. Its first director was the British biologist and writer Julian Huxley. As a scientist, he was concerned that states should not repeat the German and Japanese forays into misdirected science. He was worried about a resolution passed in 1946 by the American Anthropological Association proclaiming that efforts to formulate uniform and universal standards of human rights were bound to fail in a culturally pluralistic world.[9]

A few months after the anthropologists voiced this scepticism, Huxley authorized the circulation of a UNESCO-sponsored open-ended questionnaire asking respondents to give their views on various theoretical problems raised by the formulation of a Universal Declaration of Human Rights. The query was sent to about seventy eminent persons worldwide, including Benedetto Croce (Italian historian), Margery Fry (American penal reform expert), Mohandas Gandhi (father of modern India), Harold Laski (British political scientist), Jacques Maritain (French theologian), and Chung-Shu Lo (Chinese philosopher).[10] Huxley wanted to avoid taking normative positions based on surmise. Commenting in his book, *Freedom and Culture,* on notions of and justifications for new human rights standards, he mused: "It is no longer possible for us, as it was for our ancestors in the eighteenth century age of reason, to conceive of human rights existing in the abstract, merely waiting to be deduced from first principles by human intellect."[11]

Despite concern among some scientists in 1947 that answering Huxley's survey would unduly enmesh them in politics, UNESCO received numerous thoughtful replies. Among them were letters from Jean Haesaerts (Belgian sociologist), Pierre Teilhard de Chardin (French paleontologist), and A. P. Elkin (American anthropologist). Their concerns were notably diverse; two salient themes characterize the respondents' views of human rights and their role as scientists in the context of the new postwar era. They spoke about (1) their professional responsibility to serve constructive and not destructive politically dictated ends and (2) the need for wide-ranging freedom, to pursue both their task of truth-seeking by scientific methods and their obligations as citizens to act responsibly. Such responsibility, they said, includes criticism of the applications of their own work and that of colleagues. There is no reason to think the savants' views influenced the formulation of the Universal Declaration of Human Rights. Their ideas are worth noting here to provide early expressions by scientists of their own notions about links between human rights and scientific freedom and responsibility.

Regarding scientific responsibility, the British physiologist R. W. Gerard welcomed UNESCO's consultation with scientists of the day about a code of human rights because, "Science has created the present milieu in which . . . [human beings] must live and interact and it is creating new viewpoints as to how . . . [human beings] must live and interact."[12] He welcomed prospects for such a proclamation but conceived of human rights as a human construct reflecting human needs rather than as a set of norms deduced from eternal verities. Drawing analogies from biological evolution and feedback principles, he warned that a human rights code should be expected to change with the times, and thus should include "provisions for mandatory reexamination and reformulation at appropriate intervals."

Another well-known scientist of the day, the American chemist W. A. Noyes, reacted to the UN query commenting that science can be used for good or ill; to ensure that it benefits society, it requires some very specific social conditions to prevail.[13] Noting the possible misuse of nuclear power, he appealed for the formulation of a new sense of scientific responsibility that might serve as a linchpin connecting science and human rights to ensure the humane use of the fruits of science. Noyes wrote to UNESCO that because of their experience in developing engines of potential destruction, and their importance in warfare, scientists can no longer take for granted their status as free and independent individuals. "Whether they like it or not," he argued, "scientists are tied to the military destinies of their respective countries." From this basis, he reasoned that human rights and the rights of scientists to protect their capacity to express themselves critically have become "inextricably entangled." Much was at stake, he concluded, because in a world ever more shaped by science and technology, "The struggle of . . . scientists to maintain their freedom of action has an important bearing on the struggle of mankind for prosperity and happiness."

In response to the UNESCO questionnaire and the 1947 draft version of free expression provisions then circulating, the distinguished Dutch hydro- and aerodynamics professor J. M. Burgers reflected on scientific freedom and responsibility.[14] He said the postwar world "apparently stands before great changes, the outcome of which cannot be seen; we must accept our part in it." Burgers argued that scientists' freedom publicly to communicate their findings entails the duty to speak out critically on how well or how adversely scientific applications affect social justice and influence social relations. He concluded that, to discharge such duties, the positions in which scientists work "must afford them the necessary freedom for this." In his view, like the good parent, the scientific progenitor has a duty to criticize any errant progeny.

Another of the UNESCO respondents was F. S. C. Northrop, a Yale professor and author of *The Logic of the Sciences and the Humanities.*[15] He applauded the UN plans to devise a concrete "bill of rights" but insisted that it must possess two basic characteristics.[16] First, he argued on behalf of a charter to affirm that "all the differing ideologies of the world would gain expression." By this he meant to warn that standards of human rights that simply aped the classical French and Anglo-American models would fail because they tend to leave to chance people's economic freedom to maintain even a minimum livelihood. Such a limited concept of rights fosters a businessmen's "culture of laissez-faire values, with all the other values and aspirations of mankind left anemic and spiritually and ideologically unsustained." Thus, Northrop argued, a successful global bill of rights must give free reign to a "plurality of cultural values." Ideologically open-ended and multivalued, Northrop's new plan for global rights, he hoped, could avoid the cultural imperialism feared by the American Anthropological Association.

Northrop's second condition is both profound and complex, calling for both a philosophy of world culture and a philosophy of science. By this he meant that the new set of rights must ensure full scope for scientific research on the impact of varying cultural practices and ideologically directed systems of governments on people's human rights. Pursuing this task using social science methods, he hoped that "the philosophical premises of cultures and ideology" might prove, at least in part, to be scientifically testable. In some respects, Northrop's standards were heeded, if one reviews the menu of rights and liberties included in the Universal Declaration of Human Rights. The document supplies a range of rights and liberties, at once giving "free reign to a plurality of cultural values" as well as guarantees needed to scientifically study and critically assess the social consequences of newly defined human rights.[17]

The Architecture of Human Rights

With the view so widely prevailing in the late 1940s that the promotion of human rights might protect against tyranny and serve as an antidote to conflict, it becomes important to ask: what are human rights? Whatever the rich and ample philosophical literature on human rights says about their origins and justifications, it remains true that human rights are social constructs that take on different meaning in changing circumstances. They constitute individual and group claims for the sharing of power and other values, most importantly, equality, mutual respect, and forbearance toward others in their pursuit of survival, dignity, and happiness. They recognize human livelihood needs and the duties to facilitate them by those who hold power. They also set limits to power, specifying certain outrageous government-sponsored practices as beyond all standards of civility and totally out of bounds: torture, extrajudicial killings, interference with the privacy of family life, racial, religious, and sexual discrimination, and the like. But human rights, taken together, are not simply a list of requirements and of banned practices. They add up to more than applications drawn from an abstract field of theory. Human rights should be seen as components in a plan of action, as a field of endeavor. They require everyone's work, support, and commitment. The Universal Declaration of Human Rights constitutes history's most ambitious effort to develop standards that governments promise to abide by, standards that everyone is obliged to respect and support.

We do not have to begin from scratch in thinking about human rights because in 1948 the United Nations took the first step toward formulating internationally defined norms.[18] The Declaration sets out a charter of rights and liberties, which was described as a grand edifice by one of its framers. French Nobel laureate René Cassin said the structure of human rights can be visualized as a temple (or an Asian pagoda, or an African meeting hut) founded on four pillars.[19] First come the civil and personal rights (the right of equality; to life and liberty and security of Articles 1–11). Then come the social rights that belong to the individual in his and her relationships with the groups in which he or she participates (the rights to privacy; to family life and to marry; to freedom of movement within the national state or outside it; to have a nationality; to asylum in case of persecution; and to property and to practice a religion of Articles 12–17). The third group is that of political rights exercised to contribute to the formation of government institutions or to take part in the decision-making process (freedom of conscience, thought, and expression; freedom of association and assembly; the right to vote and to stand for election; the right of access to government of Articles 18–21).

The fourth category is that of rights exercised in the economic and cultural area (those rights that operate in the sphere of labor and production relationships and in that of education, rights to work and social security and to free choice of employment, to just conditions of work, to equal pay for equal work, the right to form and join trade unions, to rest and leisure, to health care, to education and the right to participate freely in the cultural life of the community of Articles 22–27).

Erected on these four pillars and found in the remaining three Articles of the Declaration is a fifth section, which Cassin called the "pediment of the temple." It encompassed harmonizing provisions holding the structure together, calling on governments to make arrangements in support of human rights. Article 28 lays out the right to a social and international order in which human rights can be fully realized. Charles Malik from Lebanon suggested this broad provision to overcome the Western bias that rights are largely negative, and substitutes for the view that rights depend on states doing nothing—the view that governments have duties to foster a favorable social structure within which human rights can take root, and that international duties also call on prosperous states to assist the economic development of poorer states.[20] Articles 29 and 30 further set out principles to harmonize rights, for example, that they must not be exercised in ways conflicting with other UN objectives: free speech should not be misused to disseminate war propaganda.

The image of the four-pillared temple supplies people in the sciences with an opportunity to see the links between their disciplines and human rights. Reflecting on the likely collapse of one pillar if undermined helps show how all human rights are interrelated. What are the consequences for science and for scientists if any one pillar were undercut or demolished? In this four-pillared temple of human rights, there is much of importance for the scientific enterprise: equality enough to safeguard access to scientific education for all without regard to race, sex, or other status factors (Article 3 from the first pillar); the right to privacy, often essential in medical research and for the security of scientific records (Article 12); freedom of movement necessary for scientists to attend international conferences (Article 13 from the second pillar); freedom of thought, essential for scientific creativity (Article 18); the right to information and freedom of expression central to scientific inquiry (Article 19 from the third pillar); everyone's right to enjoy the advancements of science and scientists' intellectual property rights (Article 27 from the fourth pillar); and an international order promotive of international co-operation, including technology transfer (Article 28 tying the structure together in the pediment).

Advancement of Science

The accomplishments of science over the last hundred years have enabled us to see far more deeply than ever before into the nature of matter, life, and the universe. They have also equipped us with the power to change our environment and to alter the living organisms in it in ways unimaginable to our ancestors. With such enhanced power comes increased responsibility for its intelligent use. The release of nuclear energy, one of the great turning points in human history, has thrust on us the necessity of preventing the destruction of civilization. The emerging understanding of life processes, and their application in modern biotechnology, enables us to modify living organisms in ways that can result in great benefit or enormous harm.

What kinds of such harm should we anticipate? Who will alert us to its nature and imminence? Do we have to wait, as in World War II, until political madness or accident unleash the destructive powers of which science is capable before we try to set limits on its applications? Scientists themselves are well equipped to sound such an alert, and the Nobel Laureate Henry Kendall drafted the "World Scientists' Warning to Humanity" in 1992.[21] Signed by more than 1,700 scientists from seventy-one countries and published by the Union of Concerned Scientists, it forewarns the public about atmospheric disruption, threats of water and food scarcity, and the likelihood of destruction of plant and animal species. The scientists' warnings concluded that a "new ethic is required," saying we must "enlarge our attitude toward our global responsibilities in caring for ourselves and for the earth."

In recent years, scientists' admonitions about environmental degradation and the limited population carrying capacity of our globe are beginning to overlap with alerts from social activists, policy analysts, and other scholars. Tests and taunts linking human rights to technology have multiplied beyond the imagination of the document's framers, fifty years after the adoption by the United Nations of the Universal Declaration.

Such new challenges for law and policy stormed in on us like an unexpected tornado with the advent of twenty-first-century catastrophes involving terrorism. On 11 September 2001, terrorists attacked the Pentagon complex of the U.S. Department of Defense and the twin towers of the World Trade Center in New York with the terrible loss of thousands of innocent civilian lives. Within twenty-four hours, the UN Security Council approved Resolution 1368 (2001) saying that any act of international terrorism was a threat to international peace and security. It recognized the right of victim states to collective self-defense under the UN Charter, calling on all states to bring to justice "the perpetrators, organizers and sponsors" of these terrorist acts. Moreover, it said those responsible for supporting or harboring the perpetrators "would be held accountable." Thereafter, the United States along with other countries launched an armed assault on military targets in Afghanistan because that country's Taliban regime failed to take action against the putative perpetrator, Osama bin Laden and his associates. The Allied view was that such failure effectively amounted to state tolerance of atrocious acts, human rights violations, and crimes against humanity.

Today, this kind of argument is gaining currency in human rights law and theory concerned with responsible "acts and omissions." For example, consensus is building among international governmental organizations that by virtue of tolerating their presence and acquiescing in their killings, states are responsible for civilian massacres by paramilitary groups.

Beyond these legal considerations, related policy views have entered the field of public debate. Soon after the events of September 11, 2001, the Union of Concerned Scientists (UCS) asserted that the attack on the United States tragically demonstrated the fact "long noted by the U.S. Joint Chiefs of Staff," that terrorism is a far more likely threat to the United States than an attack by long-range missiles. "The security debate has grown beyond military defense to include energy security," the UCS argued. They underscored their concern for the vulnerability of nuclear power plants and other energy facilities to sabotage, as well as the heavy American reliance on foreign oil. Bolstering their work on nuclear reactor safety, renewable energy, and clean vehicles, UCS cautioned that U.S. policy-makers should put the nation "on a path toward a safer decentralized power system and reduce dependence on oil imports."

Terrorism also prompted other Cassandra-like alerts, some highly speculative, from other science-based groups. The Nuclear Information and Resource Service (NIRS) approvingly reprinted Harvey Wasserman's hypothesis that, had one of the jets hitting the World Trade Center instead plowed into the Indian Point nuclear plant forty miles up the Hudson River from New York City, the "enduring cloud of radiation would have dwarfed the ones at Hiroshima and Nagasaki, Three Mile Island and Chernobyl." Wasserman said that because the Indian Point plant has operated for decades, its accumulated radioactive burden far exceeds that of Chernobyl, which ran only four years before it exploded. A head-on jet crash there "could have collapsed or breached either of the Indian Point containment domes," possibly creating damage sufficient to render thousands of the world's most populous and expensive square miles permanently uninhabitable."

Wasserman's alarming speculation was published on the NIRS website <nirs.org> in the context of their noting a *Sunday Times* (London) report of 21 October 2001 that terrorists may have planned to use one of the airliners on 11 September "to bomb a nuclear power station."

This is scary stuff, some would argue too alarming, and open as well to charges of "junk science." Nevertheless, we need to be alert to all contingencies as people face new and unexpected threatening adversities such as nuclear catastrophe and bioterrorism. While the "parade of horribles" gets longer, creating public fear and widespread attention in its wake, it becomes ever more important to enlist relevant scientist's advice. It was no time for the president of the United States to be without science advisors.

The counsel of scientists is needed both by policy-makers and the public to help sort out realistic fears from phantasies connecting the applications of modern science to our daily lives now and in the future. And they are many: threats to human dignity posed by the prospects of cloning; privacy issues connected to the mapping of the human genome; hate propaganda disseminated by the Internet and worldwide web; discrimination problems associated with lack of access by the poor to the most expensive high-technology medical treatments; women's issues and reproductive rights; persecution of scientific whistle-blowers who reveal dangerous threats to the environment posed by careless corporate dumping practices and secret state-sponsored nuclear waste policies. Only minutes after the Chernobyl meltdown, scientists detected increased radiation in Sweden, and then the Canadian Arctic, and then the whole earth. These are the ways science teaches us that everything is part of the same whole system. Likewise, human rights teaches us that we are all part of the same global community. The Universal Declaration of Human Rights teaches us that all human rights are interrelated and interdependent and universal. Science and human rights have something in common, and the connections between them should be made plain to everyone concerned. The challenge arises precisely at the post-Cold War juncture when international dialogue is more needed than ever to bring human rights standards to bear on science, technology, and the health professions.

Finally, it is instructive to return to the strong note of scientific scepticism about human rights voiced by the American Anthropological Association (AAA). Their statement in 1947 renounced the claims to human rights universality as overblown and failing to take cultural particularities into account. In 1999, the AAA Anthropology and Human Rights

Committee repudiated the position of 1947 announcing a "Declaration on Anthropology and Human Rights" based on large-scale membership balloting. The new declaration, described by the committee as a "complete turnaround" from that of fifty years earlier, states that the "AAA has long been, and should continue to be concerned whenever human difference is made the basis for a denial of basic human rights, where 'human' is understood in its full range of cultural, social, linguistic, psychological and biological senses."[22] The committee explained that today the AAA reflects a commitment to human rights consistent with international principles but not limited by them, because "Our understanding of human rights is constantly evolving as we come to know more about the human condition."

Conclusions

It is time to begin a fresh debate and to forge the links between science and human rights. Consider how the Universal Declaration of Human Rights was a global response to the devastating confrontation of nations in World War II. Armed struggle is generally a form of conflict based on the notion that "what I win, you lose." But that axiom is not valid when applied to the global threats to our environment described by the "World Scientists Warning to Humanity." Its message is that we are all in the same environmental boat, we will all get soaked if it leaks, and we will all perish when it sinks. This kind of thinking and the new ethic it calls for harmonize with the universalist vision built into the human rights standards and the global responsibilities they place on all of us. Scientists who have clung to the notion that adherence to human rights values will undermine their objectivity as scientists must step aside. They have had their day. As affirmed by the newly declared position of professional anthropologists, in human rights terms, we are all, inescapably, global citizens.

Chapter 2
Science in the Universal Declaration of Human Rights

Dear Teacher: I am a survivor of a concentration camp. My eyes
saw what no person should witness: Gas chambers built by learned
engineers. Children poisoned by educated physicians. So I am
suspicious of education. My request is: Help your students to
become human.

—Haim Ginott

A *New Yorker* cartoon pictures a shadowy dungeon, two prisoners chained
to the floor, with only a tiny ray of light piercing an iron grate in the ceil-
ing. One prisoner says to the other, "Now here's our plan." These two
unfortunates, stuck in an obviously hopeless situation, still come up with
a plan. While certainly no knee-slapper, the cartoon can make you smile,
appreciating a certain irony about the human condition: we don't really
know the prisoners don't have a plan; we don't know that if they do have a
plan it won't work, because we do know that human beings can be highly
creative in devising schemes to get out of trouble.

   In this chapter, I introduce the origins of the Universal Declaration
of Human Rights in its historical setting. My task is to tell a story of
people making plans in a setting of evident hopelessness surrounded by
the shadowy wastelands of Asia and Europe. From France to the Philippines, vast areas where people lived lay in rubble in 1945, and the con-
sciences of those who yearned for peace seemed shackled to endless, continuous warfare. The survivors of World War II settled on a bold plan
based on an untested theory. On the notion that human rights-respecting
governments do not war against each other, the Universal Declaration of
Human Rights was devised as a promissory note signed by UN member
states to reduce conflict. The Preamble to the Universal Declaration of
Human Rights says that the calamity of war is caused by "disregard and

contempt for human rights . . . result[ing] . . . in barbarous acts which have outraged the conscience of [hu]mankind."

The chapter concentrates on the formulation of the Universal Declaration of Human Rights, noting that some of the delegates to the earliest UN meetings thought it necessary to take account of the fact that wartime "barbarous acts" were, in their views, tied to misdirected science and its applications. In the wake of a terrible global conflict, and in search of consensus on how to avoid another world war, UN delegates did not shrink from the discussion of big issues such as the connections among science, human rights, and war and peace. In this chapter, I try to show how the framers came to link these issues in the visionary provisions of the Universal Declaration of Human Rights.

Drafting the Plan

The Universal Declaration of Human Rights emanated from the United Nations Human Rights Commission. It was set up in 1946 by the Economic Social and Cultural Council of the United Nations, to make recommendations for promoting respect and observance of human rights.[1] The eighteen members began their work in early 1947, electing Mrs. Eleanor Roosevelt to chair the commission.[2] The popular American wife of the late war leader, President Franklin Delano Roosevelt, she was appointed U.S. delegate to the first session of the United Nations by President Harry S Truman. The Human Rights Commission had two vice-presidents. One was Dr. P. C. Chang (China) who quickly demonstrated his skills as a scholar, peacemaker, and master of the art of compromise. The second was Professor René Cassin (France), a quick-witted and able speaker. His earlier diplomatic experience with the League of Nations earned him respect as a leader whose position on various issues often commanded a following. The commission's rapporteur, Dr. Charles Malik (Lebanon) was an advocate of the natural law philosophy of St. Thomas Aquinas. A professor and gifted teacher, he said that from the beginning, all the commission members knew that their task of composing a declaration of human rights was itself an educational undertaking.[3]

To use their human rights, people need to know about them. Malik made this keynote observation, arguing that the drafters "must elaborate a general Declaration of Human Rights defining in succinct terms the fundamental rights and freedoms of [everyone] which, according to . . . the Charter of the United Nations all states must promote."[4] This responsible setting forth of fundamental rights "will exert a potent doctrinal, moral and educational influence on the minds and ways . . . of people everywhere." The view that the Universal Declaration is a teaching resource is embodied in the Preamble, which says the instrument was designed as a common standard of achievement for all peoples and all nations, and therefore "every individual and every organ of society," keeping this Declaration in mind, "shall strive by teaching and education to promote respect for these rights and freedoms."

The dynamics of the process producing the UDHR are complex and intriguing. The newly organized Commission on Human Rights had at its disposal eighteen official or semiofficial drafts by the time the UN instructed it to prepare a declaration in 1947.[5] Thus, the problem for the new international organization was not to discover material from which a bill of rights could be fashioned. With no lack of draft models, the principal challenges were legal and conceptual. Thus, the commission debate centered on (1) whether the first UN human rights formulations should take the legal form of a binding treaty with enforcement institutions or a declaration addressed to public opinion and carrying only moral suasion; and (2) conceptually, what balance should be struck between political rights and social rights. Certainly, there was no question as to whether human rights were the proper business of the United Nations; that issue was settled by the Charter of the United Nations, which refers to human rights in no less than seven places.

The initial session of the commission was devoted to mapping out its functions and the scope of its work, including the nature of the proposed international bill of rights.[6] Mrs. Roosevelt felt that it should be prepared first in the form of a declaration that would guide public opinion and could be adopted as a resolution of the General Assembly.[7] So singular a vision did not win support without debate. Mr. Valentin Tepliakov (USSR) thought that any decision on the legal form of their work product was premature, while both India and Australia were impatient with an unenforceable declaration and pressed instead for a convention. Mrs. Hansa Mehta (India) argued that adequate machinery must be set up to enforce the new instrument when human rights were violated. Australia insisted on a treaty-based International Court of Human Rights. Such wide-ranging exchanges turned out to be preliminary posturing, and the commission shifted to the practical business of asking staff members to collect data to frame ideas for a first outline of a bill of rights.

The commission was fortunate to have talented staff support, headed by John P. Humphrey. He was a Canadian professor of international law, a social democrat, and a workaholic. From his vantage point as the secretariat director of the Human Rights Commission, he said the text of the Universal Declaration of Human Rights had no one dominant progenitor or inspired authors, "in the sense that Jefferson was the father of the American Declaration of Independence."[8] Nevertheless,

Humphrey's role in specifying proposed rights related to science is important because they are clustered with other socioeconomic rights, seen as problematic by some delegates who were leery of expanding the range of safeguards beyond civil and political rights. The reason the Declaration included a full menu of socioeconomic rights is not to the credit of the Soviets and their friends. Rather it is because Humphrey's draft language readily prompted pride of ownership in the delegations from Latin America, who made sure it stayed in. Humphrey found ways to signal the Latin American delegates that he admired the "Pan American Declaration" then in deliberation in Bogotá. Humphrey found the Latin American draft interesting, according to Mary Ann Glendon in her biography of Eleanor Roosevelt. He liked it because:

it represented a harvest of the main elements of the continental Europeans, as well as Anglo-American rights traditions; it accompanied its list of rights with a list of duties; it was supranational; and it proclaimed that essential rights of man are not derived from the fact that he is a national of a certain state, but are based upon attributes of his human personality.[9]

Showing how the Latin American connection was sealed, Glendon notes that one of the Bogotá framers, Felix Nieto del Rio of Chile served briefly on the first UN Human Rights Commission before being replaced by Hernán Santa Cruz, described by Humphrey as "politically left of center."

Latin Americans tended to vote as a bloc on human rights matters in the first year of the UN's existence, and this proved important in the politics leading to the UDHR's provisions relating to science. For example, Humphrey used a draft proposal from the Inter-American Juridical Committee for UN consideration. It said, "Everyone has the right . . . to share in scientific advancement and its benefits."[10] The version succinctly framed by Humphrey and submitted by Chile was accepted by the Human Rights Commission, but met a clamorous fate when passed along for final review by the Third Committee of the General Assembly.

As we will reference this committee again, we should note that the UN General Assembly has several standing committees, the first dealing with disarmament and international security, the second with economic and financial issues, and the third with humanitarian and cultural issues. Sometimes, the Third Committee meets as a "committee of the whole" with all General Assembly delegates participating. This was the case after the initial framing of the Universal Declaration was completed, and the draft Declaration was turned over to the Third Committee where voting blocs sometimes undid the work of the Commission.[11]

The Pavlov-Roosevelt Exchange

The commission benefited from Eleanor Roosevelt's diplomatic skills exhibited in her role as chair. She ensured that debate was germane, and showed flexibility and openness to differing views on how to organize the Declaration, including the provisions of Article 27 on culture and science. She occasionally stepped out of her role as commission chair and engaged in substantive debate, especially with Alexie P. Pavlov from the Soviet Union. He was known for his acumen and skill in debate and carefully researched and wrote his own speeches. A sharp exchange between the spokespersons from the U.S. and the USSR superpowers nearly sidelined the Latin American initiative on science and human rights. Relying for explanatory details on memoirs and biographies, here is an interpretive sample of some dramatic dialogue that took place in the Third Committee as the Soviets and their friends tried to bend the Chilean proposal to their own objectives.[12]

"An atmosphere of terror prevails throughout the world," the learned Russian diplomat warned the audience. "It is terror owing to the application of scientific discoveries for destructive purposes."

The voice was strong, and everyone listening recognized it was the first plank in the typically careful argument of the polished Leningrad attorney and diplomat. Delegate Alexie Pavlov knew that fear can prompt action, and several representatives to the new United Nations in 1947 nodded their heads in agreement with his proposition, perhaps thinking of grotesque Nazi medical experiments, of American responsibility for nuclear destruction in Japan, of the British blanket bombing of civilians in Dresden, and of chemical and biological warfare dreaded by everyone. The genie of nuclear science could not be re-bottled; something had to be done. Where better to deal with such weighty matters than in the fledgling United Nations in session to contemplate refining and drafting a new global bill of rights.

Pavlov pressed his advantage with a stinging argument seemingly formulated to challenge Chairperson Eleanor Roosevelt. It was an awkward moment for the lady whom members relied on to steer proceedings through rough patches, such as departures from the unwritten rule to avoid speaking specifically of shortcomings of other countries. Pavlov occasionally ignored the rule. In her autobiography, Roosevelt noted that Pavlov, was "an orator of great power, the words rolled out of his black beard like a river, and stopping him was difficult indeed."[13]

"Already American policy makers are creating a danger of extinguishing disinterested scientific research in United States universities in favor of laboratories for military purposes," the Soviet delegate asserted in an extended polemic blast. This unsubstantiated and icy swipe at American

Figure 1. Eleanor Roosevelt holding a poster of the Universal Declaration of Human Rights while visiting Lake Success, New York, in 1949. She was unbending in arguing against and helping to defeat Soviet efforts to link science and the work of scientists to ideological goals. Purged of that political content, Article 27 remains a sweeping pronouncement, saying, "Everyone has the right freely . . . to share in scientific advancement and its benefits." Courtesy of the United Nations, UNATIONS photo UN23782.

policy offended the dignified American lady who chaired the meeting, making some of those present uncomfortable. Why use a forum with the lofty goal of seeking world peace through human rights to chill discussion heretofore so cordial between Mrs. Roosevelt and Mr. Pavlov, between America's first lady and the Soviet Ambassador to Belgium, between former war allies—the United States and the Soviet Union? Did the delegates recognize in Pavlov's rhetoric a harbinger of the Cold War rivalry only beginning to unfold? And where was he going with this argument: Nazi science served destructive purposes, now Americans are mobilizing science for military purposes?

The nephew of the famous conditioned reflex scientist, Pavlov spoke solemnly. "We need to recognize and proclaim the people's rights to enjoy the applications of science mobilized in the service of progress and democracy," Pavlov boomed, adding that science also should be harnessed to "the causes of peace and international cooperation."

Mrs. Roosevelt was prepared. Asked once in a different context how to get along with the Soviets, she said succinctly: "have convictions; be friendly; stick to your beliefs; and work as hard as they do." In responding to Pavlov's challenge, Roosevelt adopted the role of the patient teacher, bringing her high-pitched voice to bear in setting the issues straight, in schooling the attentive pupils on an important lesson: "The words 'progress' and 'democracy' apply to abstract ideas, and for these ideas no uniform interpretation exists," she said, concluding sternly, "It seems dangerous to adopt a text which could be interpreted as a pretext for the enslavement of science."

"Enslavement of science"—these are harsh terms and their choice told the delegates that an animated dueling match was underway, and that the former first lady was a worthy adversary. If the Soviets had their way, then who would decide which projects of science met their standards of progress and peace? She could not agree that science should be placed at the service of politics. "Yet that might be the practical effect of the USSR proposal," to situate a newly conceived right to ideologically tainted science on the people's pedestal of human rights.

Eleanor Roosevelt was not alone. She needed support and it was forthcoming from the United Kingdom. Mrs. Corbet rallied to the American's view, responding: "Science should not be placed at the service of an ideology falsely called 'progress' as it had been recently when invoked by propagandists of a doctrine bestowing racial superiority upon Germany."[14]

Others piled on when the commission's handicraft came to the General Assembly for final review in the Third Committee. The Soviet proposal was condemned vigorously by the Belgian representative for trying "to assign to science a political mission,"[15] and most succinctly by Mr. Watt of Australia as failing to perceive that "the sole aim of science could only be the quest for truth."[16] A roll call vote mobilized the Latin Americans to vote in unison, mercifully killing the discussion and defeating the Soviet proposal by 25 to 10 with 7 abstentions.[17]

The Grand Theory

Science and human rights. What could possibly explain these two complex topics engaging global leaders in 1947? In the atmosphere of the day, many thought—perhaps naively—of the topics in terms of cause and effect as if armed conflicts could be explained as the machinations of anti-human rights politicians intoxicated by the poisoned fruits of science and technology. Reduced to its barest elements the underlying logic for a new strategic plan for world peace, said

- misguided applications of science in the hands of megalomaniac politicians = war;
- societies empowered by human rights = peaceful social structures;
- ergo science advancing in human rights-friendly societies = peace.

War left none of the UN founders untouched; they were all familiar with miseries multiplied by the products of technology. Aghast at the novel devices from scientists' drawing boards, they worried about restraining tyrants whose hands held the mechanical levers of death, the weapons of destruction, and the intention to abuse people's human rights on a massive scale. On the theory that respect for people's rights and liberties reduces the prospects of hostility, world leaders meeting to design the United Nations had sought to introduce human rights into the international commitments of member states. The most optimist among them hoped that by restraining the mailed fist, they would foil the warrior's inhumane misuse of science and technology. The resolution of the Pavlov-Roosevelt debate precluded the prospect of any science czar deciding between peace-loving versus nonprogressive science. The grand question then became how to engineer new world arrangements whereby those in power who control such weapons and who command their designers can be bridled by rational principles favoring international peace.

A cornerstone for the peace-making goals of the UN, the answer has two parts: empower people at the grass roots with a full arsenal of human rights and connect scientists by a link of responsibility to the public and its right to share in the benefits and applications of their work. As importantly, fortify with human rights those who conduct the work of science. Scientists, like everyone else, need an environment of fundamental rights and liberties so that they are no mere puppets of political authorities, while at the same time, they should be aware that their work is judged by the standard of the public's right to share in scientific advancement and its benefits.

The scaffolding for this important conceptual construct is fastened together by several provisions of the Universal Declaration. They are addressed to everyone's rights, including their right to information and freedom of thought, as well as related rights to scientific benefits and the rights of scientists. They include

Article 19. Everyone has the right to freedom of opinion and expression; this right includes freedom to hold opinions without interference and to seek, receive and impart information and ideas through any media and regardless of frontiers.

Article 20. 1. Everyone has the right to freedom of peaceful assembly and association. 2. No one may be compelled to belong to an association.
Article 27. 1. Everyone has the right freely to participate in the cultural life of
the community, to enjoy the arts and to share in scientific advancement and its
benefits.
  2. Everyone has the right to the protection of the moral and material interests resulting from any scientific, literary or artistic production of which he is the
author.

These are safeguards cognate to the needs of the scientific enterprise
because free speech, assembly, and participation as well as rights to intellectual property characterize the conditions scientists need to pursue
their professional work effectively and because these rights bear on the
public's prospects for enjoying and sharing the applications of science.

Debate on Science and Human Rights

The question of whether and how a statement of worldwide rights and
fundamental freedoms should refer to science and technology was new
to global discourse. Articulating the key concepts and finding the best
words to do so was not easy. The language and terms in Article 27 referencing science drew multiple thunderbolts of high-energy debate. The
language involved was subjected to many changes in 1947–48 during the
legislative drafting process of the United Nations Commission on Human
Rights and thereafter during the final review in the General Assembly.

  The elitist tone of the original article, appearing only to exult scientists,
was overcome by saying that everyone has the right not only to share in
the advancement of science (crediting scientists, engineers, and students
of science) but also to share in its benefits (the general public). The drafters argued vehemently before reaching this position. The thorniest concern was over whether scientists deserve special human rights consideration apart from other human beings. The Chinese representative evoked
a vision of science seen in terms of a social enterprise as he led commission members beyond a tangled maze of debating points regarding the
question of who has a right to enjoy the benefits of science. The provisions
relating to science originally said that everyone had the right to "share
in scientific advancement." Calling for additional reference to "its benefits," Chang argued with Confucian subtlety that in the arts, letters, and
science alike, aesthetic enjoyment had two sides: a purely passive aspect
when one appreciates beauty and an active aspect when one creates it.[18]
In this connection, the Chinese representative said that the expression
"participate in" or "share in" did not express this dual aspect as precisely
as it might. The text referred more clearly to creation than to passive enjoyment. He therefore advocated the addition of the words "and its bene-

fits." This proposal had the brilliant added advantage of overcoming the objections that special protection for intellectual property as a human right favored privileges of only a small proportion of society.

Professor René Cassin summarized the new consensus on Chang's final version of the measure by asserting that, "even if all persons could not play an equal part in scientific progress, they should indisputably be able to participate in the benefits derived from it."[19] This point was important because it helped to link everyone's sharing in the benefits of science with other facets of human potential, that is, in the framers' terms, everyone's right to the full development of the human personality. Here we have a notion in need of clarification. It is an important notion anchored in philosophical foundations about human nature.

It is sometimes argued that the Universal Declaration of Human Rights does not rest on a coherent theory of human nature. The contrary view is that the Preamble's recognition of the "inherent dignity and worth of the human person" is the first plank of such a theory, completed by several references elsewhere to the "right to the full development of the human personality." This arresting notion of the human being's full personality, while abstract, is important as a thematic thread running through the UDHR.[20] Its significance in framing a holistic concept of human nature as essentially free, social, potentially educated, and entitled to participation in critical decision making is bolstered by repetition at several points:

- Article 22 says everyone's rights to social, economic and cultural rights are "indispensable" for the "free development of his personality."
- Article 26 posits a right to education, and says "Education shall be directed to the full development of the human personality."
- Article 27 links sharing the benefits of science in the larger context of the right to "participate in the cultural life of the community, to enjoy the arts and to share in scientific advancement and its benefits."
- Article 29 repeats the holistic vision of human rights, saying: "Everyone has duties to the community in which alone the free and full development of his personality is possible."

The language linking these provisions in terms of "the full development of the human personality" illustrates the organic nature of the Declaration whereby diverse rights flowed from a belief in the equality of all human beings and the fundamental unity of all human rights. The often reiterated right to "the full development of the human personality" was seen by most delegates as a right reinforced by community and social interaction. It linked and summarized all the social, economic, and cultural rights in the Declaration. Given the goal of the full development of the human personality in the context of society—the only context in which this can occur—it follows that "everyone's right to share in scientific advancement and its benefits" is a social right, a social good, and a responsibility of society as a whole.

Completing our review of the origins of the UDHR, we must enter the somewhat murky field of intellectual property. In its second paragraph, Article 27 says: Everyone has the right to the protection of the moral and material interests resulting from any scientific, literary, or artistic production of which he is the author. This language was modeled on a provision on intellectual property of the American Declaration of the Rights and Duties of Man. Adopted shortly before the Universal Declaration in 1948 and written in Bogotá, Colombia, it sought to humanize and democratize science with a two-pronged standard saying, (1) "Every person has the right to . . . participate in the benefits that result from intellectual progress, especially scientific discoveries," and (2) scientists have a right to protection of their moral and material interests for their scientific works (Article 13).[21]

Intellectual property rights had not fared well as a component of the UDHR before the Human Rights Commission, where both the Soviets and the Americans had objections. But the measure took on new life when the commission's draft was finally reviewed by the Third Committee of the General Assembly. It had the final say on the draft and a much larger membership, where the Latin American bloc rallied to the Bogotá text. It served as the basis on which Mexico, France, and Cuba successfully proposed adding the language on "moral and material interests" to harmonize the wording of the two declarations. The Latin American concept of "moral interests"—not then found in Common Law countries—entitles those who produce scientific and literary works to prohibit others from tampering with their works by modification or refusing to recognize the originators.

Against a British objection that intellectual property needed no special protection beyond that afforded by property rights generally, a Dutch spokesman offered a strong rebuttal. Mr. Beaufort noted the example of the scientist Mme. Marie Curie, the discoverer of radium whose work contributed materially to advances in medical research. He said that she "had devoted her whole life to the progress of science for the good of humanity"—not a mere business venture to be protected by patents.[22] The Dutch delegate said it was wrong to consider the protection of the moral and material interests of such a creative scientist and other medical pioneers on the same level as the general right of property; the "moral interest" was more abstract and, "more than any other, lent itself to infringement."

After the General Assembly adopted the Universal Declaration of Human Rights, the Lebanese delegate Charles Malik suggested that everyone, in personal terms, should understand the UDHR to mean: "this is what my Government must have pledged itself to promote, achieve and observe when it signed the Charter."[23] To those who likewise take the Universal Declaration of Human Rights seriously as a set of hallowed claims and solemn promises, it constitutes the central document for the cause of human rights. Its influence has broadened and extended since its adoption on 10 December 1948. That day was proclaimed by the UN in 1950 to be "Human Rights Day," and it has remained as such on the international calendar.

Conclusions

In 1948, when the first winds of the Cold War began to blow, drafters of the Declaration wisely repudiated suggestions to link science to standards external to the scientific enterprise, such as gratuitous political and ideological objectives. At the same time, most students of the philosophy of science acknowledge that science is hardly value-neutral because the very choice of research projects reflects social priorities. Yet, thankfully, sectarian definitions of science are widely eschewed, and racist and sexist attempts to slant the work of science are subject to unfettered criticism. For this, in significant part, we have the Universal Declaration of Human Rights to thank. There are many ways whereby the moral fiber of the UDHR stiffens and strengthens contemporary issues on science and human rights. They are discussed in later chapters but it is not too soon to point to some of the trophies of the Universal Declaration:

- nondiscrimination norms strengthen critical attacks against racist efforts to revive the pseudoscience of eugenics;
- human rights provide a plank in advocating gender and ethnic diversity in science education;
- on principle, mobilized efforts oppose politically and ideologically motivated restrictions on scientists traveling to professional conferences in countries with regimes some find objectionable;
- indigenous peoples can make intellectual property claims against corporate prospectors for sharing some of the curative secrets of the rain forest pharmacopoeia;
- scholars, entrepreneurs, and statespersons voice strong cautions about privacy rights and issues of discrimination connected to the mapping of the human genome.

To the extent that these efforts prevail despite countervailing political and sectarian forces, it is because scientists, engineers, health professionals, and the general public support an environment of open debate and freely exchanged ideas as essential to the success of the scientific enterprise. Over fifty years of international endorsements of the Universal Declaration of Human Rights remind us of the globally accepted values on which we depend and that fortify us in efforts to implement the public's rights to "share in scientific advancement and its benefits" and related standards of scientific freedom, responsibility and accountability.

In the journey toward social justice—requiring vision and the courage to innovate—the first step is due no less honor than the most recent. The UDHR framers project completed in 1948 is often so honored. Eleanor Roosevelt's assessment of the project was both modest and forward looking. "No matter how many times we revised the Declaration," she mused, we "could always see something a little better . . . [that we] might do." She concluded, "On the whole, however, it is a good document."[24] She thought it would gradually become ever more significant for world public opinion, as indeed it has. It is a tribute to the framers' efforts that, like Eleanor Roosevelt, we can always see something a little better that we might do. Mrs. Roosevelt was also typically forward-looking in her vision, and when the drafting of the Universal Declaration of Human Rights was completed, she made a statement as if she were talking to us today:

It will be a long time before history will make its judgment on the value of the Universal Declaration of Human Rights, and the judgment will depend, I think, on what the people of different nations do to make this document familiar to everyone. If they know it well enough, they will strive to attain some of the rights and freedoms set forth in it, and that effort on their part is what will make it of value in clarifying what was meant in the United Nations Charter in the references to human rights and fundamental freedoms.[25]

Chapter 3
Science in the International Covenant on Economic, Social and Cultural Rights

> Science, by itself, cannot supply us with an ethic. It can show us how to achieve a given end, and it may show us that some ends cannot be achieved. But among ends that can be achieved our choice must be decided by other than purely scientific consideration.
>
> —Bertrand Russell

Major parts of the Universal Declaration of Human Rights enter the twenty-first century with the qualities that international lawyers call "customary international law." This is so today, partly because the Declaration has been reaffirmed so many times, and because a majority of states have incorporated it into their national constitutions. Thus it is considered much more than just a normal UN recommendation, carrying only the weight of moral suasion.

Likewise, the provisions of the UDHR on science and human rights have become law in many countries because they have evolved from the form of declaratory recommendations to treaty-based state obligations. As noted, Article 27 is the provision of the Declaration most directly referring to science and human rights. It served as the model and the basis for drafting provisions of Article 15 of the International Covenant on Economic, Social and Cultural Rights (ESC Covenant). The Declaration thereby took on enhanced legal status, formalizing its provisions in two treaties called "covenants" to emphasize their solemn importance; one pertains to civil and political rights, and the second to economic, social, and cultural rights.

In this chapter, I introduce the reader to the origins of Article 15 of the International Covenant on Economic, Social and Cultural Rights. Using two methods, I try to sharpen the meaning of key science-linked provisions, leaving some for treatment in the next chapter. My first effort to shed light on certain rights relies on the framers debates, which supply an inconclusive but appropriate place to start trying to figure out the scope and meaning of scientists' rights and people's rights to enjoy the benefits of science. Second, I adopt the "violations approach" advanced by Dr. Audrey Chapman, director of the Science and Human Rights Program of the American Association for the Advancement of Science.[1] This involves identifying the "core minimum" requirements of each right and clarifying its meaning in the light of modern day violations. Finally, I argue that scientists' rights and everyone's rights to enjoy the benefits of science, potentially at odds with one another, find balance in a "binary theory of science rights." It is a harmonizing theory that is potentially helpful in guiding policies of human rights protection, for example, in the contentious field of intellectual property rights. The chapter concludes by acknowledging that while oversight and implementation procedures within the United Nations remain weak, serious discussion is underway about how to hold states parties accountable for violations.

Words Matter

For the task of drafting the International Covenant on Social, Economic and Cultural Rights, the Commission on Human Rights agreed to be guided by the principle that the text should be clear and succinct. Because words matter, the politics of drafting new human rights language is important. The commission understood that complicating detail would undermine the new treaty; every amendment added could make ratification more difficult. Moreover, when it came time to report violations, very concrete language was needed to guide states in implementing the covenant. Unlike the provisions of a declaration, those of a convention, covenant, and treaty must entail specific legal obligations by signatory countries. Applied to science and human rights, these cautions meant that the covenant, while closely tracking Article 27 of the UDHR, nevertheless, had to use a more practical format. In specifying the "steps to be taken" by states parties, its Article 15 says:

1. The States Parties to the present Covenant recognize the right of everyone:
   (a) To take part in cultural life;
   (b) To enjoy the benefits of scientific progress and its applications;

Figure 2. Albert Einstein at Princeton University in 1954 with fellow Nobel laureate Hideki Yukawa and physicist John Archibald Wheeler. A vocal supporter of the UN, Einstein argued publicly that scientists' first duty is to remain faithful to their research and to the international pooling of scientific knowledge, but he also believed that people could bring harmony and order to the international human community. He saw fellow scientists worldwide playing key roles in striving to abolish war, promote world peace, and develop science and technology to serve people everywhere. Photo courtesy of *Princeton Alumni World* and Princeton University Libraries.

    (c) To benefit from the protection of the moral and material interests resulting from any scientific, literary or artistic production of which he is the author.

2. The steps to be taken by the States Parties to the present Covenant to achieve the full realization of this right shall include those necessary for the conservation, the development and the diffusion of science and culture.

3. The States Parties to the present Covenant undertake to respect the freedom indispensable for scientific research and creative activity.

4. The States Parties to the present Covenant recognize the benefits to be derived from the encouragement and development of international contacts and co-operation in the scientific and cultural fields. (See Appendix A)

It is worthwhile to take a close look at the opening provision, because it is both little understood and a potentially useful and important article of the Covenant.[2] Article 15 begins with the provision that "The State Parties to the present Covenant recognize the right of everyone . . . to enjoy the benefits of scientific progress and its applications."

In considering covenant language addressed to everyone's right "to enjoy the benefits of scientific progress," the Human Rights Commission reviewed the parallel language from the Universal Declaration. Despite discussion about the need most broadly to extend the benefits of science, commission members working on the draft covenant expressed dissatisfaction with the UDHR specification of a right "to share in scientific advancement." At the treaty-drafting stage, words must be prescriptive and converted into specific statements of concrete legal duties borne by states obliged to write legislation, for example, statutes to implement assured rights. It would be difficult to write laws specifying how everyone could share in the advancement of science, but less ambiguous, if somewhat subjective, to say that everyone should enjoy the benefits of scientific applications. As a consequence of commission deliberations, the less advisory and more directive tone in the Economic, Social and Cultural Covenant simply says that states recognize everyone's right "to enjoy the benefits of scientific progress and its applications."

This formulation also appeared to have the added benefit of harboring a minimalist Hippocratic injunction: first, do no harm. That inference rests on the notion that science should be addressed to beneficial ends consistent with the commitments all states make in subscribing to the UN Charter and its purposes of promoting peace, development, higher standards of living, and universal respect for human rights. The framers also acknowledged that, in the future, the United Nations Organization on Economic, Social and Cultural Rights (UNESCO) might be expected to amplify the meaning of the provision.[3]

Among the covenant framers, Mr. D'Souza from India addressed an important issue of global equity implicit in the science provisions of Article 15.[4] He said that the question of who benefits by its applications "was an essentially practical matter." And he concluded, "Undoubtedly scientific discoveries should benefit not only all individuals but all nations, regardless of their degree of development." Mr. Chaudhuri from Pakistan did not refer specifically to ideas about technology transfer, but he said the proposed article meant that "great efforts" should be made nationally and internationally "in order that countries where science had made little progress might attain the goals set forth in the proposed provision," and to meet the full realization of human rights, he cited the framers as insisting on "international assistance and cooperation"[5] among state parties (Article 2).

Core Minimum Rights

In 1990, the United Nations Committee on Economic, Social and Cultural Rights said that every state was obliged to ensure essential levels of satisfaction and enforcement for human rights, guided by the minimum core content of any given right and by the minimum obligation necessary to sustain the right.[6] They set high expectations, saying that the core obligations apply irrespective of the availability of resources of the country concerned or any other factors and difficulties. Moreover, a state claiming that it is unable to discharge its duties has the burden of proving that this is the case. A temporary closure of a particle physics laboratory due to an electrical blackout, for example, would possibly be a circumstance beyond the state's control, while the elimination of an AIDS treatment program could be an example of unwillingness by the state to fulfill its obligations and would therefore fall in the category of a violation reportable to the UN Treaty Committee on Social, Economic and Cultural Rights. Moreover, UNESCO said "a State party in which any significant number of individuals is deprived of essential foodstuffs, of essential primary health care, of basic shelter and housing, or of the most basic forms of education is, prima facie, violating the Covenant."

Four core elements of the right to enjoy the benefits of scientific progress are evident from the principles noted above, framers' discussions and related Covenant text. They concern (1) an environment of freedom, (2) protection from harm, (3) equality among beneficiaries, and (4) international cooperation. These major principles take on more clarity by way of counterexamples, which set in sharp relief a violation of the principle.

An Environment of Freedom

First, this right minimally requires a state-sponsored environment of freedom. Thus, whether people actually enjoy the benefits of scientific progress and its applications depends on related basic rights, essentially tied to free speech, access to information, participation, assembly, and association. An example from Malaysia shows the harm done to everyone's rights in this area by virtue of the suppression of a health study said to embarrass the government.[7] It is a sad story of a state suppressing fundamental freedoms, with consequent risks to health and life and denial of people enjoying the benefits of science.

In Malaysia monitoring the health and welfare of female migrant laborers has been done for years by Tenaganita, a women's human rights NGO. It sponsors drop-in counseling centers, special programs on women and AIDS, and a halfway house for health recovery including help for HIV-positive women. In 1995, the group's founder, Irene Fernandez, released her "Memorandum on Abuse, Torture, Dehumanized Treatment and Deaths of Migrant Workers at Detention Camps." The focus was on eleven secret detention camps throughout Malaysia holding ten thousand overseas workers who were undocumented or whose labor permits were lost, often arbitrarily confiscated by their employers. Add to this the predicament that those held in the camps of the Southeast Asian country had no procedural rights to contest their detention. With advice from epidemiological experts and using World Health Organization guidelines, Tenaganita interviewed detainees and revealed they did not get any medical attention even when they were sick or had a high fever or diarrhea. The report said: "The denial of proper food, water and medical care led to migrants suffering from severe malnutrition, dehydration and diseases. To allow immigrant detainees to die of beri beri, a highly treatable disease, involves serious government negligence" — a failure to fulfill its duties to advance people's human rights to the benefits of science by providing elementary health care for detained overseas laborers.

In March 1996, Fernandez was charged with "maliciously maligning the good name of Malaysia in the eyes of the world." According to the judge, the truth of published statements is not a sufficient defense if carelessness or malicious intent are involved. The NGO's work focusing on improving health conditions for overseas laborers seeks to ensure that everyone, not just Malaysian citizens, enjoys the benefits of health care and scientific advances. While Malaysia claims that conditions have improved since 1996, it denied Fernandez's right to disseminate the results of her research. It should also be noted that the environment for the free exercise of human rights in the Fernandez case violates the International Convention on the Protection of the Rights of all Migrant Workers and Members of Their Families. Referring to some of the world's most vulnerable people, it says: "Migrant workers and their families shall have the right to receive any medical care that is urgently required for the preservation of their life or the avoidance of irreparable harm to their health on the basis of equality of treatment with nationals of the State concerned" (Article 28).

Protection from Harm

Everyone's right "to enjoy the benefits of scientific progress and its applications" carries the inescapable message that this right means promoting socially beneficial applications and safeguarding people from harmful applications of science that violate their human rights. What happened in Bhopal, India, offers a striking example of state and nonstate parties shamefully neglecting their international duties.[8] On December 2, 1984, a pesticide plant of the Union Carbide Corporation (USA) in Bhopal suffered a runaway reaction. Within days, clouds of chemical poisons enveloped an area of forty square kilometers, killing thousands of people in its immediate wake. The exact nature of the gas is disputed, but consensus points to methyl isocyanate. Ultimately, Union Carbide was found to be culpable through negligence for the deaths, damage, and injuries involved. But three months after the event, the provincial government of Madhya Pradesh passed the "Bhopal Act," which arrogated to itself sole power to represent the survivors in damage litigation. In fact, the law was nothing more than a scheme to absolve the multinational corporation of all liabilities in exchange for one seventh of the original claim. This and related action are described by an NGO, the Bhopal Group for Information and Action, as a failure to protect human rights and as reflecting "willful indifference of the government evident in the course of its entire proceedings against Union Carbide." Because of failed efforts to achieve justice in India, some of the victims of pesticide poisoning sought justice elsewhere, but fought a losing battle in the United States in the case of *In re Union Carbide Corporation Gas Plant Disaster at Bhopal, India.*[9] The American court said that the issue of Union Carbide's responsibility must be settled where the accident took place and called on Indian judges to "stand tall before the world" and show they can handle this kind of litigation.[10] In fact, soon thereafter, the Indian Supreme Court brokered a settlement of $500 million on behalf of the thousands of victims.

The Bhopal case in its first round under the responsibility of the provincial government of Madhya Pradesh flew in the face of "everyone's right to enjoy the benefits of scientific progress and its applications." Indeed, the tragic disregard of the casualties by corporate and government officials is addressed in the standard of the UN Declaration on the Use of Scientific Progress (see box): "All States shall take effective measures, including legislative measures, to prevent and preclude the utilization of scientific and technological achievements to the detriment of human rights and fundamental freedoms and the dignity of the human person" (Section 8). Finally, a conference of experts in Maastricht, the Netherlands, propounded a guideline relevant to acts of omission such as were involved in the Indian case. It said violations of human rights can occur through the omission of states, such as "the failure to take into account its international legal obligations in the field of ESC rights when entering into agreements with other States, international organizations or multinational corporations" (Guideline 15.J).[11]

Equality Among Beneficiaries

The strongly egalitarian proposition that everyone has the right to enjoy the benefits of scientific progress and its applications is linked to equality

Declaration on The Use of Scientific And Technological Progress in The Interests Of Peace And For The Benefit of Mankind All States shall:

- promote international cooperation to ensure . . . the realization of human rights and freedoms in accordance with the Charter of the United Nations.
- take appropriate measures to prevent the use of scientific and technological developments, particularly by the State organs, to limit or interfere with the enjoyment of the human rights. . . .
- take measures to ensure that scientific and technological achievements satisfy the material and spiritual needs of all sectors of the population.
- refrain from any acts involving the use of scientific and technological achievements for the purposes of violating the sovereignty and territorial integrity of other States. . . .
- cooperate in the establishment, strengthening and development of the scientific and technological capacity of developing countries with a view to accelerating the realization of the social and economic rights of the peoples of those countries.
- take measures to extend the benefits of science and technology to all strata of the population and to protect them . . .from possible harmful effects of the misuse of scientific and technological developments. . . .
- take the necessary measures . . . to ensure that the utilization of scientific and technological achievements promotes the fullest realization of human rights and fundamental freedoms without any discrimination whatsoever on grounds of race, sex, language or religious beliefs.
- take effective measures . . . to prevent and preclude the utilization of scientific and technological achievements to the detriment of human rights and fundamental freedoms and the dignity of the human person.
- take action to ensure compliance with legislation guaranteeing human right and freedoms in the conditions of scientific and technological developments.

Proclaimed by the United Nations General Assembly
Resolution 3384 (XXX) of 10 November 1975

standards of Article 3 of the ESC Covenant. It stipulates that states parties "undertake to ensure the equal right of men and women to the enjoyment of all economic, social and cultural rights set forth in the present Covenant." The principle is further clarified by the UN Declaration on the Use of Scientific Progress: "All States shall take the necessary measures, including legislative measures, to ensure that the utilization of scientific and technological achievements promotes the fullest realization of human rights and fundamental freedoms without any discrimination whatsoever on grounds of race, sex, language or religious beliefs" (Section 7).

A sharply contested example of such discrimination arose in Japan involving the neglect of women's reproductive rights.[12] In 1999, Miss Akiko Domoto, an elected member of the Japanese Diet, accused her country's pharmaceutical review process of violating women's human rights. She pointed to its swift approval of Viagra for male erectile dysfunction, while banning the use of contraceptive pills for women for nearly a decade. She noted that women are especially burdened because without the pill unwanted pregnancies are common in Japan. Official statistics show that one in five ends in abortion, bringing the total to about 340,000 abortions each year—a per capita incidence far higher than in other developed countries. Japan's Health Ministry countered that birth control pills had not been approved because they would undercut the use of condoms and thereby contribute to the spread of AIDS. Nevertheless, because Japan took a mere six months to approve the impotence treatment—while the birth control pill had been languishing in red tape for nine years, Viagra's fast-track debut in 1999 "generated an uproar like never before," according to Midori Ashida. She complained, "When old guys want something, they get it, but when women want something, nothing happens." She went on, "Japan is still a male-dominated society," and her colleague, Akiko Domoto, added, "The fact that Japanese women don't have the pill, used around the world, is discrimination against women and a violation of their human rights."

International Cooperation

According to the UN Declaration on the Use of Scientific Progress, the beneficial applications promised by Article 15 rights cannot be attained among countries where science had made little progress without serious cooperative efforts at the national and international levels. That seems a fair reading of Section 5, saying: "All States shall cooperate in the establishment, strengthening and development of the scientific and technological capacity of developing countries with a view to accelerating the realization of the social and economic rights of the peoples of those countries."

Contrary to the imperatives of these principles, serious problems arise in "bio-prospecting," which, when devoid of international cooperation, is rife with North-South pretense and abuse. Corporations from industrialized countries can easily reap profits from exploiting pharmaceutical treasures hidden in rain forests while neither benefitting nor sharing earnings with those in the less developed countries whose natural resources and age-old knowledge they exploit.

Biotechnology business, booming in the industrialized world, has created a growing demand for prospecting for disease-curing living materials, primarily found in the Southern Hemisphere.[13] For example, active elements in Madagascar's rosy periwinkle cure most cases of lymphatic leukemia. Certain combinations of Asian herbs effectively treat atopic dermatitis, characterized by red, thickening, and scaling patches of skin. Unraveling the secrets of the foxglove plant led to the therapeutic use of digitalis, effective in treating heart and kidney diseases. Bioactive substances in plants that fight bacteria, fungi, viruses, and insects sometimes similarly affect the human body, fighting disease causing agents. Scientists as well as poets recognize that nature is bountiful, but modern research is sometimes undertaken unfairly even when uncovering what William Shakespeare called nature's "infinite book of secrecy."

"Bio-piracy" is unfair, according to Indian activist Vandana Shiva.[14] The practice refers to corporate and academic appropriation of the wisdom of indigenous peoples to locate and understand the uses of plants (such as the medicinally potent Neem tree in India) and even human tissue and then making the most of them commercially, but giving little or no compensation to the source. Further, using deception and duplicity, these international "bio-pirates" typically ignore privacy rights, defy consent procedures, and take advantage of the ignorance of those unwittingly enlisted as scouts to guide them to valuable medicinal plants known to traditional healers.

They also prospect for human tissue on the expectation it might supply genetic material useful through manipulation to enhance diagnostic techniques and possibly for gene therapy to avoid inherited diseases such as certain types of diabetes. Such work is surely in our future, but some preliminary research has been careless. A staple of research in microbiology is the use of cell lines involving the culturing of a living cell yielding multiple duplicate cells that are useful in laboratory research. Because a cell line is a permanently established cell culture that will proliferate indefinitely given appropriate fresh medium and space, it can be useful for a long time. In 1989, American researchers drew blood samples from twenty-four members of the Hagahai tribe (a 260-member hunter-horticulturist group in Papua New Guinea), developing a cell line from them for possible use in diagnosing adult leukemia and chronic degenerative neurologic diseases.[15] The project is one of many involved in the Human Genome Diversity Project (HGDP), a consortium of scientists in North America and Europe to secure live tissue from hundreds of unique human communities throughout the world. Indigenous nations in Panama, Ecuador, Peru, Bolivia, Argentina, and elsewhere oppose HGDP, noting that it "opens the door for potential widespread abuse of human genetic materials for scientific, commercial, or military purposes."

In 1997, UNESCO members adopted the Universal Declaration on the Human Genome and Human Rights (see Appendix C). The first international text on the ethics of genetic research, it sets universal ethical standards on human genetic research and practice. The declaration seeks to balance the freedom of scientists to pursue their work with the need to safeguard human rights and protect humanity from potential abuses.

The Genome Declaration specifically says in Article 24 that its implementation requires the International Bioethics Committee of UNESCO to develop advice on the complex nature of these problems. The committee's mandate concerns vulnerable groups "in particular regarding the identification of practices that could be contrary to human dignity, such as germ-line interventions." Moreover, and very much to the point of the work in Papua New Guinea, the Human Genome Declaration, stipulates that if "a person does not have the capacity to consent," research affecting his or her genome "may only be carried out for his or her direct health benefit" (Article 5(e)). Thus, central to science-linked rights is everyone's right to enjoy the benefits of scientific progress, not the costs and risks minus the benefits.

The Rights of Scientists

The International Covenant on Economic, Social and Cultural Rights refers not only to people's rights to benefit by the applications of scientific advances, but also safeguards scientists' rights. In its second paragraph, Article 15 of the ESC Covenant contains a provision specifically addressed to the rights of scientists. It says: Everyone has the right "to benefit from the protection of the moral and material interests resulting from any scientific . . . production of which [s]he is the author" (Article 15.1(c)).

The draft did not contain this language when the UN General Assembly convened in 1952 as the permanent Third Committee met to review the commission's proposed covenant. The omission was not because of absent-mindedness. After all, everyone knew that Article 27 of the UDHR covered intellectual property rights. Rather, the covenant's drafters avoided mention of property rights—the high-voltage third rail of human rights—because the topic marked the ideological divide between left and right. At an early stage of UN deliberations, the Soviets and their allies made a successful bid to throttle all references to property rights, including the intellectual property rights of scientists. Taking this line, the Czech delegate Mrs. Leferova argued that people's rights to benefit from the advances of science should not be equated with the property rights of scientific innovators, technological inventors, and mere tinkerers.[16] If so mixed, she concluded, the resulting article would "be obscure and there would be no unequivocal statement of the right it was meant to define." Her dismissive tone carried the message that there is no place in a charter of rights for both serious assertions of everyone's human rights and the self-serving claims of a technological elite.

On the other side of the debate, the Israeli delegate reminded the General Assembly that if scientists' intellectual property rights were overlooked, the covenant would then be weaker than the Universal Declaration of Human Rights.[17] To this formalistic argument, stronger entreaties were added on behalf of intellectual property. In a David and Goliath political gambit, the tiny countries of Costa Rica and Uruguay confronted the Soviet Union and its allies, where scientists could make no claims to their inventions.[18] The Latin Americans summoned their hemispheric compatriots to reintroduce the measure on scientists' rights, invoking their pride that the language of the UDHR was drawn from that earlier crafted in the Pan-American Declaration of Bogotá.[19] Despite the fact that the provision sponsored by the Latin Americans was rhetorically scorched by the Soviet Union and its associates, the intellectual property provisions of Article 15 won overwhelming acceptance in the General Assembly's vote.

That result left open the question of what such rights involve. The Latin American concept of "moral interests" entitles those who produced scientific and literary works to prohibit others from tampering with their works by modification or refusing to recognize the originator.[20] Nevertheless, Mr. Tejera (Uruguay) said his resolution was not intended to saddle all states with technically defined specific duties regarding "moral interests," copyright, and patents. Rather the desired effect should be "gradually to bring the legislation of contracting States into line with a minimum acceptable level specified in various international treaties," such as those proceeding from the Berne Conference of 1886 dealing with patent and copyright standards.[21] In other words, the basic right embedded in this provision is not substantively defined with precision, but points instead to a procedural right to remedies in defense of intellectual property such as arbitration and conciliation and including legislative remedies to take changing conditions into account.

The Binary Theory of Science Rights

While the former Warsaw Pact countries sought to decouple the twofold connection between scientists' rights and rights of the public, their views were rejected by four-to-one voting margins in the General Assembly. The outcome of the Latin Americans controlling these issues can be summarized in these terms.

- As argued by Uruguayan and Chilean delegates, the right of the scientist and the right of the public to share the benefits of scientific advancement are not and should not be opposed.[22] Rather they are complementary, or binary rights, because respect for the rights of authors and scientific innovators assures the public of the credibility of their claims to innovation and the scientific applications available to the public.
- Second, a core minimum feature of the intellectual property rights provisions in Article 15 lies in their assurance to the public of the authenticity of the works presented to it.
- Third, at a time when property rights were otherwise excluded from the ESC Covenant, the framers of the intellectual property norms recognized the societal benefits in protecting technological progress consistent with everyone's right to "share in scientific advancement and its benefits."
- Fourth, states minimally have a duty to participate in a treaty-based intellectual property rights regime because the producers of scientific innovations deserve protection from the expropriation of their inventions and innovations, failing which they should have a right to a remedy.
- Fifth, when intellectual property rights and people's rights to the benefits of science appear to clash, intellectual property rights claims need not be seen as absolute, but those who claim them should have access to international mediation and remedial procedures to harmonize such claims in conflict with people's rights to the benefits of science.

Astronomers speak of binary stars, referring to a stellar system of two stars orbiting in balance around a common center. Balance, not dominance, is the key to this equilibrium. By analogy, given the dual objectives of intellectual property and people's claims to the benefits of science—each orbiting around the concept of human rights at the center—the binary theory suggests that balance between the two is necessary, especially when changing circumstances appear to tilt toward imbalance.

What changing circumstances might be relevant? Today, the World Intellectual Property Organization has authority to accept a single international patent application rendering it valid in many countries. It reported that 7,000 such international applications were accepted in 1985 and 74,000 in 1999. Much of this increase reflects a boom in innovative activity, but some involves less benign change, according to the UN Human Development Report 2001. It notes, "The scope of patent claims has broadened—especially in the United States, the trend-setter on patent practice."

In the UNDP's analysis, when American patents are granted, for example, on genes the functions of which may not be clear, a problem arises because at some point patent authorities risk being seen as service providers to commercial patent applicants, shifting "traditional knowledge into private hands," and thereby undermining their role as rigorous watchdogs of the public domain. What can be done about any such tilt toward imbalance? One might reasonably argue that when intellectual property rights appear in conflict with people's rights to the benefits of science, the burden of demonstrating priority lies with property rights claimants. This presumption against property rights relies on the Declaration on the Use of Science obliging states to ensure that the use of scientific achievements should promote the fullest realization of human rights without discrimination, including that which follows from the advantages enjoyed by those asserting property rights. Where the indigenous are concerned, all the advantages in any contest are on the other side. It all comes down to the fact that because claiming, using, and defending patents is easier for private corporations than for tribal groups who have traditionally used local flora and fauna for medicinal purposes, they are vulnerable to the discriminatory result of losing control over their native pharmacopeia.[23]

International Protection

After 1976, when the ESC Covenant finally came into force, the World Intellectual Property Organization (WIPO) implemented an international intellectual property regime. Intellectual property comprises two main branches: industrial property, principally involving inventions, trademarks, and industrial designs, and copyright, chiefly referencing literary, musical, artistic, photographic, and audiovisual works.

Now a UN agency with 160 members, WIPO administers more than twenty major intellectual property treaties.[24] True to the promise of Article 15, WIPO provides legal and technical assistance on matters of intellectual property to developing countries and to previous socialist states now moving toward market economies.[25] WIPO also promotes the adoption of treaties seeking to facilitate the updating of intellectual property agreements in an age of fast-paced technology changes. In 1998, for example, WIPO hosted a forum for requests by the Coordinating Body for the Indigenous Peoples' Organizations of the Amazon Basin (COICA) to provide technical advice on issues of bio-piracy. Calling for new and much needed procedures to settle contentious pharmaceutical prospecting claims, COICA pointed to the gene-patenting of medicinal life forms with otherwise unprotected preexisting elements of traditional knowledge. They argued that the peoples of the Amazon had cultivated the sacred Yagé plant for centuries and now faced its "expropriation" without benefit or compensation for pharmaceutical purposes by the International Plant Medicine Corporation of the United States.[26] In approaching such novel issues, WIPO is supposed to initiate "international action for the achievement" of ESC rights and can do so using mediation techniques and norm-setting procedures. Some disputes might likewise end up before the UN Committee responsible for monitoring the ESC Covenant.

The most serious effort to address the tension between indigenous rights and intellectual property rights is found in the UN Principles and Guidelines for the Protection of the Heritage of Indigenous People. It calls on governments around the world to enact national laws for the protection of indigenous people's heritage. Thus Principle 23 (c) says such laws should:

deny to any person or corporation the right to obtain patent, copyright or other legal protection for any element of indigenous peoples' heritage without adequate documentation of the free and informed consent of the traditional owners to an arrangement for the sharing of ownership, control, use and benefits.[27]

It should be clear from the range and variety of science-linked rights that someone should be responsible for monitoring violations and oversight of state responsibilities. But, even in a fully developed protection regime, it would be difficult to perform this function on a global basis. After all, with scientific advances continuing at a rapid pace, their impact on human rights also changes, necessitating fresh perspectives and new responses. Heretofore, the place to conduct such critical assessment has not been the United Nations. Crippled by the politics of the Cold War, it has been unable to serve as an effective forum to examine the issues linked to the impact of technology on human rights. Nonetheless, with ideological confrontations in the United Nations abating, and with ever more states ratifying the Covenant on Economic, Social and Cultural Rights, the time is ripe for states parties to the covenant to take their reporting duties seriously, for NGOs to step forward with assertions of violations, and for the ESC Treaty Committee to critically review the reports periodically filed regarding state obligations under Article 15.

The Committee on Economic, Social and Cultural Rights is an eighteen-member body of experts empaneled to study periodic reports required of contracting states. The pattern has been for the committee members to discuss the reports with representatives of the governments concerned. Its comments aim to help them in their duty to implement social, economic, and cultural rights as well as to bring to their attention deficiencies in reports and procedures (see Appendix B).

According to Philip Alston, the former committee chair, the process historically has not been auspicious.[28] He noted wryly that "past experience shows that there is a tendency for reports to list a few pieces of legislation and some international exchange agreements and assume that the reporting requirements are thereby satisfied." Such selective games of "show and tell" hardly constitute a process of accountability.

Conclusions

Accountability refers to the lines of authority and responsibility that determine to whom persons and institutions are answerable. Strictly speaking, the scientific community is not answerable to the United Nations, but to the states ratifying the Human Rights Covenants. Thus, the accountability that the ESC Committee can help to institutionalize does not concern queries about good science versus bad science. This is largely the function of peer review, which serves both as a mechanism of scientific self-regulation that preserves the autonomy of science and a symbol of professional accountability that ensures democratic control of science. Moreover, at least for the present, it is probably beyond the capacity of the ESC Committee to lay down clear markers sorting out clashes of human rights only recently becoming evident, such as where the human genome projects may pit patent and copyright claims against allegations of corporate exploitation of human tissue research. Resolution of such conflicts await normative development based on guidelines generated by the scientific community, professional associations, the United Nations including UNESCO, and emerging legislative and judicial determinations accumulating on a case-by-case basis. Certainly, the potential contribution to the safeguarding of Article 15 human rights by the ESC Committee does not envision it becoming a "science court."

On the positive side, for the first time since the founding of the United Nations, we now have the chance to make better use than in the past of the treaty reporting system, converting it into a serious process to enhance the accountability of state parties. The potential contribution that the ESC Committee can constructively make lies in holding states parties accountable for its infractions. As the duty-bearers, they must explain and bear the burden of justifying offending

- decisions such as Malaysian mistreatment of overseas workers,
- failings such as those involved in the Bhopal disaster,
- omissions, such as those involved in unregulated bio-piracy cases.

Such accountability can be bolstered by an agenda of public query and response and informed by the reception of critical reports by NGOs. As a result, states violating their treaty duties or shirking responsibilities can be exposed for public scrutiny. This would be no mean accomplishment. It would bring a public process into play, showing that science is a socially embedded activity and that the public deserves the information needed to empower it to judge whether or not, in fact, they "enjoy the benefits of scientific progress and its applications."

Chapter 4
State Responsibilities in the International Covenant on Economic, Social and Cultural Rights

> Here, then, is the problem which we present to you, stark and dreadful and inescapable: Shall we put an end to the human race, or shall mankind renounce war?
> —Manifesto of the First Pugwash Conference on Science and World Affairs

I use the historical and "violations" approach relied on in the last chapter to carry forward the analysis of Article 15 of the International Economic, Social and Cultural Rights Covenant. In this chapter, I focus on three state responsibilities to advance science-linked rights by taking steps to "conserve, develop and diffuse science." Moreover, this chapter also looks at state duties to respect scientific freedom, including the development of international contacts and cooperation. As these obligations apply to all states that are parties to the covenant, it is important to note the ever-increasing number of countries so committed.

By 2001, 147 states, including the United States, had ratified the International Civil and Political Rights Covenant, and, with the exception of the United States and a few others, the International Economic, Social and Cultural Rights Covenant as well, totaling 144 contracting parties. In short, since 1976, when these treaties came into force, about two-thirds of all countries have formally committed themselves to the legally binding provisions of the two covenants.[1] In the face of this worldwide array of treaty-bound countries, it is no longer possible to discuss human rights as aerie ephemera or the mere wishful thinking of organized underdogs and isolated elites. On the contrary, the worldwide array of treaty-bound countries attests to the global acceptance of human rights standards. Indeed, the World Conference on Human Rights, meeting in Vienna in June 1993, solemnly proclaimed that "The universal nature of [internationally defined human] rights and freedoms is [now] beyond question."[2]

Wrongs Clarify Human Rights

Edmond Cahn, an American legal philosopher, was famous for elevating scepticism to the level of wisdom. In *Confronting Injustice*, he acknowledged that abstract concepts such as justice frequently elude our full understanding.[3] Nevertheless, observing their opposites, he thought, clarified these difficult ideas. Thus, in Cahn's terms, confronting injustice sheds light on the underlying principles of justice. In the spirit of this notion—we learn about rights by knowing about wrongs—this chapter will grapple with some of the rather theoretical provisions of the International Covenant on Economic Social and Cultural Rights by looking at concrete examples of notorious transgressions.

Consider the wrongs suffered by Dr. Carmen Hernández de Vásquez, an environmental research scientist monitoring pollution problems in Mexico in 1992.[4] Large-scale political events that year affected her adversely. Negotiations were underway then involving Canada, Mexico, and the United States in planning the North American Free Trade Agreement (NAFTA). The agreement, which went into effect in 1994, created the most extensive free trade area in the world, promoted as promising economic gains contingent on common labor, environment, and human rights standards. As the director of the civil protection office for the Tijuana region, Hernández de Vásquez initiated an inquiry into mysterious deaths of farm animals around a U.S.-owned lead smelter and battery recycling firm. She strongly suspected the firm's dumping of toxic wastes was contaminating the water supply and a contributing factor in the animal deaths. The government, fearing that disclosure of the environmental pollution would threaten prospects for Mexican participation in the NAFTA, ominously warned that her investigations and public awareness campaigns were "alarming the citizenry." Hernández de Vásquez refused to back down. It took only a few months before the Mexican government dismissed her and several colleagues from their positions in Tijuana and closed down a research institution where colleagues worked, the Mexico City based Center for Eco-development.

The World University Service (Geneva) documented the Hernández de Vásquez case and reported that the Mexican government violated numerous international norms.[5] For example, the Lima Declaration on Academic Freedom says: "All members of the academic community with research functions have the right to carry out research work without any interference, subject to the universal principles and methods of scientific inquiry" (Article 6).[6] Contrariwise, the scientific work being developed at the Mexican research center was squelched, the institution closed, and scientists dismissed by the government to avoid the dissemination of information it found embarrassing. Further, the World University Service found another principle that applied to the Hernández de Vásquez case.

"Steps to be Taken"

The second paragraph of Article 15 of the Covenent on Economic, Social and Cultural Rights states: "The steps to be taken by the States Parties to the present Covenant to achieve the full realization of this right [to enjoy the benefits of science and its applications] shall include those necessary for the conservation, the development and the diffusion of science and culture." In the Mexican case, the benefits of environmental monitoring efforts were quite the opposite of being conserved, developed, and diffused.

The UN framers used each of these three functions as steps to reach the goals of the covenant. For states to satisfy the ESC Covenant's provision regarding the "conservation of science," they must safeguard those minimal conditions supporting the integrity of the scientific enterprise including the right to academic freedom.[7] Without academic freedom, the pursuit and practice of science remain vulnerable to political whims and economic expediency.

Moreover, the UN framers of Article 15 made clear that, as with human rights, science also requires international responsibility, calling for good faith and transnational cooperation. The U.S. corporation responsible for the battery acid dumping in Tijuana was at fault no less than the heavy-handed Mexican officials trying to cover up their flagrant environmental toxic waste mismanagement. If their strategy was to win support for Mexican membership in the North American Free Trade Association, then covering up American toxic dumping was a puzzling gambit, leaving environmental activists dismayed. Indeed, the passage of the trade agreement brought little relief. NAFTA and its "side agreements" that prescribe nominal environmental and labor-rights guarantees, offered Tijuana activists a new procedure, and they took further action. Because Mexican officials and the plant's owners failed to clean up the site, community members brought their case to the NAFTA-created Commission for Environmental Cooperation (CEC). A structurally weak institution with no enforcement authority, the most the CEC can do is to make the results of its investigation public, and while that may seem a minimal step forward, it is more than the courageous Dr. Carmen Hernández de Vásquez was able to do.

Another step presented by the ESC Covenant says states are obliged to ensure the "development of science." The term "development" is often used in its organic context to mean promoting growth and advancement in a nurturing environment, and it was so referenced by the framers. It follows therefore that nurturing the development of science necessarily involves the right to education, a well-spring to actively cultivate science for the benefit of all humankind.[8] Article 13 of the covenant reinforces this principle when it advocates secondary education, "including techni-cal . . . education, [which] shall be made generally available and accessible to all by every appropriate means." It also follows that access to the scientific community and to the study of science should be equal for all members of society, free from any form of invidious discrimination, and that on the basis of ability, everyone has the right, without hindrance of any kind, to become part of the scientific community, as a student, teacher, research worker, or administrator. To get positive results in recruiting minorities into professional studies of science and engineering, a proactive program is needed, including scholarships and financial support.[9]

As gender discrimination in science education is so widely prevalent, it is important to understand that the exclusion of significant numbers of women amounts to a violation of their basic human rights.[10] Without rectifying this injustice, the state is prima facie failing to discharge its obligations under the covenant to ensure the development of science.

Such a case of discrimination in Japan is particularly instructive especially because it shows that inaction is as culpable as abusive action. Nothing in Japanese law explicitly encourages discrimination against women in the sciences.[11] Because of state acts of omission, however, women have been de facto unwelcome in scientific fields at the higher echelons of responsibility. In 1996 the Ministry of Education, Science, Sports, and Culture (Monbu Kagakusho) reported that only 6.7 percent of women in natural science faculties are full professors, compared with 29.6 percent of male faculty. While Monbu Kagakusho formally promotes women's participation in science, it stops short of providing measures to level the playing field. Even after women's complaints about these matters were publicly aired, the ministry made no effort to address overcoming informal discrimination against women in the sciences. For several years, such programs as on-site day care and facilities for nursing mothers were unknown in Japan, but improvements developed with the Monbu Kagakusho policy announced in 2001 calling for nationwide human rights education to root out problems of discrimination through "people's enlightenment."

A final step safeguarding the "diffusion of science" requires that all members of the scientific community have the right to communicate the results and conclusions of their research freely to others, publishing them without censorship. For a state to promote the "diffusion of science" refers to more than merely facilitating the interaction of scientists; it also must expand and make available the benefits of science to everyone. The egalitarian phrasing of Article 15 leaves no doubt that the human right to the benefits of science are not only for scientists, but that "everyone has the right to enjoy the benefits of scientific progress and it applications."

An American case sharply illustrates discrimination in the "diffusion" of the benefits science.[12] According to the Federal Health Resources and Services Administration, a 1997 survey (conducted by the New York HIV Health and Human Service Planning Council) found that 33 percent of white respondents compared to 12 percent black and 19 percent Hispanic used the new "cocktail combination" of protease inhibitors that have restored the health of thousands of people with AIDS. Those people considered most in need of such advanced treatments were not getting the best treatment drugs, even though the disease is increasingly prevalent among them. "Problem drug use" and living in unstable housing conditions were associated with lower use of the more effective combination drugs among blacks and Hispanics. While these factors might explain much about the differential distribution of medical benefits, more is expected. According to a guideline clarifying government duties as specified in the UN Declaration on the Benefits of Science (see Chapter 3, p. 47).

All States shall take the necessary measures, including legislative measures, to ensure that the utilization of scientific and technological achievements promotes the fullest realization of human rights and fundamental freedoms without any discrimination whatsoever on grounds of race, sex, language or religious beliefs. (Section 7)

Interlocking Steps

There is an important omnibus context in which all three "steps to be taken"—the development, conservation, and diffusion of science—are integrally bound together in the process of teaching human rights to students of science, mathematics, engineering, and the health sciences. If the institutions, norms, and socially beneficial practice of science are to advance by the framers' steps, then policies supporting human rights education are needed, such as those initiated in 2001 by the Japanese Ministry of Education, Science, Sports and Culture. It called for an annual report to the Japanese Diet on "measures the Government has implemented to promote human rights education and human rights awareness raising."[13] Moreover, socially responsible education is needed in technical fields of study and in the development of informational resources. Initial efforts along popularly accessible lines include valuable Internet websites connecting science and human rights. For instance, the University of Texas posts a website titled "Human Rights, Science and

Technology Monitor," <www.cwrl.utexas.edu>, and the Harvard University School of Public Health sponsors the "Health and Human Rights" website of the François-Xavier Bagnourd Association, <www.//fxb.org>. The "Science and Human Rights" website of the American Association for the Advancement of Science is especially informative, offering a directory of human rights resources on the Internet, reporting current cases of human rights abuses of scientists, and describing projects undertaken by the Science and Human Rights Program, <shr.aaas.org>. UNESCO sustains a science and human rights agenda, which can be accessed on its website, <www.unesco.org>. Reflecting its wide ranging concerns, they published an important study in 1991 on *Women in Science: Token Women or Gender Equality.*

Taking all these resources into account, it nevertheless remains true that science, technology, engineering, and the health professions have been slow to integrate human rights materials and issues into their curricula and continuing educational training programs. Such educational programs have done little to align their fields of study with human rights norms and institutions despite standards of scientific freedom and responsibility alluded to in introductory textbooks.

Nevertheless, Caroline Whitbeck, professor of engineering ethics at the Massachusetts Institute of Technology, has shown a human rights component can be highly instructive especially in science and engineering ethics classes.[14] Some examples to which Whitbeck draws attention are the application of molecular biology to the forensic sciences, employing medical science for the care of torture survivors, and the implementation of the right to health based on civil engineering projects providing for clean water and sanitation systems. The human rights framework applied to such projects would eschew discrimination to ensure no one is denied the benefits of such programs. These kinds of issues aptly lend themselves for discussion of case studies. Engineering and science students take pride in being problem solvers, and so a problem-oriented approach to teaching ethics is a natural one for their classes "by engaging students in learning by doing." Certainly on the most fundamental level of scientific and engineering ethics, students in such technical fields need to be alerted to the essential requirements of scientific freedom necessary for the flourishing of their professions. Further discussion of this issue is presented in Chapter 10.

In 2000, MIT launched a Program for Human Rights and Justice sponsored by the Department of Urban Studies and Planning and the Center for International Studies. The initiative is premised on recognition that the impact of technology on human rights is profound in terms of the dangers to human security, whether in information technology, biotechnology, or energy systems. Moreover, human rights standards are beginning to be taken into account in other areas as well, transforming techno-logical and industrial planning in areas as divergent as hydroelectricity, mining, oil exploration, nuclear energy, defense, and extractive indus-tries. In view of these developments, one of the aims of the program is to promote the examination and analysis of the ethical and normative im-plications of modern science and technology in relation to human rights of individuals and communities. The MIT website is useful in learning more about the program, <web.mit.edu/phrj/homepage.html>.

Preserving Scientific Freedom

Let us now return to the covenant. The framers insisted that "The States Parties to the present Covenant undertake to respect the freedom indis-pensable for scientific research and creative activity" (Article 15.3). Such a straightforward proposition may appear self-evident. A review of the de-bate that raged around its formulation, however, reveals the hair-splitting objections that had to be overcome.

In the General Assembly, Mr. Vela (Guatemala) pointed out an ap-parent ambiguity in the provision.[15] He felt that the word "indispens-able" should be deleted because it could be interpreted in a restrictive sense. The Malaysian delegate agreed, urging dropping the word "indis-pensable" because it could be read as only that minimal freedom indis-pensable for scientific research need be respected.[16] Sir Samuel Hoare (UK) saved the original wording by insisting that it had been given the most careful deliberation in the Commission on Human Rights, where it was seen as enlarging the realm of freedom, even while recognizing that scientists could not be given absolute freedom in all of their work. For example, he said limitations could be set by disarmament agree-ments. Having acknowledged legitimate but limited state concerns for national security, the British delegate concluded that: "The Commission had recognized that the core of the right was protection extended to the kind of freedom indispensable for scientific research and creative activity, and that the provision should be directed to the protection of that free-dom."[17]

The scientific freedom embedded in Article 15 of the ESC Covenant is like a ship's anchor on which scientists daily depend, a mainstay for freedom of information, association, and inquiry. Sometimes taken for granted, when captains of state "haul anchor," setting scientific freedom adrift, its impact is quickly felt in democratic countries as well as those under authoritarian regimes. A modern-day example from Cuba and fur-ther on one from the United States show why scientific freedom should be broadly defined in terms of human rights.

In 1992 the physicist Leonardo Rodríguez Perez was expelled from his position at the Metallurgy Research Center in Havana.[18] He was among twenty professors and academics dismissed for signing or supporting a "Declaration of University Professors" to back the Universal Declaration of Human Rights, including academic freedom and freedom of association. According to the American Association for the Advancement of Science, Rodríguez Perez was but one of several scientists, engineers, and health professionals condemned to lengthy prison terms in Cuba, while others have been denied travel visas and otherwise harassed. In addition to violating Rodríguez Perez' Article 15 rights, the Cuban action also flew in the face of the Lima Declaration on Academic Freedom: "Every member of the academic community shall enjoy, in particular, freedom of thought, conscience, religion, expression, assembly and association as well as the right to liberty and security of the person and liberty of movement" (Article 4).

Sharing Science

To do their job, scientists must be able to freely interact with their colleagues through unrestricted communication and travel. The fourth and final paragraph of Article 15 says: "The States Parties to the present Covenant recognize the benefits to be derived from the encouragement and development of international contacts and co-operation in the scientific and cultural fields."

A revealing debate in the United Nations sheds light on the scope of the states parties' obligation to recognize the benefits of international contacts and cooperation in the scientific and cultural fields.[19] The original text called for "mutual contacts between scientific and cultural experts." Some asked: why only experts? If one is judging the quality of a house, to borrow Aristotle's analysis, then two types of knowledge are important: the expert knowledge of the architect and the assessment of those who live in the structure. In the same vein, covenant framers asked what about those of us who are not scientists but who enjoy the applications of their handiwork or suffer from their misuses. The "elitist" reference to experts was abandoned in favor of the phrase "in the scientific and cultural fields," to make clear that rights bearers are not only scientists and technical experts chosen by governments, universities and research laboratories. As explained by Mr. Hstad from Sweden, the change was necessary to show "that cultural and scientific relations between nations would not be in the hands only of experts chosen by the Governments and would therefore be as extensive and free as possible." The egalitarian phrasing of the measure reinforces the radical nature of the proposition that "everyone has the right to enjoy the benefits of scientific progress and its applications." The appeal of these principles applied to science was borne out in November 1957, when the entire article on science-related rights was adopted by the reviewing committee of the UN General Assembly by a unanimous vote.[20]

As against the precepts already set out, consider this counterexample of an abuse of the canons of Article 15. While the United States is not a party to the ESC Covenant, a well-documented blunder illustrates a clear violation of its international norms.[21] In 1994, the U.S. Department of State denied permission to Dr. R. Copote Noy, a Cuban nuclear physicist working on a research contract for the International Atomic Energy Agency, to attend an IAEA meeting in Oak Ridge, Tennessee. The IAEA is an international organization under the umbrella of the UN that fosters and guides the development of peaceful uses of atomic energy and establishes standards for nuclear safety and environmental protection. The meeting to which Dr. Noy was invited was, in fact, to review and discuss his work and the findings of eight other IAEA contractors doing research on related subjects. Because of the American refusal to allow the Cuban scientist's entry into the United States, the IAEA sought and found a new location for the meeting in another country. In pursuing this policy, the United States ignored the UNESCO Recommendations on the Status of Scientific Researchers,[22] which say

Member States should actively promote the interplay of ideas and information among scientific researchers throughout the world, which is vital to the healthy development of science and technology; and to this end should take all measures necessary to ensure that scientific researchers are enabled throughout their careers, to participate in international scientific and technological gatherings and to travel abroad. (Section 26)

Duties under Section 4 of Article 15 oblige states to recognize the benefits to be derived from the encouragement and development of international contacts and cooperation in the scientific and cultural fields. Where science is concerned, this obligation is closely connected to and doubly reinforced by the provisions of Article 15, mandating respect for the diffusion of science. As a minimum guarantee, scientists should have the freedom to maintain contact with their counterparts worldwide as well as the freedom to pursue the development of their educational capacities. By virtue of the right to cooperate freely with colleagues at home or abroad, members of the science community should enjoy freedom of movement within their country and freedom to travel outside and reenter their country. Such freedom should not be restricted unless absolutely necessary in a democratic society on grounds of national security and in accordance with international human rights law. If prohibiting Dr. Capote Noy from presenting his research in the United States con-

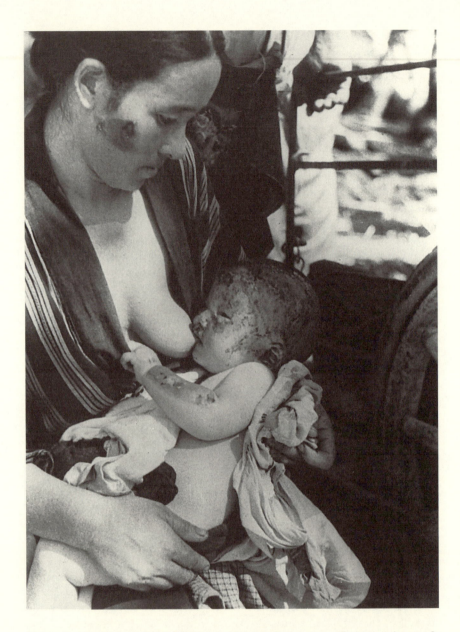

Figure 3. A mother and child in Nagasaki struggling to go on living on August 9, 1945, the day after the United States dropped an atomic bomb on the city. The attacks on Hiroshima and Nagasaki killed an estimated 110,000 Japanese and injured 130,000. By 1950 another 230,000 had died from injuries or radiation. The two cities were nominally military targets, but the overwhelming majority of the casualties were civilian. Courtesy of the United Nations, UN photo 149440 by Yosuke Yamahata.

stituted a threat to national security, the State Department did not meet the burden of justifying their exclusionary action.

Far from granting visas as a reward for the favored, states and intergovernmental organizations should actively promote cooperation between members of the scientific community as a good in itself, and as a means to ensure that the results of scientific and technological achievements are used cooperatively for purposes consistent with the UN Charter. Among such purposes identified in the Charter are several having the broadest potential impact on the lives of all people worldwide, that is, economic and social development, the realization of human rights and freedoms, and the strengthening of international peace (Article 55).

International Scientific Cooperation

Bringing people of diverse backgrounds together to discuss serious policy issues relating to international peace and security is the objective of the Pugwash Conferences on Science and World Affairs, as envisioned by its creators Albert Einstein and Bertrand Russell.[23] Noting that there exists no universal code of ethics for scientists, they sought to address this ethical void in 1955 by outlining the risks of thermonuclear war. This led to the Pugwash Movement, financed by Cleveland industrialist Cyrus Eaton, to provide a forum for scientists and others to analyze and promote the cause of international peace.

Pugwash meetings were organized, convening scientists and nonscientists to share views in the spirit of the framers of Article 15 who promoted inclusiveness for popular participation. The framers of Article 15 deliberately turned away from stipulating that a right to international contacts was exclusive to scientists, and Einstein and Russell saw no threat to the integrity of science or to the role of scientists by including nonprofessionals. Every few years, Pugwash participants assemble from around the world: young science and nonscience students and scholars and public figures concerned with the specter of nuclear harm, reducing the danger of armed conflict and seeking cooperative solutions for global problems.

While nongovernmental in makeup, Pugwash Conferences have occasionally relied on intergovernmental dissemination. Meeting in private as individuals, rather than as representatives of governments or institutions, Pugwash participants exchange views and explore alternative approaches to arms control and global tension reduction with a combination of candor and flexibility seldom attained in official East-West or North-South discussions and negotiations. Yet, because of the stature of many of the Pugwash participants in their own countries (including nuclear testing and arms advisers to governments and key figures in academies of science and universities), insights from Pugwash discussions often disseminate to the appropriate levels of official policy-making.

The first twenty years of Pugwash's history coincided with some of the most frigid years of the Cold War, marked by the Berlin Crisis, the Cuban Missile Crisis, the invasion of Czechoslovakia, and the Vietnam War. In this period of strained official relations and few unofficial channels, the forums and lines of communication it provided played useful background roles in helping lay the groundwork for the Partial Test Ban Treaty of 1963, the Non-Proliferation Treaty of 1968, the Anti-Ballistic Missile Treaty of 1972, the Biological Weapons Convention of 1972, and the Chemical Weapons Convention of 1993. In 1995, the Pugwash Conferences on Science and World Affairs was awarded the Nobel Peace Prize.

With the end of the Cold War, irresponsible nuclear energy policies, so frequently discussed in Pugwash Conferences, continue to harass humankind. For example, during the early 1990s, the nuclear power industry in Europe was engaged in the international transfer of costs and risks associated with the use of fissionable materials to generate energy.[24] With little or no market left for nuclear plants in the West, Western nuclear vendors marketed their products and services in Eastern Europe, financially benefitting because of minimum regulation. Among many examples, the *Bulletin of the Atomic Scientists* revealed that Hungary invited bids for two thousand megawatts of new capacity, twice its projected need. In turn, Western partners received electricity with neither the expense nor the risk of operating, fueling, or decommissioning the generating plants. Meanwhile the Eastern partners, underbudgeted and historically saddled with low-technology disposal systems, accepted not only the costs of fuel, but the hazards of nuclear waste disposal with all the health liabilities that meant for hundreds of employees. The situation seemed to reflect the nightmare conditions of a world without rules, as if Article 15 were nonexistent. It clearly means that the applications of science should not be engineered in ways that jeopardize other fundamental rights. But that is precisely what happened soon after the collapse of socialist regimes, endangering rights to life and health in Eastern Europe because of Western nuclear marketing strategies.

Advancing Article 15 Rights in the Future

To be effective, especially in response to complex issues like nuclear energy trades disadvantaging Eastern Europe, the ESC Treaty Committee requires substantive, analytical, expert research support because the issues they address are complex. Yet the committee is hobbled by a very small staff and historically low budget. Consequently, the committee members complain of inadequate staff research to provide an independent basis on which to conduct critical assessments of state reports. To fill the gap, NGO participation in the activities of the committee is important (see Appendix B, fourth objective). For example, under the terms of the state reporting system, NGOs are able to make "shadow reports," filing critical challenges addressed to the committee to draw offending governments into a process of query and response to explain or defend their short-comings.[25] In 1993, the Committee on Economic, Social and Cultural Rights sought more active NGO participation, saying it "reiterates its long-standing invitation to NGOs to submit to it in writing, at any time, information regarding any aspect of its work."[26] To the extent that NGO critiques of state reports reflect careful independent research, the committee's work can become more effective. If this goal is achieved, despite countervailing political and sectarian forces, it is because scientists, engineers, health professionals, and the general public support open debate and freely exchanged ideas as essential to the success of the scientific enterprise in the new millennium.

We live in a world of ever more rapid technological change, the globalization of national economies, and the shrinking role of the state. These challenges serve only to emphasize the importance of the UN capacity to deal with technological issues and the public's role in taking a heightened interest in the promotion and safeguarding of Article 15 rights. In 1996, Osman El-Hajjé presented a working paper to the United Nations calling for an annual report to the General Assembly designed to keep the organization and the public's eye on human rights issues adversely affected by technological developments.[27] The recommendation is certainly constructive, but presupposes an institutional capacity to receive, critically assess, and act on such information. According to one observer of the UN, its use of science knowledge historically has been problematic. In 2000, Calestous Juma, a Harvard University specialist on science policy, argued that most UN agencies are not well organized to tap into advisory services and independent sources of information on science and technology.[28] Without specifically referencing the ESC Committee, he noted the particular needs of treaty committees to provide opportunities for NGO participation as a way of rallying the input of the scientific and technological community to the benefit of the UN goals. Interest in the full spectrum of interrelated human rights requires that NGOs, science and health professionals, and the public become cognizant of their Article 15 rights so that they can take on more responsibility in holding states accountable for transgressions. It follows that NGOs, scientific associations, and other nonstate knowledge–based organizations must become more alert and prepared to offer treaty committees the benefits of their technical expertise.

Conclusions

The emerging debate over science accountability involves many hotly contested positions and perspectives. On the one hand, there are those who argue pragmatically that the potential contribution that the ESC Committee can realistically make lies in holding states parties to account as the duty-bearers. They bear the burden to explain offending decisions and failings, to account for the obstacles to overcoming human rights violations, and to respond to allegations by NGOs of state violations of human rights under the Covenant on Economic, Social and Cultural Rights. This prospect will remain unrealized unless NGOs become fully active in monitoring ESC rights violations, filing reports challenging presentations required of states parties, and assembling data-based indicators, including indicators showing trends over time, helpful in forming critical judgments by members of the ESC Committee. The committee will need to rely on such technical information if they choose to play an advisory role in prompting states parties to improve their record of compliance with Article 15 rights.

A more visionary perspective regarding the future of science and human rights was formulated by Judge C. G. Weeramantry of the International Court of Justice.[29] Appropriately wary of regulation affecting the scientific enterprise, he points out, "as one travels up the scale from internally induced self-awareness to externally imposed rules of conduct, there is a progressive erosion of the autonomy of the profession." "Ideally," he concluded, "all regulation should come from within." At the same time, Weeramantry is an ardent champion of the Economic, Social and Cultural Rights Covenant. Thus, he calls for implementation of Article 15 by initiatives that "come from within"—reflecting programs of human rights implementation without "externally imposed rules of conduct." By this logic, the optimal situation would involve "externally adopted standards" (international human rights) gradually infusing themselves by education into the internal consciousness of people, including the general public, and scientists and scientific professional associations with updated codes of ethics with specific links to human rights. In the real world, this is less likely to happen if such codes do not reference human rights, if science education inadequately emphasizes human rights, and if NGOs fail to mobilize effective challenges to practices that threaten Article 15 rights. On all of these fronts, progress is needed. Otherwise, states will continue as they have routinely to present self-serving reports to the UN Committee on Economic, Social and Cultural Rights where too little is heard of everyone's right "to enjoy the benefits of the advancements of science and its applications."

II
Issues

In 1993 the World Conference on Human Rights meeting in Vienna acknowledged that certain advances, notably in the biomedical and life sciences, as well as in information technology "may have potentially adverse consequence for the integrity, dignity and human rights of the individual."[1] In 1996, a UN unit followed up on this view when the Sub-Commission on the Prevention of Discrimination and Protection of Minorities called for a study on the "potentially adverse consequences for human rights of scientific progress and its applications."

Mr. Osman El-Hajjé published his working paper for the United Nations in 1997, calling for international watchfulness lest scientific and technological advances bring with them "disaster or misfortune."[2] At the same time, the author noted the counterbalancing need for "respecting scientists' rights to freedom and dignity." The working paper pinpointed issues arising under the heading of science and human rights, noting they do not lend themselves easily to classification. The reason is that scientific activity is extremely wide ranging and encompasses all aspects of human life. With that in mind, the author nevertheless argued that there are some areas of scientific activity "which appear more risky than others and which require constant attention: (1) medicine and health, and (2) computing and internet technology." These areas of problematic issues correspond to the topics presented, respectively, in Chapters 5 and 6.

Medicine and Health

In Chapter 5, "Health and Medical Ethics," I offer as background on this broad topic a recapitulation of the early years of the United Nations and the original formulation of the right to health and medical care found in the Universal Declaration of Human Rights. Using a historical perspective, the chapter then recounts the famous "Nuremberg Doctors' Trial," the results of which foreshadowed standards formalized in codes of medical ethics, with particular attention to prohibitions on practices violating human rights. Chapter 5 elaborates specific examples of such abuses, including the imposition of unfair risks on subjects in clinical studies, medical experimentation without informed consent, and violations of physician-patient confidentiality. The chapter concludes with some discussion of standards of "medical neutrality" under wartime conditions.

The UN working paper identified health and medical issues emerging on the horizon in 1997 and noted the hazards they could pose to human rights and fundamental freedoms. These include potentially adverse consequences for human rights arising from recent medical developments. Because such issues take on concrete definition in the real world and first gained notice as issues spotlighted by activists and human rights advocacy groups, I locate my discussion of them in later chapters. For example, my discussion of psychiatric treatment for torture survivors is in Chapter 7 where it illustrates "science activism" at its best. That chapter also reviews developing public policy on cloning and the human genome. Public attention to another category of problems was first sparked by NGOs, and for that reason, the challenge of securing access to pharmaceutical treatments for persons suffering from HIV/AIDS is spotlighted in the profiles of two private groups, Doctors without Borders, and the Southern Center for Human Rights, both discussed in Chapter 8. Chapter 5 introduces the United Nations Special Session Declaration of Commitment on HIV/AIDS. An analysis of human rights problems linked to biomedical patenting and genetic research figures in my account of the heroic campaign of British women concerned with the identification of genetic markers for breast cancer, explored in Chapter 9 where the focus is on citizen activism.

Computing and Internet Technology

The UN working paper referenced above said that while the Internet and worldwide web potentially provide many benefits for the cause of human rights, these advances also "broaden the gap between rich countries equipped with computers and others which are not," unless specific help is provided for them to catch up. In addition to that problem, one harmful effect of the Internet, according to El-Hajjé's paper, is that it "surreptitiously introduces an 'outsider' into the family circle," for example, by providing pornography accessible to children, presenting threats to privacy rights, and spreading messages of hatred.

Chapter 6 discusses the Internet and related privacy issues, noting expanding efforts to bring Internet technology to less-developed countries. The use of the Internet to transmit data on human rights violations leads into a discussion of the ways whereby statistics, the workhorse of scientific methodology, can supply a useful tool applied to human rights issues. The chapter discusses the important new development of quantitative approaches to human rights, showcasing a model Central American example of the constructive use of information systems and data analysis applied to human rights cases. Under the heading of technological abuses, the chapter also notes an example from the Pinochet regime in Chile in which the government sought to invade the secrecy of a human rights data collection, and another from the Marcos regime in the Philippines when statistical data were manipulated by the government to soft pedal its record of human rights abuses. Finally, insomuch as the 1993 Vienna action plan of the World Conference on Human Rights called for efforts such as statistical indicators to measure progress toward realizing economic, social and cultural rights, Chapter 6 concludes with a discussion of such indicators.

The UN paper identifying troublesome human rights issues linked to science and technology concluded by sounding a note of caution, saying that, on the one hand, excessive regulation of science might readily hamper progress, while on the other hand, practices that are dangerous for human health and freedom may become too commonplace.[3] In search of a middle ground, avoiding burdensome international regulations, the working paper called for the establishment of an International Committee of Ethics concerned with human rights to monitor emerging problems and to "draw up an annual report on the state of science and technology for submission to the General Assembly." While the suggestion seems constructive, it begs the question of whether such annual reports, perhaps followed by sharply crafted declarations, can keep pace with the advance of technology.

Chapter 5
Health and Medical Ethics

It is the privilege of the medical doctor to practice medicine in the
service of humanity, to preserve and restore bodily and mental
health without discrimination as to persons, to comfort and to ease
the suffering of his or her patients.
 — The Declaration of Tokyo, World Medical Association, 1975

In this chapter, I depict some of the history behind UN efforts to define
international standards for everyone's right to health and to medical care.
I also invoke historical memories of the atrocious medical experiments
by Nazi doctors to show how the Nuremburg Doctors' Trial contributed
to shaping globally recognized standards of medical ethics that incorpo-
rate human rights norms. Consistent with the violations approach employed in earlier chapters, instructive cases are profiled of abuses of these
standards. Finally, I reference the tragic Balkan wars of the 1990s to remind the reader of the relevance of humanitarian law, which supple-
ments human rights standards, extending protection to health professionals performing their life-saving duties under conditions of armed
conflict.

Formulating the "Right to Health"

In 1941, U.S. President Franklin D. Roosevelt announced his Four Freedoms plan (freedom of speech and expression, freedom of worship,
freedom from want, and freedom from fear).[1] "Freedom means the su-
premacy of human rights everywhere," Roosevelt announced, concluding that such a world "is the very antithesis" of that "which the dictators
seek to create with the crash of a bomb."

Soon after the war's end, work began on proclamations of rights by labor, religious, and civil rights groups. Moreover, the Conference of American States meeting in Bogotá in early 1948 prepared a bill of rights that later placed Latin American countries in support of UN efforts favoring social, economic, and cultural rights, including provisions relating to health, medicine, and science. On these topics, the American Declaration of the Rights and Duties of Man served as a model for the later United Nations Universal Declaration of Human Rights.[2]

As chairperson of the Human Rights Commission, Mrs. Eleanor Roosevelt worked closely with Canadian professor John P. Humphrey, the agency's director. His role on science-linked rights was noted in Chapter 2, and his behind-the-scenes influence was important on health rights as well. He admired the concept of the Four Freedoms and his sympathies linked him to the Latin Americans with their expansive ideas of human rights. Various NGOs formalized plans for a human rights-friendly world. It was Humphrey's job to review such recommendations, and he noted his confidence in the work of a Western NGO, the American Law Institute (ALI), describing it as "the best of the texts . . . and I borrowed freely from it."[3] For example, reflecting provisions from the ALI brief, his draft proposed articles saying: "Everyone has the right to medical care"; and "The State shall promote public health and safety." Another specified, "Everyone has the right to social security; the State shall maintain effective arrangements for the prevention of unemployment and for insurance against the risks of unemployment, accident, disability, sickness, old age, and other involuntary or undeserved loss of livelihood."

The ALI measures avoided ideological shoals by saying that the satisfaction of health and medical care rights "leaves full scope to private initiative, in countries where it is considered desirable." Nevertheless, according to the NGO, whether health rights depend on state and/or private sponsorship, duty-bearers should direct their efforts to several objectives. They should try to raise standards of health, prevent sickness and accident, and provide medical care wherever needed, including for maternity cases. Based on these views, the drafting committee produced a document with strong guidance for public health policy. It gave the right to health a priority profile, emphasizing that its realization not only required access to medical care, but also to adequate food, nutrition, clothing, and housing.[4]

Debate over social and economic rights sparked arguments about duties and duty-bearers. This, in turn, led to a decision to bifurcate drafting efforts into a declaration—stipulating the menu of human rights—and a convention—specifying the duties of states and others. In the light of that series of decisions, Mrs. Roosevelt made the case for the avoidance of detail in the declaration.[5] She said that such a document—necessarily simple and concise—has two functions:

1. To serve as basic standards to guide the United Nations in achieving, within the meaning of the Charter, international co-operation in promoting and encouraging respect for and observance of human rights and fundamental freedoms for all;

and

2. To serve as a guide and inspiration to individuals and groups throughout the world in their efforts to promote respect for and observance of human rights.

With Roosevelt's strong leadership and with consensus developing about what kind of document it was formulating, the drafting committee appointed by the commission rapidly completed a preliminary version of a declaration worth circulating.

Optimism drove most of the framers of the Universal Declaration from June 1947, when the Commission on Human Rights first considered a preliminary outline of a human rights charter until all UN delegates meeting as members of the permanent Third Committee reviewed it, and then in December 1948 the General Assembly adopted and proclaimed the Declaration. In a time-consuming exercise in the age of slow-moving communication, the text prepared by the Drafting Committee and revised by the commission was sent to every member government for its comments and suggestions. Thereafter it wound its way through the full commission, the Economic and Social Council, and 81 meetings and 168 proposed amendments of the General Assembly's Third Committee before ending up substantially changed in the case of health provisions. Finally, the draft Declaration was sent to the General Assembly convening in Paris in September 1948. There, despite vetting over the preceding two years, the General Assembly's Social, Humanitarian and Cultural Committee tore it apart once more and revised it line by line and even word by word.[6]

Connecting Health and the Right to Medical Care

The language and terms used in Article 25 of the Universal Declaration of Human Rights finally settled into this language:

1. Everyone has the right to a standard of living adequate for the health and well-being of himself and of his family, including food, clothing, housing and medical care and necessary social services, and the right to security in the event of unemployment, sickness, disability, widowhood, old age or other lack of livelihood in circumstances beyond his control.

2. Motherhood and childhood are entitled to special care and assistance. All children, whether or not in or out of wedlock, shall enjoy the same social protection.

Elements of the debates and dynamics of the drafting process responsible for this language help to clarify its meaning. For example, the International Labor Organization played a leading role in promoting the concept of an "adequate standard of living" as the hook on which to hang the right to health. Mrs. Roosevelt, in her capacity as the U.S. member, supported this approach, despite Soviet thrusts and parries to pin health rights to government funding and related programs of "social security" and "social insurance."[7] Alexie Pavlov's effort was doomed by the demonstration that the meaning of these terms referring to social programs differed greatly in various countries. On point, Geoffrey Wilson (UK) said he could not accept the Soviet conception of pervasive state responsibility because in Great Britain, social insurance was the charge of the state, employer, and the worker, and the Declaration should not embody "text which compel a country to alter completely a system of social insurance which was entirely satisfactory."

Having lost the commission members willingness to go along with him in tying social and economic rights too closely to state sponsorship, Pavlov, nevertheless, successfully gathered support for a right to medical care.[8] He fought persuasively in support of the phrase "well-being . . . including . . . medical care." His argument was that, absent any reference to social insurance or security programs, the right to health by itself did not sufficiently imply a right to medical care. With endorsements from René Cassin and several delegates who routinely followed his lead, Pavlov's notion of an independent right to medical care was then accepted in a new version linking "health and well-being" to "food, clothing, housing and medical care." When these provisions were later debated in the General Assembly, the Soviet delegate again garnered consensus for his view that "medical assistance was not merely an item in an adequate standard of living but a specific right."

The Chinese delegation showed diplomatic and drafting skill in settling the first paragraph of the article into its final form. Peng-chun Chang's omnibus draft language rejected Soviet efforts to turn "the right to security" into a "right to social security" (already specified elsewhere in the Declaration). The votes behind this move opened the way to a more general notion, "the right to security in the event of unemployment, sickness, disability, widowhood, old age or other lack of livelihood." Finally, focusing on the phrase "in circumstances beyond his control," the Norwegians asked for its deletion but lost by a vote of 20 to 6, after Chang argued that "it would be well to include the words because they would tend to encourage self-reliance."[9]

Article 25 of the Universal Declaration of Human Rights calls for the protection of mothers and children. Following a recommendation of the Commission on the Status of Women, Mrs. Roosevelt explained to the General Assembly that a special paragraph should focus on this topic.[10] It met no objection but did prompt a debate on how to ensure that references to the child would equally include rights of the "child born out of wedlock." Again, the Chinese omnibus proposal finessed this issue by dropping language about the rights of mothers and children of whatever social status in favor of the more abstract assertion that "motherhood and childhood are entitled to special care and assistance." This reification of women and children into an abstract category distressed the Yugoslav and Norwegian delegations, who garnered support for the additional proposition: "All children, whether born in or out of wedlock, shall enjoy the same social protection." Mohammed Habib (India) summarized the discussion by stating "the firm conviction that the sins of the parents should not be visited upon the children."

The "Covering Article"

The United Nations formulation of a right to health linked to medical care was a landmark achievement, but it was not meant to be read alone, taking on added meaning from related provisions. Article 25 is supposed to be read in tandem with Article 22, which the General Assembly discussed as the "covering article" recommended by the Human Rights Commission. The "covering" feature consists in supplying additional overall context for all social, economic and cultural rights. Article 22 says:

Everyone, as a member of society, has the right to social security and is entitled to realization, through national effort and international co-operation and in accordance with the organization and resources of each State, of the economic, social and cultural rights indispensable for the dignity and the free development of his personality.

As can be seen in this text, the right to social security was not defined. Nevertheless it takes on elaborated meaning in Article 25 by reference to the "right to security in the event of unemployment, sickness, disability," and the like. Correspondingly, the right to health is supported by social security claims stipulated in Article 22. Yet this entire framework of interdependent rights is conceded to vary with state capacity relative to national resources and augmented by "international cooperation."[11] Such international cooperation includes collaboration and support among governmental, intergovernmental, and nongovernmental organization and professionals societies working in support of human rights across national boundaries (see examples in Chapter 8).

The Right to Health in the Covenant

The health and medical care provisions of the Universal Declaration of Human Rights are tracked in comparable measures in the International Covenant on Economic, Social and Cultural Rights (see Appendix A). Here the language emphasizes the responsibilities of those who are treaty-bound by the covenant:

Article 12. (1) The States Parties to the present Covenant recognize the right of everyone to the enjoyment of the highest attainable standard of physical and mental health. (2) The steps to be taken by the States Parties to the present Covenant to achieve the full realization of this right shall include those necessary for: (a) The provision for the reduction of the stillbirth-rate and of infant mortality and for the healthy development of the child; (b) The improvement of all aspects of environmental and industrial hygiene; (c) The prevention, treatment and control of epidemic, endemic, occupational and other diseases; (d) The creation of conditions which would assure to all medical service and medical attention in the event of sickness.

In the drafting of Article 12 of the covenant, discussion within the Third Committee of the General Assembly shows its framers saw the right to health as embracing a wide range of socioeconomic factors that promote conditions in which people can lead a healthy life, and extends to the conditions affecting health such as food and nutrition. This expansive concept of the right to health was significantly elaborated in 2000.

That year the Committee on Economic, Social and Cultural Rights issued important guidelines "based on years of experience in examining States Parties reports." As noted in Chapter 4, such reports are required to ensure states' accountability to the treaty committee, which in turn seeks to assist them in implementation. According to UN staff attorneys, guidelines issued in General Comment Number 14 are increasingly seen as the authoritative interpretation of the content of the right to health.[12] It is consistent with the World Health Organization's definition of health as "a state of complete physical, mental and social well-being and not merely the absence of disease or infirmity."[13]

The committee's comments on the "normative content of Article 12" explain that the right to health should not be seen as a right to be healthy. Rather it is best interpreted as containing both freedoms and entitlements. The freedoms include the right to control one's health and body, including sexual and reproductive freedom, and the right to be free from interference, such as the right to be free from torture, nonconsensual medical treatment, and experimentation. On the other hand, the entitlements include the right to a system of health protection that provides equality of opportunity for people to enjoy the highest attainable level of health, consistent with available national resources.

Comment 14 explained that the right to health should be interpreted as an inclusive right. That means that it extends not only to timely and appropriate health care but also to the underlying determinates of health, such as:

* access to safe and potable water and adequate sanitation;
* an adequate supply of safe food, nutrition, and housing;
* healthy occupational and environmental conditions; and
* access to health-related education and information, including on sexual and reproductive health.

Finally, the committee said the right should be interpreted to carry the meaning that people have a right to participate in health-related decision making.

In 2001, an international group from more than fifty countries of health care workers, ethicist, and representatives of civil society undertook the development of a "Draft Declaration on Human Rights and Health Practice." It seeks to bring the significance of Comment 14 home to health practitioners, pressing emphatically for the professional responsibility to promote human rights as a condition for people's health and well-being. In so doing, according to one of those involved in the initiative, the interdependence of human rights is the key concept of the Draft Declaration. Vincent Iacopino, M.D., argues that we need a better understanding of the fact that human rights violations have consequences for people's health, as is plain when one considers the health-wasting results of war, rape in armed conflict, torture, famine, and forced migration. In Iacopino's memorable terms, "the entire Universal Declaration of Human Rights is a platform for the right to health." Health professionals must become human rights advocates.[14]

A year after the General Comment 14 was published, the UN Human Rights Commission drew attention to the new interpretation of the right to health, saying it bears directly on the HIV/AIDS pandemic, which in 2001 took a toll of 5,000 lives daily. With the exception of the United States, which abstained from voting, the fifty-three members of the Human Rights Commission acknowledged that the right to health includes access to "facilities, goods, services and conditions necessary for the realization of the highest attainable standard of health," and this means that providing resources to address the catastrophe is a matter of human rights, seen not in a spirit of humanitarian generosity, but as a responsibility. The commission also called on governments to protect those who reveal their HIV status and to combat the stigmatization of "women, children and vulnerable groups" afflicted with the disease.[15]

The Universal Declaration of Human Rights and parallel provisions of the Human Rights Covenants represent a triumph of the pen over the sword. Where the right to health is concerned, its formulation in UN instruments has gained influence in scope and over time. For example, beyond the four pillars and pediment of the UDHR, the document's health provisions intersect with other international norms. They correlate with and in some instances they are even embedded in standards of medical ethics and humanitarian law.

The Nuremberg Doctors' Trial

The framers of the Universal Declaration of Human Rights closely followed developments in the postwar trial in Nuremberg of Nazi war criminals. It influenced the debate on how or whether to connect human rights, medicine, and science in the Universal Declaration.[16] Indeed, several fundamental standards of medical ethics are anchored in human rights norms. For example, in unqualified language, the Declaration rebukes the cruelty attested at Nuremberg and suffered by millions during the war years saying: "No one shall be subject to torture or to cruel, inhuman or degrading treatment or punishment" (Article 5). The Preamble to the Universal Declaration of Human Rights says that it was formulated for many reasons, including humankind's "outraged conscience" over "barbarous acts" resulting from "disregard and contempt for human rights."

On that point, the International Covenant on Civil and Political Rights codified the Declaration's provisions in a solemn international treaty to which most countries are parties, including the United States. Article 7 of the 1976 Covenant repeats the language of the Universal Declaration of Human Rights forbidding "torture or cruel, inhuman or degrading treatment or punishment." But the covenant goes further, stating that "no one shall be subjected without his free consent to medical or scientific experimentation." The UN delegates participating in the drafting of the covenant attached strong significance to the second sentence as a result of the atrocities of the Nazi experimentation and so agreed it deserved a special provision, even at the risk of repetition of the first sentence.[17] The result is that medical experimentation without informed consent is a violation of Article 7 of the International Covenant on Civil and Political Rights and therefore a violation of international law.

The historical predicate for this provision was documented after the war when the allied powers initiated a succession of criminal proceedings that detailed Nazi atrocities. Its most famous sessions in Nuremberg involved military officers of the Third Reich. Other trials implicated soldiers, industrialists, and politicians. The separate "Doctors' Trials" presented ghastly images of physicians trained in the pseudoscience of eugenics and undertaking concentration camp experiments on unwilling prisoners.[18] As explained by Brigadier General Telford Taylor, the trial of the twenty-three defendants fully laid out the details of science and medicine run amuck under Nazi sway. Taylor was the chief counsel for the trails of war criminals, and he made the opening statement in the "Case against the Nazi Physicians" on December 9, 1946, saying:

The defendants in the dock are charged with murder, but this is no mere murder trail. . . . These defendants did not kill in hot blood, nor for personal enrichment. They are not ignorant men. Most of them are trained physicians and some of them are distinguished scientists.[19]

Accused of war crimes and crimes against humanity, fifteen of the twenty-three defendants were found guilty. Seven were found not guilty, and one was acquitted of the charges of having performed medical experiments but was found guilty of SS membership. Among those condemned was Edwin Katzenellenbogen, erstwhile member of the faculty of Harvard Medical School.

The legacy of the Nazi doctors' trials is found in the Nuremberg Code, which summarizes the rules that all medical researchers must follow when conducting experiments on humans. The voluntary consent standards of the code are spelled out here in combination with a modern-day example of their violation.

The first principle of the Nuremberg Code deals with informed consent.

The voluntary consent of the human subject is absolutely essential. This means that the person involved should have legal capacity to give consent, should be so situated as to be able to exercise free power of choice, without the intervention of any element of force, fraud, deceit, duress, overreaching or other ulterior form of constraint or coercion; and should have sufficient knowledge and comprehension of the elements of the subject matter involved as to enable him to make an understanding and enlightened decision.[20]

Although some of the principles in the code rely on utilitarian standards, that philosophy does not clarify the entire code. For as Dr. Ruth Macklin points out: "If utility were the only fundamental ethical principle, there would be no need to obtain informed consent from research subjects when the research is likely to yield great benefits to future patients while posing little risk of harm to the patients themselves."[21] Rather the principles of Immanuel Kant echo through the code, in

Figure 4. Kosovar Albanian doctors in Mitrovica protesting "ethnic discrimination" in 1999. They were squeezed out of the hospital where they traditionally
practiced but which was on the Serb side of the Ibar River. Calling for UN intervention, they publicly protested violations of medical neutrality in Kosovo, align-
ing themselves with the standards of the World Medical Association. Courtesy of
Physicians for Human Rights USA.

Dr. Macklin's view. Professor of bioethics at the Albert Einstein College of
Medicine, she summarizes the Kantian principle of respect for the person
as incorporating "at least two ethical convictions: first, that individuals
should be treated as autonomous agents, and second, that people with
diminished autonomy are entitled to protection." On the principle that
human beings should be treated by each other as ends not means, the
UDHR Preamble begins by emphasizing that international human rights
are premised on the "recognition of the inherent dignity and . . . the equal
and inalienable rights of all members of the human family."

Human Rights and Medical Ethics

The early, specific and direct influence of the Nuremberg Code on the
medical profession is well documented. In various international normative formulations, the principles enumerated in the code have been am-

The Declaration of Geneva
At the Time of Being Admitted as a Member of the Medical Profession:

- I Solemnly Pledge Myself to Consecrate My Life to the Service of Humanity;
- I Will Give to My Teachers the Respect and Gratitude Which Is Their Due;
- I Will Practice My Profession with Conscience and Dignity;
- the Health of My Patient Will Be My First Consideration;
- I Will Respect the Secrets Which Are Confided in Me, Even After the Patient Has Died;
- I Will Maintain by All the Means in My Power, the Honor and the Noble Traditions of the Medical Profession;
- My Colleagues Will Be My Sisters and Brothers;
- I Will Not Permit Considerations of Age, Disease or Disability, Creed, Ethnic Origin, Gender, Nationality, Political Affiliation, Race, Sexual Orientation, or Social Standing to Intervene Between My Duty and My Patient;
- I Will Maintain the Utmost Respect for Human Life from its Beginning Even under Threat and I Will Not Use My Medical Knowledge Contrary to the Laws of Humanity;
- I Make These Promises Solemnly, Freely and upon My Honor.

The World Medical Association, 1948, 1968, 1983

plified: informed consent, physician responsibility, welfare of the patient and research subject, and risk-benefit analysis. The World Medical Association (WMA), founded in 1947 soon after the Code was promulgated, determined that ethical guidelines were urgently needed, including an elaboration of the Hippocratic Oath in the Declaration of Geneva (1948, see box).

The Nuremberg principles have numerous progeny in terms of the development of modern standards. The WMA Declaration was reformulated and expanded, for example, in the International Code of Medical Ethics and the 1975 Declaration of Tokyo, which forbids doctor attendance in torture sessions. It quite deliberately echoes language prohibiting torture from the Universal Declaration of Human Rights and alludes to the Geneva Conventions. It says that doctors:

shall not countenance, condone or participate in the practice of torture or other forms of cruel, inhuman or degrading procedures, whatever the offense of which the victim of such procedures is suspected, accused or guilty, and whatever the victim's beliefs or motives, and in all situations, including armed conflict and civil strife.

Today there are several foundational ethical guidelines for human subjects protection that build on the Nuremberg tradition and are now found in medical association codes of ethics. Simply identifying the topics involved in such codes helps one to appreciate the broad and complex scope of this important field. Ethical guidelines cover the following:

- informed, voluntary consent;
- the right to withdraw from participation in a research project;
- caution in using recruitment incentives for such participation;
- disclosure of alternatives;
- problems of proxy consent or community consent;
- the use of placebos;
- risk-benefit balance in research and treatment and fair distribution of risks and benefits;
- protection of vulnerable participants;
- research participant confidentiality;
- institutional or other committee review boards;
- conflict of roles;
- physician referrals; and
- innovative therapy versus research.

The continuing relevance today of these standards are demonstrated by several modern examples. Below are contemporary cases of violations of medical ethics and human rights concerning abuses of informed consent requirements, and violations of norms protecting doctor-patient confidentiality. The first example, from the United States, imposed grossly unfair risks on the research participants; the second, from Sub-Saharan Africa, involves medical researchers culpable of professional wrongdoing; and the third, from Turkey, implicates government officials in cruelly abusing the care givers of torture victims.

Unfairly Imposed Risks: The Tuskegee Study in the United States

Between 1932 and 1972, the U.S. Public Health Service (PHS) conducted a notorious long-term study of the tertiary effects of syphilis. The participants were 399 poor African American men infected with syphilis and living in rural Alabama. PHS researchers kept the participants in the study from knowing the nature of their disease, telling them instead that they were being treated for "bad blood." In exchange for free treatment, the participants were discouraged from seeking any alternative medicines, and they were denied penicillin in the 1940s when it became useful.

Public health historians Amy L. Fairchild and Ronald Bayer concluded that the Tuskegee study serves as a standard of research abuse, violating multiple elements of professional ethics and the Nuremberg Code.[22] The study

- relied on deception regarding the very existence and nature of the inquiry into which individuals were lured;
- entailed social vulnerability to recruit and retain the participants; and
- featured a willful effort to deprive subjects of access to appropriate and available medical care to further the study's goals.

On May 16, 1997, President William Clinton formally apologized to the families of the deceased and to the eight surviving subjects, who were invited to the White House. In addition to acknowledging that the PHS conduct of the study was "profoundly, morally wrong," the president also announced support for the establishment at the Tuskegee Institute in Alabama of a bioethics museum combined with a research and health care center "to ensure that medical research practices are sound and ethical."

The Absence of Informed Consent in HIV Research in Africa.

A shameful violation of the principle of the Hippocratic Oath—"first do no harm"—concerns the transfer of health risks to Sub-Saharan Africa. The circumstances giving rise to the African scandal were detailed by Michael Day in *New Scientist,* showing that the sheer density of HIV infection in Sub-Saharan Africa lured large-scale studies of vaccines and drugs by Western drug companies and medical researchers . . . "taking ethical short cuts in poor countries."[23] In 1997, Michael W. Adler, M.D., reported in *The Lancet* on harmful medical investigatory procedures in early research on HIV infections.[24] Expatriots along with local nationals took blood samples from infected persons in Sub-Saharan African countries using methods that would not be allowed in Europe or North America. Adler said techniques of gathering blood samples amounted to "coercive and unethical research, which was done without proper information and consent procedures." Further, according to Adler, the research involved had no immediate relevance to local communities. "People were no more than arms to be bled, forgotten about once the needle was removed." Indeed, he characterized the research using persons infected with the HIV virus as "grab and run freezer-filling work."

These practices run headlong into the first Nuremberg principle which says the voluntary consent of the human subject is absolutely essential. Day and Adler concluded that those contributing blood did not "have sufficient knowledge and comprehension of the elements of the subject matter involved as to enable [them] to make an understanding and enlightened decision." Using clarifying language in 1964, this standard was elaborated in the World Medical Association's Declaration of Helsinki: "In any research on human beings, each potential subject must be adequately informed of the aims, methods, anticipated benefits and potential hazards of the study and the discomfort it may entail" (Section 1.9). The WMA also said those offered placebos for research purposes should not be left untreated: "In any medical study, every patient, including those of a control group, if any, should be assured of the best proven diagnostic and therapeutic methods" (Section II.3).[25]

Among the ethical and human rights problems involved in the situations described by Day and Adler, was the injustice done to those who bore the risks and burdens of investigation but did not share the benefits. Moreover, as a matter of "everyone's right to enjoy the benefits of science," the HIV research under fire by Day and Adler was inconsistent with guidelines from the UN Declaration on the Use of Science (1975; see Chapter 3, box). Referring to international cooperation for beneficial purposes, it says, "All States shall cooperate in the establishment, strengthening and development of the scientific and technological capacity of developing countries with a view to accelerating the realization of the social and economic rights of the peoples of those countries" (Section 5). This standard for international cooperation has largely been honored in the breach, with a salutary exception in 2001.

That year the UN constructively initiated the formation of UNAIDS, an organization empowered to negotiate with drug companies to respond to the African situation. As a result several European countries volunteered support, and in the United States, Bristol-Myers Squibb Company, Merck & Company and Abbott Laboratories were the first to announce their willingness to sell AIDS medicines "below cost" to Sub-Saharan African countries. They also pledged to allow South Africa to bypass company patents on related drugs. Not commenting on the time and lives lost by unethically undertaken blood sampling during the 1990s, UNAIDS greeted these developments saying "the pharmaceutical companies are now very seriously seeking to improve further the affordability of their medicines."[26] An important international feature of the UNAIDS program is a commitment to strengthen international regional cooperation,

in particular North/South and South/South transfer of relevant technologies suitable to the environment in the prevention and care of the
afflicted.

The call to action was premised on recognition of the human right to
health and medical care.[27] Thus, the UN Declaration of Commitment on
HIV/AIDS said international action was needed, among other reasons,
because:

- Sub-Saharan Africa . . . is currently the worst affected region where
  HIV/AIDS is considered as a state of emergency. In that area, it threat-
  ens development, social cohesion, political stability, food security and
  life expectancy and imposes a devastating economic burden . . . [in
  need of] urgent and exceptional national, regional and international
  action;
- the access to medication in the context of pandemics such as HIV/
  AIDS is one of the fundamental elements to achieve progressively the
  full realization of the right of everyone to the enjoyment of the highest
  attainable standards of physical and mental health;
- the prevention of HIV infection must be the mainstay of the national,
  regional and international response to the epidemic; . . . prevention, care, support and treatment for those infected and affected by
  HIV/AIDS are mutually reinforcing elements of an effective response
  and must be integrated in a comprehensive approach to combat the
  epidemic.

The resulting plan of action demanded widespread international moral
and financial support. It is a long-term multifaceted plan, laying out
strategies for prevention, care, support, and treatment. Special attention
is addressed to empowering women to reduce their vulnerability, and to
assistance for orphaned children. National policies are required to respect the dignity of persons living with and affected by HIV/AIDS.

Under UNAIDS strictures and guidelines in the field of research and
development, human rights must be respected in programs of clinical
trials and monitoring. As if taking into account the kind of slapdash work
first described by Day and Adler in 1997, UNAIDS calls on participating
governments, organizations, and health professionals to ensure that all
research protocols for the investigation of HIV-related treatment, including antiretroviral therapies and vaccines, must be based on international
guidelines and best practices. Moreover, such research and related treatment must be evaluated by independent committees of ethics, in which
persons living with HIV/AIDS and caregivers for antiretroviral therapy
participate.

The Turkish Attempt to Violate Physicians' Confidentiality

In 1996, the International Council for Rehabilitation of Torture Victims (ICRT, Copenhagen) complained of Turkey's record of torture by police.[28] The country's dreadful human rights record was propped up by an Anti-Terror Law permiting persons arrested under it to be held in solitary confinement for as long as thirty days, leaving ample opportunity for abuse of detainees. The same year, the Council of Europe's Committee for the Prevention of Torture found convincing evidence of torture practices by law enforcement officers in Turkey, even uncovering torture instruments during their inspection tour of prisons and detention centers. According to the ICRT, the country's Foreign Ministry was stung by the European report. Taking a "kill the messenger" approach, they convened a meeting to decide on shutting down the ICRT affiliate clinic, the Human Rights Foundation of Turkey (HRFT). By 1996, HRFT had established four treatment and rehabilitation centers where eight doctors, three psychiatrists, and three social workers had treated some 3000 torture survivors. Fearing exposure, the ministers suspected that the HRFT regularly reported torture cases to international organizations, thereby drawing criticism from NGOs as well as European and NATO officials.

Having tolerated the existence of these centers for six years, the Turkish Ministry of Justice convened a criminal trial disingenuously invoking two propositions: (1) torture is a crime in Turkey and (2) it is a crime not to report a crime. Using these norms as a legal trap, Turkish prosecutors began a harassing practice in 1996 of filing criminal charges against HRFT personnel, charging them with "disobedience to the orders of officials authorities" and "negligence in denouncing the crime of torture." The "disobedience" alluded to was the justifiable refusal of administrators and health professionals to let authorities look into medical records of persons who were treated at the HRFT's Adana Rehabilitation Center. In bullying tactics, the police demanded detailed information on the patients and their medical records, which presumably contained information about police torturers. Over time, Turkey brought to trial many of the founding members of the HRFT and physicians from the Istanbul and Adana branches, accusing them of operating illegal medical facilities, all the while continuing state-approved torture to prop up a shaky regime.

Any demands for government access to medical records is contrary to universal principles of doctors' professional secrecy as formulated, among others, by the World Medical Association, of which Turkey is a member. To no avail, the provisions of the Hippocratic Oath were ex-

plained in the Turkish trial, for example, the physician's traditional promise: "What I may see or hear in the course of treatment . . . I will keep to
myself holding such things shameful to be spoken about." Clumsy, crude,
and even violent attempts by government officials to elicit information
from physicians and desecrate the confidentiality of medical files strikes
at the heart of universally accepted standards of doctor-patient privacy.
Such privacy is essential for the healing, trusting relations necessary between client and care provider during rehabilitation. The Turkish trials
continuing through 2000 were a source of international embarrassment,
among other reasons because numerous NGOs sent trial observers, including the Center for Victims of Torture (Minneapolis), International
Rehabilitation Council for Torture Victims (Copenhagen), the Danish
Amnesty International Medical Group, and the International Federation
of Health and Human Rights Organizations.

The Turkish case shows that scientific professionals and societies of
health care providers have worked out response strategies to human
rights abuses and related violations of medical ethics. These include
procedures borrowed from human rights groups and reflect techniques
more common to human rights organizations like Amnesty International
to promote protective urgent action on behalf of human rights victims,
including fellow professionals.

Care for the Care-Givers

With the end of the Cold War, but with no end in sight of multiple hot
wars, the troubled dawn of the twenty-first century emerged with multi-
farious limited hostilities, flashpoints of civil strife, genocidal conflict,
terrorist attacks, and ethnic rivalry. Such circumstances necessarily have
an impact on the right to health and medical care. In the early 1990s,
the dogs of war were unleashed with shocking fury in the Balkan conflicts engulfing the former Yugoslavia. In this context, the United Nations
awarded its Human Rights Prize to the staff of the Kosevo Hospital in
Sarajevo, Bosnia. In 1993 the prize singled out medical workers there for
their courage in the face of continuous attacks and indiscriminate sniper
firing, and artillery shelling directed at the hospital from nearby territory
held by Bosnian Serbs. Many civilians lost their lives, including nurses on
duty at the Kosevo hospital.[29]

Tragedies such as attacks on hospitals and the killings of the Kosevo
nurses while on medical duty involve a "grave breach" of humanitarian
law. From its inception, this field of law—previously called "the laws of
war"—has mandated the protection of health workers. And for good reasons: no medical professional serves the victims of war or enters a field

Regulations in Time of Armed Conflict

1. Medical Ethics in time of armed conflict is identical to medical ethics in time of peace, as established in the International Code of Medical Ethics of the World Medical Association. The primary obligation of the physician is his professional duty; in performing his professional duty, the physician's supreme guide is his conscience.

2. The primary task of the medical profession is to preserve health and save life. Hence it is deemed unethical for physicians to:
   a. Give advice or perform prophylactic, diagnostic or therapeutic procedures that are not justifiable in the patient's interest.
   b. Weaken the physical or mental strength of a human being without therapeutic justification.
   c. Employ scientific knowledge to imperil health or destroy life.

3. Human experimentation in time of armed conflict is governed by the same code as in time of peace; it is strictly forbidden on all persons deprived of their liberty, especially civilian and military prisoners and the population of occupied countries.

4. In emergencies, the physician must always give the required care impartially and without consideration of sex, race, nationality, religion, political affiliation or any other similar criterion. Such medical assistance must be continued for as long as necessary and practicable.

5. Medical confidentiality must be preserved by the physician in the practice of his profession.

6. Privileges and facilities afforded to the physician must never be used for other than professional purposes.

World Medical Association 1956, 1957, 1983

of combat without a strong sense that he or she is a noncombatant and must be seen as performing professional duties that are neutral in relation to the battle that may be raging all around. The principle of medical neutrality is a protective shield on which doctors, nurses, medics, and all personnel assigned to health services rely during wartime. The protection of human rights standards and of humanitarian norms are not sepa-

Figure 5. Eric Stover (center) participating in the exhumation of the remains of hospital patients who were evacuated at gunpoint from a Croatian hospital on 20 November, 1991 and executed by the Yugoslav People's Army. Forensic evidence by pathologists, anthropologists, and archaeologists verified the identities of the victims and confirmed that they had been shot with semi-automatic weapons and buried in a mass grave. This proved to be important evidence in the criminal proceedings before the Hague International Criminal Court for the Former Yugoslavia. Courtesy of Gilles Peress Studio, photo by Gilles Peress.

rate efforts but are joint and concerted goals and concerns.[30] This "convergence" of human rights law and humanitarian norms means the two sets of rules are not mutually exclusive, and both may be fully operative, especially when viewed through the health professional's lens of medical neutrality.

Medical neutrality is a somewhat ambiguous term. It requires health professionals to avoid partisanship in giving professional assistance without discrimination, but it does not call for neutrality in the health practitioner's duty to promote and protect human rights. The requisite neutrality concerns issues of both rights and responsibilities. As such, any systematic effort to classify violations of medical neutrality should take into account abuses of rights guaranteed by medical neutrality and abuses of responsibilities required by medical neutrality. In the schematic presentation in the next box, rights and responsibilities form an important basis for distinguishing between various kinds of abuses of medical neutrality.[31]

Principles of Medical Neutrality

A. Abuses of rights guaranteed by medical neutrality
    1. Infringements against medical personnel, wounded and civilians
       Killings or disappearances of wounded, sick, and medical personnel
       Torture or cruel, inhuman, or degrading treatment of the above
       Serious harassment impeding medical functions
       Punishment for treating the sick and wounded, including punishment for upholding medical confidentiality
    2. Infringements against medical facilities and services
       Bombing or shelling of hospitals and clinics
       Incursions into hospitals and interrupting necessary medical care
       Preventing medical services in conflict areas by delaying delivery of supplies and free passage of medical personnel where needed
B. Abuse of responsibilities required by medical neutrality
    3. Abuse of medical facilities
       Use of hospital/clinic/ambulance for military purposes
       Abuse of medical emblem (red cross, red crescent)
    4. Abuse of medical skills
       Torture, cruel treatment, or military interrogation by medical personnel
       Selective and discriminatory treatment of wounded combatants or civilians on nonmedical grounds
       Medical treatment given according to military instruction rather than clinical indications
       Breach of medical confidentiality

Physicians for Human Rights, 1996

The principles linked to medical neutrality reflect a noble effort to alleviate the suffering caused by war, and to protect civilians from risks of armed conflict. For example, the Geneva Conventions of 1949 and the Additional Protocols of 1977 establish rules for wartime conditions, strictly obliging states to provide humane support for the sick and wounded. They must be afforded medical treatment "to the fullest extent practicable and with the least possible delay" (Prorocol II, Article 7.2). Moreover, states must respect and protect all health professionals in the performance of their medical duties regardless of the persons benefitting therefrom" (Prorocol II, Article 10). Consistent with the UDHR, everyone, irrespective of their wartime partisanship, has a right to medical care.

Strictly speaking, humanitarian law extends rights to medical professionals not as doctors, nurses, or medics and not as individuals, but as medical practitioners. Such professionals are protected by humanitarian law, not on the basis of their credentials, but on the basis of the functions they are performing at any given time. As stated by one specialist, "The status of the medical profession during war has never been looked at independently, but has always been considered from a functional point of view, that is to say, in regard to the need to protect the wounded.[32] A physician who undertakes nonmedical functions in a field of armed conflict cannot claim the protection of the rules of war while not acting in support of the wounded and sick. Therefore, Dr. Che Guevara, in his political role in Latin America, would not have been able to claim any of the rights associated with medical neutrality. Likewise, as the leader of break-away Bosnian Serbs in the 1980s, Dr. Radovan Karadžić, can hardly claim the rights linked to health professionals under the rules of war.[33] Ironically, troops under his command consistently shelled the Kosevo Hospital in which he had served for several years as a psychiatrist in Sarajevo.

Since the mid-nineteenth century, the International Committee of the Red Cross has fostered the maturation of humanitarian law, and for their part, medical professional associations have made normative contributions as well. For example, humanitarian law links recognition of the neutral status of health professionals tied to nondiscrimination standards important in medical ethics. The World Medical Association's "Regulations in Time of Armed Conflict" specifies that, "In emergencies, the physician must always give the required care impartially and without consideration of sex, race, nationality, religion, political affiliation or any other similar criterion." In 1973, the International Council of Nurses affirmed support for Red Cross Rights and Duties of Nurses under the Geneva Convention of 1949, and in 1975, the same group resolved that nurses must ensure that without any discrimination the sick and wounded in wartime "shall be treated humanely and cared for by the Party in conflict in whose power they may be."

Conclusions

The rights to health and medical care proclaimed in the Universal Declaration of Human Rights lay the basis for people's rights as well as for care-givers' duties and responsibilities. Invidious discrimination is never an option open to a health professional—neither in peace nor in war. In fact, during periods of armed conflict, humanitarian law comes into play reinforcing the Universal Declaration of Human Rights by affording protection and the status of a neutral to health professionals. Nevertheless, the correct attitude for such a care giver is always to behave as he or she would if a completely free agent in peacetime. No wonder that the UN Human Rights Prize was awarded to the staff of the Kosevo Hospital in Sarajevo, Bosnia, who courageously honored patients' rights to medical care even at the cost of their own lives.

Since the UN adoption of the Universal Declaration of Human Rights, its canons have become globally pervasive, influencing related areas of law and professional standards, including medical ethics and policy analysis. The Declaration helps us see how various violations undermine the right to health and thus contribute to improved understanding of public health issues.[34] It calls on us to apply a human rights perspective to public health issues.

A human rights perspective applied to public health scrutinizes inequalities in the distribution of health resources and identifies institutional discrimination against disfavored minorities and immigrants. It prompts us to ask whether medical research funds are allocated fairly to issues of women's health, contributing to morbidity, mortality, and lack of well-being. The UDHR reinforces our understanding that among the essential steps in responding to the AIDS pandemic is recognizing and ensuring the human rights of those at risk. Human rights analysis calls on us not only to look at war with abhorrence but to monitor the extent to which modern war and civil strife take a toll on civilians, including children. In short, human rights analysis, drawing on internationally defined standards, disclose how rights violations contribute to ill-health and even undermine the right to life.

Over a half century after the adoption of the UDHR, we see the gap between, on the one hand, its promises on which people rely and, on the other, persistent offenses against human rights that must be acknowledged. Conditions under which the right to health is hampered have proliferated far beyond that imagined in 1948. In addition to the related violations of human rights with which we are all familiar, the framers of the UDHR could not have foreseen such present-day issues as the maldistribution of medical services for life-saving drugs based on ethnic, racial, and national differences; police state invasions of doctor-patient relations; DNA testing without regard to privacy; gene patenting that does not benefit gene contributors; pharmaceutical fraud and dumping in less developed countries; arbitrary restrictions on scientific freedom and abuse of scientific whistle blowers; and discrimination of access to education in science, technology, and medicine. For these and myriad other such contemporary problems, we look to the UDHR to begin but hardly to conclude inquiry into applicable normative standards and enforcement mechanisms.

Chapter 6
Information Technology and Statistics

Statistics must have a clearly defined purpose, one aspect of which is scientific advance and the other, human welfare.
—P.C. Mahalanobis, Indian Statistician

Introduction

This chapter discusses one of the wonders of applied science, the new information technologies, used both to gather and disseminate information and, with new software technologies, to analyze data as well. I acknowledge serious problems of mal-distribution of Internet facilities, nevertheless, noting concerted responses are underway to the North-South divide affecting electronic transmission of information. Linked to these developments are both problems of censorship and the infringement of privacy rights. The chapter notes that Internet transmissions are increasingly relied on to help build a database at various NGO headquarters or in safe havens overseas. In this process, the new methodologies for monitoring human rights violations have increasingly come to rely on two kinds of technical guidance, that of information specialists on the use of encryption to safeguard the privacy of their transmissions, and that of statisticians on how to assemble and analyze a useful human rights database. Statistics applied to human rights problems has come of age in effectively and reliably helping people to vindicate human rights violations and to improve public policy. Its use in recent years supplies a significant example of science in the service of human rights.

The New Information Age

When Johannes Gutenberg invented the printing press, he gave the world a device that expanded the mind without the need for travel. History shows us that one of the consequences of movable print publishing was that English Levelers in the seventeenth century turned political pamphleteering into a cottage industry. The writings and petitions of politically minded Puritans and other dissident groups were broadcast. These ideas served to undermine the legitimacy of the Stuart monarchy, contributed to the Glorious Revolution, and justified complaints leading to the English Bill of Rights of 1689.[1]

Thomas Jefferson was among the first to recognize that rights and liberties have global implications. In a 1787 letter from Paris to James Madison in Virginia, he wrote: "a bill of rights is what the people are entitled to against every government on earth."[2] It took that letter, traveling by ship from France to Virginia, two months before it reached Madison.

Today, we can look forward to a twenty-first-century world of instant communication served by satellite dishes, super-range radio, computer networking, worldwide fax service, microelectronic computing, fiber optics, and the Internet. These and more cyberspace advances yet to come serve as mind-broadening technologies that should give tyrants much to fear. In the hands of those resisting oppression, their high-tech media devices defy frontiers to expose human rights abuses. Further, globe-belting "human rights friendly" technology makes available international human rights norms to which to repair in complaining of political acts of barbarism, and to which to turn in judging the legitimacy of political regimes. As this process advances, lowering the shield of traditional state sovereignty, we face a new format for global politics. On the horizon is a global society in which individuals and groups become greatly empowered actors, taking on roles which historically have been reserved for states and diplomats.

Scholars and policy-makers are only now beginning to speculate about the impact of the Internet on world affairs.[3] Just as the new technology of the printing press served pamphleteers' ideas about natural rights in the seventeenth century, so today's communications technologies engender a broader social consciousness of rights and responsibilities of governments, groups and individuals. Indeed, it is safe to say that we are moving toward to a new model of world affairs.

According to global politics specialists like James Rosenau, John Burton, and Marvin Soroos, the emergence of a better informed and a more critical public is developing a new perspective on international relations—the "global society model."[4] No longer must our understanding of international relations be limited by focusing nearly exclusively on the behavior of nations and of international organizations composed of states. Modern communication and transportation, as well as the evolving international division of labor and the globalization of capital are rendering obsolete the classical notion of world politics where the sphere of independent sovereigns was all but impenetrable to anything but pressures from other states. Territorial boundaries, however bolstered by doctrines of sovereignty, no longer stand impregnable; they are, indeed, downright porous. Of great importance for human rights, the new channels also empower NGOs to disseminate information and ideas. Before turning to that positive development, we must recognize some negative effects: pollutants, drugs, and terrorists penetrate these pores in state sovereignty, and pornography and hate propaganda easily traverse the Internet.

The promotion of intolerance and hatred on the Internet is particularly troubling.[5] This does not mean that censorship is a solution. In 2001 the Southern Poverty Law Center estimated that the Internet carried 350 "hate sites" on the worldwide web, each spewing a destructive philosophy of hatred, prejudice and violence. Such sites can not only reach millions of children, but reach them in the privacy of their own rooms, where, as Morris Dees, Director of the Center says, "they will be assaulted with hate in its most raw and corrosive forms." Dees reported that the Center's study of this problem showed that one of the sites directly promotes human rights violations, telling teenagers how to start violent confrontations that "provoke racial minorities and gays into throwing the first punch." To respond to this abuse of international communications, the Southern Poverty Law Center has set up its own site: Tolerance.org. It provides users a "truth tour" of hate sites where the lies of such groups are exposed, where parents and others find advice they can use to raise tolerant families, and where teachers learn methods for using Tolerance.org in their classes. The website, which is in Spanish and English, will enable visitors to view a searchable "hate map" showing where hate groups operate across the country and a "human rights map" with links to hundreds of groups that promote tolerance. Visitors can take an interactive psychology test to measure hidden biases. Pop-up "truth panels" will debunk the propaganda of infamous hate sites.

Tolerance.org enters the "marketplace of ideas" by confronting ignorance with knowledge, an approach consistent with human rights standards. But some governments insist on more direct and heavy handed techniques for countering what they do not like. For example, it is clear that the government of the Peoples Republic of China seeks to control the international free flow of information. According to Chinese law, the Internet can only be accessed through the state-owned service provider, ChinaNet, and in 1999 officials ordered the closure of the country's most outspoken and popular Internet forum, Richtalk. Likewise, tighter controls were ordered at the growing number of cybercafes in China. In 1998, Lin Hai, a Chinese software engineer was charged with "inciting to over-throw state power," and tried in secret in Shanghai. He was sentenced to two years in prison for providing 30,000 Chinese e-mail addresses to a U.S.-based pro-democracy newsletter. Despite such repression, the flow of information is persistent, and continuing news about censorship in the People's Republic of China is available from the Digital Freedom Network, <www.hrichina.org/Xinwenming/index.htm>.

By delivering cheap access to information, and by providing forums for debate in countries where the media are monopolized, the Internet offers the disenfranchised an opportunity to participate in responding to their own misery. The Internet can be used to mobilize people locally. For example, electronic mail campaigns against corruption influenced Korea's 1999 elections and played a key role in publicizing the corruption that ultimately deposed President Joseph Estrada of the Philippines in 2000. E-mail and the Internet can also break international barriers. NGOs, working within and outside countries with tyrannical regimes, can use communications technology to bypass government control and communicate directly with ordinary citizens. Where governments exert too tight a control over Internet use by their own citizens, as in Vietnam or Burma, websites communicate with expatriate communities, sympathetic foreign audiences, and also with internal groups who are able to access the Internet illegally by dialing out of the country using mobile telephony.[6]

With access to the Internet available in 2001 for over 400 million people, The United Nations *Human Development Report* estimates the figure at one billion by 2005, but distribution will probably continue to show the North greatly advantaged over the South.[7] The report comments, "Connecting a major portion of the population will be a challenge in developing regions. But the digital divide need not be permanent if technological adaptations and institutional innovations expand access." Responding to fears that the Internet will not serve less developed countries, OneWorld and the Dutch development aid agency Hivos have joined forces to help organizations based in developing countries to use the Internet for sustainable development and human rights.[8] The initiative includes helping hundreds of South-based NGOs to go on-line, connect to sources of support and training, and build online gateways promoting regional perspectives from civil society in Africa, Latin America and South Asia.

Through technological changes, the "international community" invoked so often in rhetoric, is becoming a reality and a challenge. It is a challenge shaped by the new global environment and a challenge to an ever broadening circle of conscientious professionals concerned with human rights everywhere. If adherence to human rights is to be the foundation for the international community, new patterns of cooperation must be developed. Such cooperation is needed among professionals across the boundaries of many disciplines to make progress in so broad a field as international human rights. Certainly, human rights workers need the combined counsel of lawyers and scientists in the documentation of rights violations. But more exotic forms of expertise are useful as well. For example, human rights NGOs seeking to use fax, electronic mail and Internet transmissions to help build a database in a safe haven overseas need the technical guidance of information specialists about the use of encryption and other techniques to safeguard the privacy of their transmissions.

Privacy International (New York, London, and Sydney) offers such advice to human rights groups worldwide, and the Electronic Privacy Information Center (EPIC, Washington, D.C.) monitors government policy designed to undermine privacy on the Internet. Together with other groups such as the Global Internet Liberty Campaign, they canvass privacy law and Internet issues worldwide <www.gilc.org/>. Their reports point to an ominous trend. They conclude that

- the Internet is coming under increased surveillance;
- legal authorization to do so is regularly abused, even in democratic states;
- and "the main targets are political opposition, journalists, and human rights activists."[9]

In 2001 the Global Internet Liberty Campaign flagged policy proposals aired within the European Union (EU). The EU developed and circulated for ratification a wide-ranging Cybercrime Treaty.[10] It requires logs of activities on the net to be retained. Operators and service providers in turn, must respond to police demands for telecommunications data, including electronic mail and records of Internet usage. The treaty requires domestic companies to comply with foreign investigators, even when they are looking into activities that are not crimes on domestic soil. Privacy International and EPIC alerted their campaign colleagues and list-serv members about the Convention's provisions, arguing that they were vague and posed threats to personal privacy, allowing police to conduct broad sweeps of international communications.

Of course most countries place at least some restrictions on Internet usage. That was the finding of a major report released by Freedom House (New York) in 2001. The survey found that Internet freedom exceeds levels of press freedom in most countries, including some closed societies governed by censorious regimes. Of 131 countries eligible for the study,

58 (44 percent) are considered to have Least Restrictive access to the Internet; 55 (42 percent) are considered Moderately Restrictive, and 18 (14 percent) are rated Most Restrictive. Comparing the data between the Internet study and the results of the larger survey on the press, it is clear that Internet freedoms outpace press freedoms. Many repressive governments—among them Iran, Pakistan, Uzbekistan, Saudi Arabia, Syria, and Zimbabwe—place fewer restrictions on Internet access than they do on print and broadcast media. Leonard Sussman, the survey's author, explained this finding: "The Internet's relative openness in some closed societies reflects the dilemma posed by the opportunities on the web for economic development, international trade, cultural advances."

Among the study's other findings were

- There is a strong correlation between a free press and open Internet access.
- Yet some of the most repressive and closed societies restrict content on the Internet "least" or "moderately."
- Some major democracies (Australia, UK, U.S.) restrict freedom on the Internet, ostensibly to maintain state secrets, investigate terrorism, or bar pornography.
- Countries such as China with Internet access considered Most Restrictive generally allow only state-run Internet service providers to operate.

The entire *Survey of Press Freedom*, containing country-by-country reports and an interactive press freedom map, is available online, <www.freedom house.org/pfs2001/pfs2001.pdf>.

The prevalence of human rights violations everywhere makes the process of reporting infringements a moral imperative, and changing technologies including electronic messaging also make such action feasible. While censorship and stifling of communications are standard fare for human rights violators, their gag orders cannot always or easily catch up with the pace of technical change. We now live in a global environment that exponentially expands opportunities to disseminate information, including information about gross violations of human rights. Information, whether sent instantly by the Internet or quietly from one country to another by diplomatic pouch, is essential in developing facts about human rights issues. But a problem built on the scaffolding of information transmission remains: how to analyze information received. The skills of statisticians can be critically important in this task, especially because vast amounts of information about human rights issues traverse cyberspace. Often such data call for careful statistical analysis.

Statistics as a Tool for Human Rights Analysis

In 1941 the Dutch ambassador to Germany reviewed reports of numerous deaths among Jews deported to Polish "labor camps." The extraordinary number of nearly simultaneous deaths due to "heart failure" listed in each report led him correctly to deduce the true cause of these simultaneous deaths was systematic killing. In this case, the evidence was overwhelming and the ambassador could reach a sound conclusion without technical knowledge. In a less clear case, for example, one showing a variety of causes of death, the ambassador would have needed assistance from a statistician to draw scientifically reliable inferences from the data. Based on the record he reviewed, there is no doubt that a statistician would have confirmed his judgment on technical grounds, agreeing with his conclusion based on knowledge of the situation in Europe, well-founded suspicion, and the evidence of the data eliciting his concern for others.

As the workhorse of science, statistics is becoming increasingly important in the analysis of public policy, including issues of human rights. Properly employed, statistical analysis is a powerful tool to dig out the truth on many subjects. And it is especially important in the human rights field, because reliably produced information based on hard evidence can be a key element in securing a remedy for violations.[11] Scientifically analyzing data regarding human rights violations is not always necessary, as the Dutch ambassador's judgment suggests, but it is often very useful. Statistics is the science of collecting, analyzing, and interpreting numerical data relating to an aggregate of individuals (or for that matter relating to crop yields, temperature trends, and many other phenomena). The information on which the numerical data are based sometimes derives from anecdotal qualitative news. Of course, the first step in collecting information requires accuracy to establish the credibility of the data on which analysis and interpretation depend.

An International Case Study

Human rights monitors and activists are acutely aware of the urgent need for developing verifiable information about violations of human rights. The power and impact of systematic data collection can be seen in a case from Southeast Asia. This case highlights the fate of one victim in the context of a nationwide profile of victimization. Its resolution did not require sophisticated statistical methods, but it demonstrates the effectiveness of responding to tragedy at the grassroots level by launching a process of planning, collecting, analyzing, and disseminating information. In this instance the process of statistical data collection and analysis linking it with an internationally generated remedy should encourage professionals to give serious thought to the value of statistics in human rights.

Our Southeast Asia case starts when a corrupt chief executive (Ferdinand Marcos) in the Republic of the Philippines set up a police state and derailed democracy. A year after he suspended civil liberties in 1972, religious leaders surveyed their members throughout the 7,000 island nation "to gain an objective picture of the effects of martial law."[12] The study revealed pervasive political detention without criminal charges and the routine practice of torture by the military performing police functions in all regions of the country.

In January 1974 religious leaders established the Task Force Detainees of the Philippines (TFDP), a nongovernmental organization, "to provide moral and spiritual support through regular detention camp visits." Consulting with volunteer cooperative attorneys and statisticians, the TFDP created a network of national, regional, and local units to gather data on torture and other human rights violations in the over one hundred political detention centers throughout the Philippine archipelago. TFDP analytical reports, denounced by the Marcos government as subversive, were distributed locally to relatives of the victims and circulated internationally through church channels and human rights networks. By 1976, the Task Force had developed carefully documented dossiers to identify nearly 6,000 persons as imprisoned without the benefit of habeas corpus or other legal recourse. By analyzing these cases by region, group, gender, and other categories, they made a credible case of widespread gross violations of human rights based on a statistical analysis of sound data. This accounting of a baleful continuing attack on the citizens of a former democracy attracted a great deal of attention from international organizations and the media

Anecdotal Fact-Finding in the Philippines

Consider one of the TFDP reports detailing the tragedy of Mrs. Trinidad Herrera.[13] On a day in April 1977, as she walked down a street in Quezon City, she could not help notice that a car full of men was following her. Finally, one of them called out her name. Stopping to find out what they wanted, she was hustled into the car and arrested on grounds of illegal assembly. Herrera had led protest meetings on the right to housing and against government plans with World Bank support to relocate squatters in order to make way for the construction of tourist hotels in Manila. In fact, she was the president of the Zone One Tondo Organization (ZOTO), an umbrella association for several hundred small groups throughout the Tondo slum area where she lived.

Hours after her arrest, Herrera found herself facing interrogation at

Camp Crame, a sprawling military compound used to corral political prisoners. Answering the questions shouted at her, she denied that she was a member of the Communist party, acknowledged knowing two persons about whom she was asked, gave her correct address, and explained the relationships among several groups within ZOTO. Nevertheless, one of the interrogators suddenly shouted, "You are not cooperating!" Thereupon all but two or her tormenters slipped out of the room; the remaining officers uncovered a box containing an army crank telephone with clipped wires. Stripping Herrera of all her clothing, the uniformed men attached wires to sensitive parts of her body. Without regard for her responses, they would turn the crank on the field telephone to give electrical shocks. The jolts were so severe, she could not help urinating from the intense pain and finally agreed to sign any confession put before her.

On 5 May 1977 Herrera was transferred to the Bicutan Rehabilitation Center. Inmates and religious visitors smuggled out reports to her family that, unable to feed or bathe herself, she would merely sit and stare blankly with tears in her eyes. At that time, despite political risks to his military career as a medical officer, Lieutenant Ladislao Dialo bravely filed a report confirming the existence of scars from electrical abuse. On May 14, Trinidad Herrera was released on orders from President Marcos. He was embarrassed by U.S. congressional hearings focusing on human rights abuses in countries receiving American military assistance. The public airing of this issue in 1977 revealed that the Philippines had received hand crank telephones from the United States. One Representative summarized the impact of the Herrara case and concluded from the hearings that human rights violations in the Philippines were serious and numerous.

The numbers here are disturbing, and instances of torture have increased so rapidly that even the World Bank threatened postponement of a $15 million resettlement loan to the Philippines at the suggestion of Canadian Director Earl Drake. Drake was concerned with the arrest of Trinidad Herrera, a Manila slum leader. Mrs. Herrera had been detained by authorities after having expressed some concerns about aspects of the World Bank project in Manila's Tondo slum district.[14]

U.S. congressional hearings reviewed thousands of TFDP documented cases. It is likely that the shocking human rights degradation suffered by Trinidad Herrera would not have been enough by itself to spark Canadian, American, and World Bank attention and concern. Seen as representative of a consistent pattern of gross violations of human rights under the Marcos regime, however, the Herrera case in combination with others prompted a high-level policy response. Also, the careful documentation of many such victim files by the TFDP formed the basis of reports prepared by Amnesty International and the International Commission of

Jurists. Were it not for these carefully substantiated accounts, the case of Trinidad Herrera would not have gained international attention and would have remained unremedied.

Statistical Analysis

The documentation of Herrara's case is not a statistical example by itself. Rather, as a well-documented file, it is the necessary first step, reflecting good database design and documentation in the field, essential for fact-retrieval and setting an audit trail, all needed for effective information system work. As illustrated below, such work is relied on when the database is used for analysis helpful in calling violators to account. In fact, the Herrara case was combined with thousands of others used in statistical analysis in a civil suit filed in U.S. Federal District Court in Hawaii.

President Marcos was driven from office as a result of the "people power" revolution in the Philippines in 1986. He fled the country in disgrace, taking refuge in Hawaii, where he was served with complaints by many Filipinos like Trinadad Herrara seeking damages for human rights abuses against them. By 1991 nearly 10,000 such complaints had been combined in a civil suit with multiple plaintiffs called a "class action" and filed under the title of *Hilao v. Estate of Marcos*.[15] The U.S. Alien Tort Act (discussed in Chapter 8 of this book) served as the basis for the Filipinos' action for recovery of damages from those responsible for torture,[16] extra-judicial killings, or "disappearances."

The court certified the case as a class action, defining it as all civilian citizens of the Philippines who, between 1972 and 1986 fell into any of three categories: those who were (1) tortured, (2) summarily executed, or (3) "disappeared." Marcos died in Hawaii while the case was still pending and his family representatives were substituted as defendants. The details of the Marcos regime and its human rights abuses were presented to the court, which acknowledged the credibility and reliability of the database so meticulously assembled by the TFDP during the years of dictatorship. Eventually it decided that the evidence warranted a judicial order on behalf of Filipino victims for awarding damages assessed against Marcos properties, real estate, and other assets in the United States and elsewhere.

The Filipino human rights victims filed several law suits against the estate of the wealthy dictator, and both compensatory and punitive damages totaling $2 billion were eventually awarded. Statistical analysis was used to determine one part of the award, the compensatory damages. The process involved illustrates how such work can serve the cause of justice on behalf of human rights victims. To assess compensatory damages for the thousands of claims filed, the federal district court allowed the use of a sample of the three categories of the enumerated claims—torture, nonjudicial executions, and "disappearances." James Dannemiller, an expert statistician, was responsible for the method used, testifying that the onsite examination of a random sample of 137 claims would achieve "a 95 percent statistical probability that the same percentage determined to be valid among the claims would be applicable to the 9,541 valid claims filed."

The court appointed an expert administrative aide, a "special master," to serve as a technical advisor. He traveled to the Philippines taking sworn statements from the 137 randomly selected claimants and their witnesses. Taken under penalty of perjury, the claim forms and depositions were completed by November 1994. On reviewing the evidence to ensure the violations fell within the three named categories and that they took place between 1972 and 1986, the special master recommended that 6 claims of the 137 in the sample should be found not valid, leaving 131 claimants.

On the basis of past torture cases and other considerations, the special master recommended an amount of money necessary to compensate the victims, considering many factors. For example, what was the victim's age? Was torture physical as well as mental? What methods were used, and for how long? What were the victim's actual losses, including medical bills? In the cases of summary execution and "disappearance," the master considered whether torture took place prior to death or disappearance; the nature of the actual killing or disappearance; the victim's family's mental anguish; and lost earnings, computed according to a formula established by the Philippine Supreme Court and converted into U.S. dollars. The recommended damages for the 131 valid claims in the random sample totaled $3,310,000 for the 64 torture claims (an average of $51,719), $6,425,767 for the 50 summary execution claims (an average of $128,515), and $1,833,515 for the 17 "disappearance" claims (an average of $107,853).

A jury trial on compensatory damages was held in January 1995. Dr. Dannemiller testified that the selection of the random sample met the standards of inferential statistics, that the successful efforts to locate and obtain testimony from the claimants in the random sample "were of the highest standards" in his profession, that the procedures followed conformed to the standards of inferential statistics, and that the injuries of the random-sample claimants were representative of the class as a whole. The jury heard testimony from the 137 random-sample claimants and their witnesses, and also heard the special master's testimony. Deliberating for five days, members of the jury had been instructed that they could accept, modify or reject the recommendations. In fact they found invalid only two (instead of six as recommended) of the 137 claimants in the random sample. As to the sample claims, the jury generally adopted the master's recommendations, and the district court subsequently followed the jury's determination in the amounts awarded to the victims. In addition to the compensatory damages as described above, "corrective" or punitive damages were also awarded in very large amounts. In 1996 a U.S. Court of Appeals reviewed the decision of the federal court, including the statistical methodology used to guide the jury. Judges Betty Fletcher and Harry Pergerson upheld the lower court's decision and its procedures in *Hilao v. Estate of Marcos*[17] but Judge Pamela Ann Rymer dissented. Basing huge compensatory damage awards on statistical inferences, she said, left her "with profound disquiet." Unhappy with the class action nature of the suit, she felt due process required a real trial for each plaintiff, not simply a statistical sampling of thousands of victims: one plaintiff, one trial, one remedy.

A Model of Quantitative Analysis

Each violation of human rights and fundamental freedoms deserves individual attention and universal condemnation. No one seriously interested in applying statistical science to monitoring human rights violations would argue that "if you can't count them they don't count." However, those who work in the field of human rights know that fixing the responsibility for violations requires an assessment of how, how much, and why human freedoms are curtailed or endangered. A model of excellence in analyzing large scale human rights violations is the report *State Violence in Guatemala, 1960–1996*, by Patrick Ball, Paul Kobrak, and Herbert F. Spirer.[18] The report combines historical analysis with statistics from the International Center for Human Rights Investigations (CIDH) to present a compelling history of the deliberate and sustained violence committed by state forces during Guatemala's domestic armed conflict.

The Guatemala study, subtitled *A Quantitative Reflection*, relies on a database meticulously assembled covering 43,070 violations against 16,265 victims, of whom 13,527 are victims whose full identity is known. The statistics present a clear picture of the period 1959–94. These were decades of unrelenting Guatemalan state reliance on extrajudicial violence to maintain political control in a divided nation. Data analysis by the authors credibly supports the view that state terror over time expanded in both intensity and in the scope of its victims, from selective assassinations of militants in the armed insurgency to an ever widening attack on members of the political opposition. The report also inquires into the methods and agents of violence, including state use of civilians to attack other civilians, a policy that contributed to the long-term militarization of Guatemalan society. Analysis of database information shows how violence rose and fell across all presidential regimes, military and civilian. Human rights violations are analyzed by the gender, ethnicity and age of the victims, and regional differences show the ever increasing penetration of violence into rural areas.

What distinguishes the *State Violence in Guatemala* report from many other NGO presentations of criminal catastrophes is that the authors systematically explain the methodologies they use, supplying the reader an instructional resource as well as an historical document of importance. Another feature of the report is that it examines how violence was reported in the press and thus understood at the time. For much of the period of insurgency, the Guatemalan press avoided placing blame on the military, but did report on the evidence of state violence. The statistical profile of such violence shows that a record number of over 800 killings and disappearances per month took place during 17 months of President José Efrain Rios Montt's incumbency (1978–82). Nevertheless, because of increased state censorship and intimidation of the media by killings of journalists and attacks on media offices and equipment at that time, fewer government killings were reported during his regime. The press blackout coincided with Reagan administration lobbying to restore military aid to Guatemala cut off by the U.S. Congress in 1977. Thus the question of how people do or do not get timely information about human rights violations has a strong bearing on how they can respond to such abuses.

Statistics in the Service of Human Rights

Interdisciplinary cooperation is not without difficulties. Quite different professional vocabularies and often seemingly incompatible methods of analysis are used by lawyers, social scientists, statisticians, medical specialists, technicians in all fields, humanists, and community activists. Still, when all concerned share a determination to make progress on problems of global importance, there are inducements for specialists from widely diverse fields who have found ways to work together, for example, in assessing the status of human rights worldwide and to direct quantitative approaches to specific problems of human rights observance. In his Presidential Address to the American Statistical Association in 1984, I. Richard Savage set a novel goal for statisticians. The Yale University professor alerted them to the possible contributions of statistical science and asked them to attend to the quantitative features needed to understand and help eliminate the causes and results of human rights deprivations.[19]

Thomas B. Jabine, a fellow of the American Statistical Association and an expert in applied statistics, responded to President Savage's challenge, becoming a leader in what he calls the "field of human rights statistics." Jabine differentiates between uses of human rights data for advocacy purposes and uses for enforcement and implementation of individual rights and freedoms. He says "The line of demarcation is not always sharp; many kinds of data can serve both purposes."[20] For example, the statistics included in mandatory reports to the United Nations by countries that have ratified international human rights treaties are intended to be used for the implementation and enforcement of specific human rights covered by the treaties. The reports are reviewed by the UN committees, which then make recommendations to the countries involved on how to improve their human rights policies and practices. However, Jabine concludes, some people who are directly involved in the UN human rights reporting system or have examined it from the outside have come to the conclusion that its most effective use is to publicize violations and failures to make progress, thus empowering human rights advocacy groups in each country to exert pressure on their own government to do better.

Most national governments try to gather, analyze, and publish data relevant to economic, social, and cultural progress by the people of their countries. National governments and international bodies, such as the UN Statistical Office, have collaborated on the development of concepts, definitions, and operational procedures for the production of statistics on income, expenditures, health, education, housing, labor force activities, and other aspects of the welfare of their citizens.

Of course, statistics can be distorted, and sometimes maliciously so. During the 1970s, the Marcos regime used fraudulent public health data to support the claim that the Philippines could not afford both "bread and freedom." As the martial law government curtailed free speech and press freedoms, it falsely reported ever-improving health, nutrition and education data to the Asian Development Bank, arguing that suppressing civil liberties facilitated such improvements in society as reduced crime, as well as better health and education. Thus, governments are able to withhold data or tinker with the results in attempts to improve their images. However, the notorious Marcos government use of fraudulent data was addressed by the new Philippine Constitution of 1987, promulgating a people's right to public access to information used by agencies in formulating public policy.[21]

Descriptions of human rights abuses and crimes against humanity often originate with the national and international news media. Information also comes from single-issue organizations and specialized private groups interested in various aspects of human rights. It is disseminated by political solidarity and refugee groups with diverse motivations. Direct reporting, occasionally at great risk, comes from victims and their families as well as from human rights workers with various support groups, all of whom may be vulnerable to government reprisals. For example, during the last year of the Pinochet regime in Chile, a military prosecutor attempted to seize the medical files of the Vicaría de la Solidaridad, a human rights organization of the Catholic church in Santiago.[22] When Prosecutor Sergio Cea arrived at the Vicaría on February 15, 1989, Auxiliary Bishop Sergio Valech informed him that the files had been removed from the premises and refused, on grounds of conscience, to say where they had been taken. Even after the Supreme Court issued a ruling upholding the government's seizure order, Bishop Valech said that compliance "violates one's conscientious duty to safeguard the moral and legal rights protected by professional secrecy [confidentiality]." The documents contained medical evidence of torture by government officials of the Pinochet government.

Governments sometimes report on the human rights records of other countries, as in the case of the U.S. State Department *Country Reports on Human Rights Practices*. The premise for U.S. government human rights reporting was explained in 1979 by Deputy Assistant Secretary Warren Christopher.[23] Testifying before the House of Representatives Committee on Foreign Affairs, Christopher explained, "The assessment of human rights conditions is not an exact science. There are inevitably some questions of judgment on which reasonable people will differ." Nevertheless, Christopher concluded, "I believe we can have confidence in our overall appraisals and in our identification of trends. And that is an essential predicate for an effective human rights policy." The main policy objective for Canada, the Netherlands, Norway, and the United States attempting to produce standardized assessments of international human rights has been to provide an objective basis for relating foreign assistance to human rights performance in recipient nations.[24]

Data for Advocacy and Implementation

NGOs are important sources of anecdotal information on human rights violations, and they sometimes rely on statistics in their advocacy programs. Because of the dominance of lawyers in human rights NGOs, they do not depend on statistics as much as they could. An exception is the Women's Learning Partnership (WLP), a North-South coalition of women's groups devoted to sharing information across borders. It seeks to form patterns of cooperation among women's groups on a global basis. In 2001 their Internet website featured a "Human Rights Facts and Figures" presentation with diverse statistics on women and education (70 percent of the world's 855 million illiterate people are women); health (of 8,000 fetuses aborted at a Bombay clinic, 7,999 were female); and gender violence (domestic violence is the leading cause of injury and death for women worldwide), and so forth. WLP considers the Internet a primary tool for advancing women's human rights beyond national boundaries, so their Internet site is an important resource for advocacy and for sharing the kind of information useful in dealing with women's issues, <www.learningpartnership.org/WLP/facts/human.html>.

To date, the chief antidote to unreliable information in the field of human rights reporting and fact-finding derives from the multiplicity of independently published assessments by nongovernmental organizations. The Lawyers' Committee for Human Rights and Human Rights Watch occasionally publish critical reviews of the U.S. *Country Reports* if they see evidence of lack of objectivity favoring a "client state." Voluntary groups independently publishing human rights reports are many and include Amnesty International, Survival International, the International Commission of Jurists, the Minority Rights Group, the Ligue international des droits de l'homme, Crimes of War, and scores of others. Human rights advocacy groups are proliferating worldwide and hence the sources of information are increasing. The Human Rights Internet (Ottawa) and the Science and Human Rights Program of the AAAS (Washington, D.C.) publish directories enumerating and profiling NGOs active in international human rights throughout the world. All of these organizations greatly increase the number of people who are engaged globally in monitoring international human rights. In other words, the international law of human rights has an attentive global constituency.

While the reliability of the reports of such NGOs is often reputed to be very high, taken in their entirety they do not provide systematic and comprehensive coverage of human rights violations. Each group operates under the constraints of its respective mandate and resources, leaving holes in geographic, topical, and temporal coverage. This adds to the haphazard rather than systematic nature of public reporting. The resulting gaps in human rights data collection impede the goal of systematically and, when appropriate, statistically measuring change in human rights observance over time. Moreover, many human rights groups lack statistical knowledge and consequently they may see their reports seriously challenged. No matter how solid the eye-witness depositions and documentation, if information on clustered cases of abuses are presented inconsistently, allegations of official culpability may be challenged by government malefactors. No matter how well intentioned NGO monitors, if they present insufficient quantitative support for claims of widespread human rights abuses, they may miss opportunities to analyze trends over time, including those that serve to demonstrate government failings to eliminate and remedy violations. If an NGO follows data collection techniques that use haphazard or unnecessarily diverse protocols, they may inadvertently forfeit the opportunity to analyze comparable data showing convincingly how abuses represent policy and not just ad hoc aberrations.

The problem of haphazard and methodologically inconsistent data gathering by NGOs is sometimes overcome by cooperation. An outstanding example of a collaborative project with statistically powerful analysis is *Political Killings in Kosova/Kosovo.*[25] It focused on Serbian efforts to suppress Albanian insurgents who, in 1990, declared Kosova/Kosovo an independent republic within Yugoslavia. Concerned with Belgrade's abuses of Albanians, the report was a joint project of the Science and Human Rights Program of the American Association for the Advancement of Science and the Central and East European Law Initiative of the American Bar Association. The Bar Association, in turn, drew from an alliance of Albanian NGOs who came together as The Center for Peace Through Justice. In a statistical tour de force concerning the killing patterns of the 10,500 Albanians in 1999, the report argues:

> If killings are a means of intimidation used to facilitate mass forced evictions, then refugee flows and killings would logically occur together. The fact that the increases in the number of reported killings fluctuate in unison with refugee flows is consistent with the proposition that there was a coordinated campaign targeting ethnic Albanians.[26]

The report offers a useful illustration of the strengths of statistical analysis and the advantages of sharing data in the framework of NGO cooperation.

To ensure that NGOs improve their skills in monitoring human rights violations and in statistical analysis of their resulting data, technical help has become available in recent years. Three examples follow.

1. Training in information systems management.
The difficulties faced by NGOs regarding information systems management is the concern of Human Rights Information and Documentation Systems, International. HURIDOCS is a global network of organizations concerned with strengthening the information handling capacities of human rights organizations in over 150 countries.[27] It does not collect information but rather tries to facilitate human rights documentation work by developing tools and techniques for information handling (such as formats for the recording and exchange of information on documents, organizations, and human rights violations) organizing training courses and workshops on human rights information handling in cooperation with organizations involved in the network. It also provides advice and support for the establishment and maintenance of documentation centers and information systems. In 2001, HURIDOCS published two manuals in their Human Rights Monitoring and Documentation Series. They take divergent conceptual paths: a "what is" guidebook providing an overview of various topics, and a "how to" manual meant to impart specific tech-

nical skills. *What Is Monitoring* is available on the HURIDOCS Web site
<www.huridocs.org/tools.htm>. It deals with the purposes, methods and
types of monitoring and data analysis.

2. Truth telling in cases of large-scale abuse.

In 2000, the Science and Human Rights Program of the American Association for the Advancement of Science published a 300-page manual
for human rights activists and monitors facing problems of collecting testimonies from a wide range of deponents, designing the computer data
entry screens for information processing personnel, and structuring data
to support complex analytical queries. It is entitled *Making the Case: Investigating Large Scale Human Rights Violations Using Information Systems and
Data Analysis*.[28] The edited volume brings together reports by ten experts
who worked on data processing, database representation, and generating
analytical reports as well as documenting large-scale human rights violations and the like. They tell how they created and used information systems to serve the purposes of truth telling in four countries—El Salvador,
Guatemala, Haiti, and South Africa—over the seven-year period 1992–
99). Edited by Patrick Ball, Herbert F. Spirer, and Louise Spirer, the volume is readable, practical, and a landmark technical contribution to the
cause of protecting human rights worldwide. Interest in the book goes
beyond the human rights community, evidenced by the fact that *Making
the Case* serves as a resource in college courses on information systems.

3. The development of statistical indicators.

The use of statistical indicators is helpful in research on economic and
social development.[29] The UN *Human Development Report* is the resource
to watch as it yearly improves its methodologies and presentation of development indicators for countries around the world.[30] A human rights
indicator is a piece of information (often a composite of several categories of data) used in measuring the extent to which a legal right is being
fulfilled or enjoyed in a given situation. For example, Oxfam, a British-
based NGO, has developed a pilot model of a human rights indicator, the
Education Performance Index (EPI).[31] Designed to measure implementation of the right to education, it is an aggregate indicator monitoring
primary school enrollment rates, gender equity, and school completion
(students beyond grade 4), divided by the country's Gross Domestic Product per capita. The lower the score the deeper the educational depriva-
tion. By this complex measure, we learn that the poorest countries are not
necessarily the worst offenders. On the other hand, the data involved are
insufficiently broken down—"disaggregated" to use the technical term—
making it difficult to tell whose rights are being shortchanged. Using per-

pupil average expenditures on education may be a helpful indicator but lacks precision for human rights purposes without reliable data on whose needs are unmet.

Jabine and Johnston contend that the real value of human rights indicators is as a comparative tool. For example in the field of economic, social, and cultural rights they report that such indicators will acquire value by identifying problems "in particular areas or among particular population groups in comparison with other areas or groups." More important, they conclude, these indicators, when available in time-series form, can reveal trends, and hopefully they can thereby permit "valid judgments as to whether conditions are improving or worsening over time."[32] Data-based indicators are especially convenient measures to chart trends for any given country in its efforts over time to implement the right for which measures are reported. From a baseline, the indicator would also highlight backsliding in rights performance. This kind of information could be helpful to the UN treaty committees that monitor human rights performance and to NGOs seeking to point to shortcomings (see Appendix B). Several human rights NGOs have tried to develop statistical indicators useful for monitoring the progressive realization of various social, economic, and cultural rights (see Appendix B, fifth opjective). Nevertheless, the surge toward producing data-based human rights indicators has faltered because of a lack of conceptual clarity with regard to the specific contents of the major economic, social and cultural rights.

In 2000, with the problem of conceptual clarity in mind, Stephen Hansen of the AAAS Science and Human Rights Program produced a comprehensive *Thesaurus of Economic, Social and Cultural Rights*.[33] About the same time, the World University Service-International (Geneva) joined with the American Association for the Advancement of Science and HURIDOCS to explore the possibilities for identifying the components of sophisticated and useful indicators relating to the progressive realization of the right to education. The right to health has also been broken down into component elements by the AAAS *Thesaurus*.[34] With the scope of that right so identified, states parties to the International Covenant on Economic, Social and Cultural Rights could begin the task of formulating health care indicators (data-based summaries) and benchmarks (points aimed for and measured from the first reporting year to show forward or backward movement). In 2000 the UN Committee on Economic and Social Rights asked states parties to adopt this analytical tool, calling for its application to the right to health. The Committee said the development of benchmarks and indicators will help it cooperate with reporting States to identify "targets to be achieved" over the five-year period between mandatory reports, supplying a basis on which "to consider whether or not the benchmarks have been achieved, and the reasons for any difficulties that may have been encountered." In adopting this new approach, the UN treaty committee monitoring socioeconomic rights is aware that the development of human rights indicators is unfinished work. Even when effectively designed, human rights indicators will never tell "the full story" because they do not and perhaps cannot tell enough. Left untold is the full historical, social, political, cultural, and economic context within which human rights transgressions take place, answering the question: who benefits, and who is left out? (see Appendix B, second and fifth objectives).[35]

Conclusions

People who work in the field of human rights come from every level of educational attainment. For example, those who staff human rights advocacy groups are often well educated in the humanities, social studies, and the law. Increasingly, they are well trained in computer uses and Internet procedures. As is often the case, they are not trained in statistics. Thus human rights activists may be doubtful about statistical applications to their field of work, arguing that a numeric presentation may capture the facts but not the truth. This may be correct, depending on how we test for the truth and what we expect from it. From one point of view, when the Task Force Detainees visited Trinidad Herrera in the Philippine detention camp, they served the truth as a witness to her pain. Truth in the context of witnessing connotes direct observation of the facts in a spirit of solidarity, verification and attestation. When Physicians for Human Rights (USA) dispatched an urgent action alert on behalf of Muslim health professionals facing abuse in Bosnia, they served the truth in the context of calling on members to take action. When Americas Watch reported that the Reagan administration's human rights report on Guatemala soft-pedaled the murderous behavior of client militias, media editorials said they were "telling truth to power."

Statistics is all about the pursuit of truth, but truth defined largely in terms of the mathematics of probability. This sounds technical, arcane, and cold. The truth couched in statistical terms cannot, by itself, serve the role of truth as witness, truth as a call for action, or truth saying "shame on you." But it does serve the truth in other profoundly important ways. Many statisticians offer their services to human rights groups on a consulting and even a pro bono basis, and when they do they help such groups organize data collection, attend to the technical requirements of information systems management, and analyze and make inferences from data. Statisticians also find common ground with the human rights groups they serve by agreeing that analysis supported by reliable data must be developed in a historical context. In this sense, statistical expertise in the service of human rights can greatly enhance the capacity of NGOs and policy-makers, especially in meaningfully sorting out voluminous data collections, setting the record straight, and calling for policy changes based on an assessment of the way things are going .

To know the way things are going, it helps to adopt the attitude of Martin Luther King, Jr.'s "I Have a Dream," focusing on a goal, however distant. Viewed in the long term, the implementation of human rights calls for markers along the way toward their progressive realization. For this purpose, we need to know how to assess progress in terms of which rights are being abused and how frequently, who the victims and violators are, and how these elements change over time. Generally, NGOs lack the expertise and financial resources needed to sustain statistical programs that meet professional standards. Under the circumstances, the accomplishments of these organizations are laudable, but they need additional support for the important mission of informing the world about progress or the lack of it in the field of human rights.

III
Politics

Part I of this book introduces and seeks to clarify internationally defined standards that link science and human rights, showing conceptually that UN norms cover both scientists' rights and those of the global public to enjoy the benefits of science. Part II gives detailed attention to the two areas of science and human rights identified by the Vienna World Conference on Human Rights in 1993 as most problematic, namely, health and medical ethics on the one hand, and cyberspace and information technology on the other. In Part III I turn from norms defined and issues assessed to politics pursued.

Individuals and private groups have important roles to play in redressing human rights injustices. If they do not join the human rights struggle, governments and other social institutions will succeed in their disregard of simple human respect. Part III is replete with profiles of such individuals and groups. One such example is the Minneapolis-based Center for the Victims of Torture, which supplies psychiatric therapy for torture survivors. Another example of individual heroism involves the Russian marine biologist Alexie Nikitin, who, at the risk of imprisonment, blew the whistle on Soviet nuclear dumping in the White Sea. The initiatives of groups and individuals such as these are essentially political, in the best sense of that word. Since the time of Aristotle, politics has been defined in terms of people pursuing constructive efforts on behalf of the common good.

Conflict and cooperation are the stuff of politics, whether we look at the processes of people responding to conflicts or their patterns of working out cooperation, as in myriad kinds of human rights problems connected to science, technology, and health. Thus broadly characterized, politics marks the ground covered in each of the remaining chapters, differentiated on the basis of the actors discussed: scientists (Chapter 7); nongovernmental organizations (Chapter 8); citizens at the grassroots community level (Chapter 9); and transnational organizations, including corporations and professional societies (Chapter 10). Despite this differentiation among chapters, there is naturally some overlapping, for example, as individual actors interact with advocacy groups and transnational organizations. In all of these chapters, the topics and issues presented range widely, some concerning challenges to scientific freedom and intellectual property rights, some involving the misuse of technology in ways that violate human rights, and some selected to demonstrate the utility of scientific and technical methods applied to human rights issues, whether concerned with civil, political, social, or economic rights. In short, examples of many sorts illustrate the diverse links between human rights and science.

Chapter 7, "Scientists as Human Rights Activists," lionizes the heroic response of scientists in defense of human rights. Their initiatives include not only their own claims to scientific freedom but also action on behalf of the human rights of others, bringing technical expertise into the service of everyone's human rights. For example, forensic anthropology proved its usefulness in the cause of human rights victims in Argentina, where courts accepted these scientific findings in prosecutions against military officials responsible for the deaths and disappearances of thousands of victims of the Argentine Junta's "Dirty War" (1976–83).

Chapter 8, "NGO Activism in Science, Technology, and Health," profiles diverse public interest groups, both those composed of science and health professionals such as Physicians for Human Rights (PHR) and general membership groups such as Amnesty International. The technical work done by PHR is not only admirable, it also effects results helpful to specific people. In 1996, they set up a molecular genetics laboratory at the University of Washington in Seattle capable of analyzing samples obtained from its forensic investigations.[1] When first established, the lab obtained DNA fingerprinting for children and relatives from El Salvador. Twelve years earlier, the Salvadoran military abducted hundreds of children and infants, placing them in foster homes or giving them up for adoption. As a result of the DNA fingerprinting, many families found their lost children. Chapter 8 portrays valuable work done by Amnesty International, for example, investigating and monitoring the human rights abuse of a heroic medical doctor in Paraguay whose son was tortured by officials of a right wing police state suspicious of the physician's offering free treatment for the rural poor.

Chapter 9, "Grassroots Activism in Science, Technology and Health." gives many illustrations of community activism, concerned both with members of the general public who risk their jobs to report the misuses of technology (whistleblowers) and with others who enlist scientific support in facing serious local problems. One example, involving "participatory research," is set in Woburn, Massachusetts, where people combined to investigate their polluted water supply. They suspected it was at the root of many ailments especially among children, and they investigated the cause of illness following advice from experts at the Harvard School of Public Health on how friends and neighbors could effectively conduct their own epidemiological study.

Chapter 10, "Emerging Governance Among Transnational Organizations," brings the politics of international human rights to the global level, where transnational organizations, including multinational corporations, international environmental groups, and professional societies, are all involved in responding to the new pressures of globalization by redesigning their codes of conduct to take human rights into account. In diverse ways, the examples given all tie science and technology together with human rights. I argue that in taking this route these institutions are moving toward common modes of governance designed to align them better than in the past with international standards of human and environmental rights. I focus on a Cambodian case to show the new "global compact" standards applying to corporations and taking into account the UN Human Rights Commission finding that illicit toxic waste dumping is a threat to the human rights to life and health.

Throughout the world, the recognition of internationally defined human rights and the need for adherence by public authority to domestic and international law are acknowledged. They are also ignored as governments give higher priority to perceived national security needs, economic gain, and political advantage. These perennial forces within our global political economy will not change only because of appeals to conscience or excessive trust in new international rules and institutions. To keep such negative forces in check, people must organize to pursue common objectives, fashion new modes of governance, and work out human rights respecting accommodations to conflicting interests. Where the topic of this book is concerned, this means, among other actions, vindicating human rights by the persistence of NGOs in "telling truth to power"; the heroic grassroots level action by individuals asserting their human rights; the vigilance of professionals demanding the political space necessary to exercise their commitments to scientific freedom and responsibility; and the willingness of scientifically trained people to offer their expertise when needed in the service of human rights.

Chapter 7
Scientists as Human Rights Activists

> It is now both morally and technologically true that we can no longer ignore the way people are treated in their human rights from one country to another.
>
> —Andrei Sakharov

This chapter opens with a historical nod to Galileo and more contemporary counterparts such as Andrei Sakharov who have suffered the wrath of lesser men enthralled with political power. Today professional societies regularly mobilize support for politically abused scientists. In fact, the relatively recent development of organized defense of scientific freedom has been paralleled by enlarged commitments as well to scientific responsibility. The concluding section depicts scientists, technicians and health professionals bringing their expertise into the service of human rights and thereby showing that such good citizenship takes many forms.

The Historical Abuse of Scientists

For centuries scientists have suffered repression on account of their work. The two classic examples of Archimedes and Galileo in the history of Western science have become legendary. Archimedes' fate illustrates a "blame the inventor" mentality, and Galileo ran headlong into the condemnation of deviation from accepted orthodoxy.

According to the historian Plutarch, the great mathematician Archimedes was executed by Roman soldiers in 212 B.C. while experimenting with the use of mirrors to concentrate solar energy on the sails of Roman warships.[1] Plutarch's account of the Punic Wars between Rome and Carthage suggests that the celebrated student of geometry had it coming to him because combatants used his ideas. Worse still, in Plutarch's colorful description, his advanced catapults put to shame "the hundred handed giants of mythology." Thus caught up in the cross play of power and politics, Archimedes paid for his science with death, the dreaded fate of a combatant but unworthy indemnity for a scholar.

The other classic case is dated 1609, when Galileo of Padua aimed his recently constructed telescope at the surface of the moon and the satellite moons around Jupiter. He concluded that his observations supported Copernicus's heliocentric theory.[2] Galileo's book, *The Messenger of the Stars*, brought down on him the condemnation of church authorities. He argued that it would be "a terrible detriment for souls if people found themselves convinced by proof of something that it was made then a sin to believe." But to church officials at the time, Galileo's thinking threatened the social order because it questioned the orthodox view of humankind in the universe. It did not take long before Galileo found himself confined to house arrest and his work suppressed. It took a lot longer before Pope John Paul II conceded in 1980 that Galileo had been badly treated by church authorities in the seventeenth century.[3]

Today's historians of science continue to chronicle the fate of those who contribute to our cumulative scientific knowledge despite the political quirks of their day. Two books in particular tell this story well.[4] For Great Britain, William McGucken's *Scientists, Society, and the State,* and for the United States, Peter J. Kuznick's *Beyond the Laboratory: Scientists as Political Activists in 1930s America* trace the origins of the modern role of the citizen scientist.

McGucken and Kuznick trace the increasing concern of scientists regarding the impact of their work on society, and society's infringements on scientific freedom, beginning in Britain in 1931 and reinforced in the United States only somewhat later. In various journals such as *Nature* and *Science,* and in meetings of the British Association for the Advancement of Science and the American Association for the Advancement of Science, members debated such politically volatile issues as the misuse of science by corporate interests in the West and Lysenkoism in the Soviet Union.

Lysenkoism illustrates how politics dictates the outcome of scientific experimentation. Trofim Lysenko, one of Stalin's political favorites in the mid-1930s,[5] was a biologist who controlled scientific research, bending laboratory results to suit ideological expectations about reshaping human nature under the beneficent conditions of socialism. With Stalin's approval and without supporting scientific evidence, Lysenko insisted that acquired characteristics could become inherited characteristics, and he thereby coerced biologists to reject modern genetics, which held that changing the environment will do nothing, whether for humans, laboratory rats, or wheat germ, to change genetically determined characteristics. In fact, the abuse by Stalin became internationally notorious because those who disagreed with Lysenko's "proletarian science" suffered banishment and imprisonment. By the hundreds, they paid for expressing skepticism that giving people a better environment would enable them genetically to pass on to subsequent generations the beneficial effects promising the new "socialist human nature."

In the pages of the journal *Science and Society*, some British scientists such as J. D. Bernal "toed the USSR line," according to Andrew Huxley, and others on the European political left paid scant attention to Lysenko's victims but decried the Western dependence of science funding on corporate interests, profit motives, and preparations for war inspired by nationalism.[6] Public debates carried the critical voices of dissenters who spoke up against the perversion of medicine and persecution of scientists in Nazi Germany, the use of mustard gas in Ethiopia by Italy, and other contemporaneous events that jarred scientists into debate over and reassessment of their role in society. We owe much to the ferment of pre-World War II debate and to the activist scientists of the 1930s who helped bring to science their concern for social justice.

The discovery of uranium fission atoms was a transforming experience for many scientists in the late 1930s and thereafter. A nuclear physicist, Joseph Rotblat, was living in his native Poland in 1939 when he read that the uranium atom, impacted by a neutron, would break into two particles, releasing energy. He joined American scientists working on the development of the atomic bomb, but in 1944, when he learned that the Germans had abandoned their nuclear weapons plans, he resigned and left the Manhattan Project. He said the use of the atomic bomb was unthinkable for any but deterrent purposes. Speaking in biographical terms, he explained the larger principles that brought him to that decision and his concept of scientific responsibility. "From my early youth, I wanted to be a scientist. I was also conscious of the social responsibility of science. I believed that although the primary impulse for pursing scientific research is the intellectual satisfaction of enlarging knowledge and understanding the laws of nature, science could also be of service to the community."[7]

Rotblat wrote that he had a stunning awakening when he learned that the atomic bomb had not only been tested, as he had hoped it would be, but also used, as he feared, against a civilian population in Japan. "I realized the enormous political significance of this event," he said, convinced it would lead to a disastrous international arms race. He joined with a number of other scientists involved in nuclear weapons projects after World War II, and as he explained, "we organized ourselves in groups like the Federation of American Scientists in the United States and the Atomic Scientists Association in Great Britain." These groups tried to educate the public, warning them about the dire consequences of an inevitable international arms race, and, as Rotblat said, hoping "thereby to influence governments." He lamented, "Of course, the governments ignored our warnings, and as we foresaw, nuclear weapons development escalated."

Rotblat demonstrated a level of civic-minded independence that was unusual in the 1950s, when Senator Joseph McCarthy's investigations and those of other U.S. congressional committees chilled academic and scientific freedom. Nevertheless, he signed on the Russell-Einstein Manifesto and chaired many meetings of the Pugwash Conferences on Science and World Affairs. In 1995 Joseph Rotblat and Pugwash were awarded the Nobel Peace Prize.

Today, many scientists who have endured political abuse have also spoken out plainly about the human rights of all persons worldwide. Prominent examples are the late Nobel laureate Andrei Sakharov and the Chinese astrophysicist Fang Lizhi. The thoughtful premise of their perspective is that technically trained professionals are human beings first, and only second scientists, engineers, health professionals, and so on. Of course, as Rotblat, Sakharov, and Fang Lizhi all learned, politicians may try to bring scientists to heel if their public utterances go against the political grain. Some personally suffered because they took their free speech rights seriously in the mid-1970s. Two examples are mathematician Yuri Orlov, punished for setting up a Helsinki Human Rights Watch Committee in Moscow, and statistician Carlos Noriega, abducted in front of his wife and three children for organizing an Argentine Committee on Scientific Freedom and Human Rights. The President of the U.S. National Academy of Sciences at that time, Philip Handler, said in an interview in *BioScience* that "tortured shoemakers hurt quite as hard as tortured scientists."[8] He explained that his statement was intended to avoid any suggestion of imputing special privileges for social elites or insinuations of rights peculiar to scientists. Nevertheless, members of the science community occasionally do become special targets for human rights abuses particularly because their professional activities make them more visible. In Handler's memorable terms, "Protesting only for scientists doesn't quite fit with my own beliefs about all of this. Scientists happen to be a little bit more visible. The world knows about them. The shoemakers are taken off behind the barn and shot."

Of course, the shoemaker is hardly shot for making shoes, but the scientist might very well be harassed for pursuing his or her professional work. Given the environment within which scientists work, they must recognize their need for the protection of formal guarantees of freedom, lest fear of them by insecure politicians turn them into doomed targets. This need for protection has an obvious explanation and some subtle elements. Any effective modern government needs the participation of scientists in the shaping of policy for science and of policies based on applications of science. Scientists as a group can therefore possess a significant degree of latent political power. Since scientists are not so easily managed by administrators and politicians, they may rouse a "fear of scientists" as an elite group.

This subtle notion of latent political power connected to science drew commentary from the president of the Brazilian Society for the Advancement of Science, José Goldemberg.[9] Speaking at some political risk in 1980 about the Latin American dictatorships then engulfing the Southern Cone of the hemisphere, and pointing to censorship attempts directed against Brazilian scientists for questioning the wisdom of government plans associated with nuclear energy, Goldemberg generalized that military regimes want docile populations. In a workshop in Toronto on Human Rights and Scientific Cooperation, he observed: "Scientists are not docile, generally speaking, and the better they are, the more independent they are. Therefore, they are a breed to be watched with suspicion by government authorities." Goldemberg went on, "Just by being scientists, they are likely to be seen as a threat and therefore a special target of repression." He concluded: "In this sense, science and scientists cannot be separated from politics."

Activism for Scientific Freedom

In professional circles, polemics about scientists actively promoting human rights involve no tea party banter but heated disputations reflecting fear about science being undermined by politics. For example, in 1977, Sir Andrew Huxley tried to dissuade the British Association for the Advancement of Science from passing a resolution condemning the persecution of scientists in various dictatorships in Latin America and Asia.[10] Thus Roger Posadas, then the only nuclear physicist in the Philippines, was jailed by the Marcos regime for public criticism of its excesses; likewise, Dr. Joel Filártiga was harassed in Paraguay for giving free medical care to the rural poor and other scientists in the Southern Cone of Latin America have paid for openly faulting dictators by being locked out of their laboratories, dismissed from academic posts, and sometimes joining the ranks of the disappeared. Huxley said of Soviet dissidents like Yuri Orlov and scientists in detention without charges in Latin America and the Philippines that these are people "suffering not for their scientific opinions but for political acts unrelated to the fact that they are scientists." He said that scientists who were concerned should join Amnesty International, but should not commandeer the science academy to undertake political work.

Dr. John Edsall, Harvard biologist and founder of the Committee on Scientific Freedom and Responsibility of the American Association for the Advancement of Science, responded to Andrew Huxley by insisting that "Bodies such as the British Royal Society or the United States National Academy of Sciences, have not only a right but a responsibility to concern themselves with the defense of human rights of scientists."[11] Fortunately, Edsall's view has become the accepted standard. He reasoned that when scientists overseas are deprived of their jobs because authorities dislike their social commentary or are denied access to scientific literature for political reasons, and the like, then "it is wrong to pretend that all of this is none of our business as scientists." In his appeal for solidarity with persecuted scientists, Dr. Edsall pointed to the compelling case of Andrei Sakharov.

In the late 1950s Sakharov boldly called for a unilateral ban on nuclear testing. Because the Soviet Union's premier nuclear physicist was also father of their hydrogen bomb, his views commanded global attention. He urged scientists and statesmen to do whatever they could to terminate the dangerous arms race, arguing for peaceful coexistence with the West to avoid destruction of civilization.[12] Sakharov explained that after Nikita Khrushchev exposed the human costs of Stalin's totalitarian rule he began to give critical thought to his own links to the Soviet military-industrial structure. The great physicist insisted his work as a scientist and human rights activist was connected: "My views were formed during the years I spent on nuclear weapons, my struggle against testing of these weapons in the atmosphere, underwater, or in space; in my civic activity and writing; in the human rights movements."[13] In the 1970s, Sakharov openly argued for changes in the Soviet Union, advocating the need for rule of law, greater contact with the West, and the development of a "parliamentary democracy." As one of the founders of the dissident movement in the Soviet Union and because of his outspoken criticism, he was ordered into "internal exile" far from Moscow, away from his laboratory and confined to house arrest in Gorky. He was prohibited from traveling to Stockholm to accept his Nobel Peace Prize, but even under these restraints he wrote eloquently about the importance of global activism, saying, "The defense of human rights is a clear path toward the unification of people in our turbulent world, and a path toward the relief of suffering."[14]

In the United States, Sakharov's appeal elicited a response in the National Academy of Science (NAS). In the mid-1970s, Lipman Bers and other members launched a campaign for the creation of a human rights committee within the NAS. It was planned as an organized initiative to use the prestige of the institution and its members to pressure governments to resolve the cases of disappeared, imprisoned, and threatened scientific colleagues. By 1976, the committee was functioning and had publicly denounced the treatment of eight colleagues in three countries: Argen-

Figure 6. Andrei Sakharov, 1979. In 1975 Sakharov spoke out critically on the product of his own scientific work, the Soviet hydrogen bomb. In his Nobel address he said he envisioned a future in which international human rights would serve the cause of global peace, be enhanced by ever more technologically sophisticated communications systems, and evolve into a worldwide movement enlisting the support of everyone including scientists. Courtesy of AAAS Archives, photo by Jeri Laber, Helsinki Watch.

tina, Uruguay, and the Soviet Union. Bers, one of the modern founders of
the branch of mathematics called complex analysis, often reminded colleagues they must never take freedom for granted. His convictions were
expressed in what he coyly called the "international language of science
—heavily accented English."[15] In successfully demanding an Academy
public statement in support of Andre Sakharov, Bers said, "When Sakharov began speaking out about victims of injustice, he risked everything,
and he never knew whether his intervention might help." Bers concluded
in his appeal to the Council of National Academy of Science, "Should we,
living in a free country, do less?"

Sakharov's heroic boldness challenged scientists everywhere to speak
their minds and to respond in solidarity to their calls for free expression.
Fortunately, his appeal took on salience at a time when the reach of science and technology had come to affect every quadrant of our globe. Sakharov envisioned an international human rights movement enhanced by
ever more technologically sophisticated communications systems.

Today cyberspace validates Sakharov's vision and has provided us with
beneficial technological advances. Instant global communications can
alert people everywhere to human rights violations. Increasingly, affinity
groups, such as lawyers, religious clergy, teachers, health professionals
and other scientists, have organized human rights monitoring activities
showing that the abuse of their colleagues overseas is their professional
business. The trend connecting human rights with diverse professions
affects science as well. Since 1978, the AAAS Program on Science and
Human Rights has sent scores of investigative missions to countries of
every political stripe to look into reports of governmental intrusions into
scientific freedom and other allegations of mistreatment of members of
the science, health, and engineering communities.

The American Association for the Advancement of Science publicizes
cases of abuses of scientists relying on a Science and Human Rights Action
Network. Called, AAASHRAN, the electronic network provides timely
distribution of information and continuous updates or alerts as received
by the AAAS operating over the Internet, <shr.aaas.org/program/shr.
htm>. The docket of cases is also analyzed annually in a *Directory of Persecuted Scientists, Engineers, and Health Professionals.* In 1995, when Turkish
engineers suffered more than any other group on which AAASHRAN reported, it detailed the case of two Turks, Yavuz Onen, an engineer, and his
research assistant Fevzi Onen. They were charged with criminal violation
of the "Law to Fight Terrorism" because of their participation in organizing The Turkish Human Rights Foundation. It drew official attention
by publishing a report called the *File on Torture, 1980–1994.* Nevertheless,
showing the efficacy of urgent action, the foundation was able to say, "As a
result of the international outcry that followed their arrest, the two were

acquitted one week later." The AAAS *Directory* concluded, "It is important to recognize that individual and group actions let governments know that the repression of individual human rights does not go unnoticed."[16]

Not surprisingly, the tallying of reliable reports of persecuted scientists has given birth to a Science and Health Professional's Electronic Mail Alert Network. Members are urged, in the manner of Amnesty International, to write or fax government officials in offending countries to express concern. The instant transmission of information by electronic mail and the Internet is important, according to the AAASHRAN, because, as the cases of the Turkish engineer and research assistant show, rapid action can pay off, minimizing harm to the victims.

Activism for Scientific Responsibility

In our complex, fast-paced society, it is not unusual for highly educated people to know little about developments in fields outside their own. Few scientists, engineers, technicians, or health professionals are familiar with international human rights declarations and covenants. While scientists may score low on human rights legal literacy, nevertheless, as individuals and members of professional associations, they have shown sensitivity regarding the rights of scientists to freedom as citizens and in their work. More problematic is widespread appreciation for everyone's right to enjoy the benefits of scientific progress and its applications.

Of course, the proposition of the Universal Declaration of Human Rights that everyone should "share in scientific advancement and its benefits" is quite a daunting postulate. Who is to say whether the applications of science are harmful or that everyone shares its supposed benefits? And to which benefits are people entitled? Answers to questions such as these are the province of no science czar but rather require that the public play some role in assessing whether, in their view, the applications of science are beneficial. In fact, some steps in this direction have been developing since the 1970s, when a kind of populist science emerged in the United States.

At this time, a group of scientists who were also political activists developed support among other professionals to take a stand for what they called "public interest science."[17] They sought to advance the cause of scientific responsibility by criticizing American military involvement in Southeast Asia, government programs for crop destruction and defoliation in Vietnam, the development of nerve gas stockpiles, and the deployment of anti-ballistic missile systems. Public interest science said that scientists and the public must join forces to oppose misuses of science and redirect technology to benefit everyone in ways that are consistent with human rights. Its advocates warned of the dangers of leaving the exploitation of technology in the effective control of special industrial and governmental interests.

Those promoting public interest science acknowledge many obstacles, including a disturbing trend they see that can undermine science for the common good. Professor Maurice Gibbons and colleagues argue that the typical post-World War II academic mode of knowledge-production is being systematically replaced by a process taking away from scientists decisions about the goals of their research.[18] On one hand, expensive research in government laboratories is increasingly subject to financial ceilings, for example, the American closing down of the Superconducting Super Collider. On the other, scientists in industrial companies may face new limits on their ability to report research results as firms privatize knowledge—for instance, gene patenting that benefits business objectives—on the basis of corporate officers identifying research results as their "intellectual property." Based on these kinds of examples, Gibbons et al. see ever more capital intensive research abandoning the traditional academic mode of knowledge production.

Displacing that model are new decisional patterns resulting in the agenda for scientific innovation being set by corporate and government policy-makers, as well as wealthy funders preoccupied with technological, commercial, and political concerns. Consequently, the tendency today of transforming public knowledge into intellectual property does not necessarily advance public interest science in the service of people's rights to enjoy the benefits of science. According to Professor of Physics John Ziman, science risks losing objectivity when research results that an academic scientists would have published immediately in the past are increasingly being identified by those paying for the work as "intellectual property" that may be kept secret for commercial reasons.[19] According to Ziman, what is lost under these new conditions is adherence to the principle of "public knowledge"—traditionally the linchpin of academic science. Given the dynamic nature of the scientific enterprise, Ziman, Gibbons, and others remind us of the importance of scientists cultivating self-critical perspectives to identify negative trends. On the other hand, there are some new positive trends.

Public Interest Science in the Service of Human Rights

Public interest science has taken a proactive step in organized efforts bringing science into the service of human rights. To understand this important development, a look at its origins in the 1970s is necessary. It was then that the spread of autocratic dictators throughout Latin America resulted in a crisis for international science. In Argentina, Paraguay and Chile, those under suspicion by their governments began to "disappear," victims of extrajudicial executions. Scientists worldwide heard dire tales from these countries of fellow scientists being sanctioned and dismissed from their posts for criticizing their own repressive regimes. Debates flourished among scientific membership groups worldwide as to whether to boycott international conferences held in capitals such as Rio de Janeiro, Santiago, and Buenos Aires.[20] The Argentine Junta seemed oblivious to the brain drain its self-proclaimed "dirty war" on dissidents caused, as floods of scientists and other scholars fled the countries of the Southern Cone in the mid-1970s and early 1980s.

Scientists and health professionals from all over the world who attended the Cancer Congress in Buenos Aires in 1977 heard reports of especially widespread disappearances in Argentina at the time. Two groups of brave women protesters, the Mothers of the Plaza de Mayo and later the Grandmothers of the Plaza de Mayo, formed to pressure the government. When a new civilian government finally replaced the Junta in 1983, it appointed a national commission to conduct a wrenching investigation of human rights abuses under the prior regime.[21] This event marks the beginning of cooperative efforts among scientists, not only in Argentina, but later worldwide, to bring the expertise of their respective disciplines to the support of human rights causes. For the new direction in science activism, Eric Stover deserves much of the credit, beginning with his initiatives as director of the Science and Human Rights Program of the American Association for the Advancement of Science. Freshly recruited to the AAAS in 1981 from the London Secretariat of Amnesty International, Stover became the pivotal figure in fostering the mobilization of scientists and technical experts to serve the cause of advancing human rights. Later, as director of Physicians for Human Rights, he inspired the same level of dedication to activism, recruiting and heading up teams of forensic pathologists and other health professionals dedicated to monitoring the medical consequences of human rights violations. Here are four such examples of science in the service of human rights, beginning with the seminal case from Argentina.

Forensic Anthropology and "No-Name Graves" in Argentina

In 1983, when democracy replaced a violent dictatorship, forensic techniques became central to determining the manner of death of thousands in Argentina, many of whom were finally found buried in graves marked *Ningun Nombre* (no name). Two members of the staff of the National Commission on the Disappeared, Marita Vera and Maria Julia Bihurriet, recruited six university students to begin the grim task of opening mass graves and meticulously sorting out and documenting what they found. Under the direction of American forensic anthropologist Clyde Snow, skeletons were exhumed and analyzed by the methods of forensic anthropology to confirm execution-style killings and, in many cases where soft tissue remained, to discern the signs of partially healed injuries from torture.[22] Dental and medical records were used to identify the victims, and in a number of cases forensic examination of the human remains refuted the claims of captors that the victims had died of natural causes or in "shoot-outs." Forensic methods also were employed in attempts to link living children to their putative grandparents when parents of the children had been executed. (Children of murdered parents had often been secretly adopted, at times even by those who had carried out the tortures and executions.) Moreover, by the mid-1980s molecular biologists led by Mary Clair King (University of California, Berkeley), in collaboration with Ana María Di Lonardo and other Argentine specialists, brought the power of blood-typing and later mitochondrial DNA sequencing to reunite kidnaped children with their separated families.[23] These techniques, in a process of human rights technology transfer, were later used in Brazil, Guatemala, Honduras, Iraq, Kurdistan, Mexico, the Philippines, and the former Yugoslavia.

Psychiatric Care for Torture Victims

The consequences of political oppression linger on many years after the dictators have expired. Torture victims may suffer from the symptoms of post-traumatic stress syndrome. Their lasting pain is vividly described by Jacobo Timerman in his *Victim Without a Name, Cell Without a Number*.[24] By the year 2001, there were 155 treatment programs for such people in 71 countries. Many of them depend on funding from the United Nations Voluntary Fund for Victims of Torture. In the course of clinical practice, health professionals have the unique opportunity to recognize the physical, psychological, and social health consequences of human rights abuses, and with some training to participate in appropriate treatment interventions.[25] Following the lead of the Copenhagen-based International Council for the Rehabilitation of Torture Victims, such training is provided in the United States by the Center for the Victims of Torture, serving over 25 treatment programs affiliated with the National Consortium of Torture Treatment Programs. Moreover, diagnostic training is supported by Physicians for Human Rights (USA) and Physicians for Human Rights (UK) in their continuing medical education programs offered at numerous medical colleges and universities.

    In the United States, the importance of teaching health professionals about treatment methods for torture survivors is especially relevant because between 1980 and 2000 more than two million documented refugees and asylum seekers came to the United States many of whom having experienced traumatic human rights abuses. Dr. Allen Keller said in 1996 that a growing number of his patients at the New York University Medical Center came from Bosnia, some of them survivors of torture in detention camps, others beset by assorted traumas from the long Balkan war. In response to legislative proposals to require foreigners seeking asylum to file applications within thirty days of entering the United States, Keller told Physicians for Human Rights (USA) that many of those he sees are so traumatized by the horror they endured that it can take months, even years before they can talk about it. "As a physician who examines survivors of torture," he reported, "I appreciate the difficulty that torture victims have recounting their traumatic experiences. I can only imagine the psychological devastation at being required to recount these events in a foreign language upon arrival." [26] Unfortunately, such reluctance can be mistaken for a lack of "credible fear" of persecution—a showing required by U.S. law to qualify for political asylum.

Pro Bono Statistical Analysis on Behalf of Rape Victims in Bosnia

At the invitation of the United Nations, a team of medical experts spent two weeks in 1993 in the former Yugoslavia. Their mission was "to investigate reports concerning the widespread occurrence of rape and in particular, allegations that rape was being used in a 'systematic' way, especially in Bosnia and Herzegovia." [27] The team collected data from hospitals and medical centers on pregnancy rates, birth rates, abortion rates, and the number of pregnancies reportedly due to rape. They also received direct testimonies on rape from victims and eyewitnesses. The group was in constant telephone touch with Herbert Spirer, professor of statistics at the University of Connecticut and member of the register of consulting statisticians for human rights associated with the American Statistical Association. With Spirer's assistance, the UN team used estimation procedures with assumptions clearly spelled out. For example, they documented 119 cases of pregnancy resulting from rape. Relying on medical studies that showed that of 1 of every 100 incidents of rape results in pregnancy, the team estimated that these 119 cases represented roughly 12,000 incidents of rape. They concluded, moreover, that "the majority of the rapes that have been documented have been committed by Serb forces against Muslim women from Bosnia and Herzegovina." They filed their report with the UN Special Rapporteur on Torture and presented it to the International Tribunal for the Former Yugoslavia in the Hague.

Promoting Public Participation in Science Policy

In 1986 a group of international law experts met in the Netherlands to consider the nature and scope of the obligations of states in the field of economic, social and cultural rights. The twenty-nine participants agreed unanimously on a set of standards, called the "Limburg Principles," to guide the implementation of these rights, including those related to everyone's right to enjoy the benefits of the advancement of science. One such principle says that nongovernmental organizations can play an important role in promoting the implementation of human rights.[28] "This role should accordingly be facilitated at the national as well as the international level."

There are many examples in the health sciences of NGO efforts to reach out to the grassroots to implement the people's right to enjoy the benefits of advancements of science. The Medical Action Group in the Philippines regularly sponsors community workshops on the right to health, including the promotion of popular knowledge about alternative medicine, helping people to understand the value and limits of herbal remedies that are accessible, inexpensive, and pharmaceutically trustworthy. This is especially helpful in a poor country where remote areas are otherwise medically underserved.

In another example involving health and human rights, Physicians for Human Rights (UK) has published a *Course Guide on Medicine and Human Rights*, including a bibliography. This resource is globally accessible on the Internet, <www.dundee.ac.uk/med&humanrights/SSM/admin/ad-guide.html>. Moreover, specialized scholarly journals are beginning to emerge, such as *Health and Human Rights*[29] and the electronic journal *Medicine and Global Survival* <www2.healthnet.org/MSG>.

Beyond the health sciences, there are also apt examples involving nongovernmental initiatives to bring nonprofessionals into the orbit of science. The British Association for the Advancement of Science is active in efforts to develop and diffuse science, including programs to promote popular participation. Thus the British Committee on Public Understanding of Science (COPUS) employs "outreach programs," publications, and activities to popularize science and advance public understanding and enhance public debate about science policy, thereby adding to the understanding of science a new dimension, namely, "an awareness of the public's point of view."[30] In pursuing this goal, the British Association is in admirable harmony with Limburg Principle 11, which says:

A concerted national effort to invoke the full participation of all sectors of society is . . . indispensable to achieving progress in realizing economic, social and cultural rights. Popular participation is required at all stages, including the formulation, application and review of national policies.

Public Participation and Education

To extend the benefits of science and its applications to everyone, science policy should be enlivened by more democratic participation. Critics of elite decision-making in science policy argue that complex issues linked to technology too often end up on the desks of experts with policy biases. In *Politics and Technology*, John Street asserts that, if all experts are partial—and many are in the context of our modern "corporatist structure," and if their advice is biased, then there has to be some way of checking or countering elite judgment by reliance on democratic participation.[31] Hence the need for widespread education to promote scientific knowledge even as it becomes increasingly sophisticated and specialized and even as the public's reliance on experts appears to grow since most individuals are unable to assess scientific claims for themselves.

The urgency for citizen action and public criticism of the applications of science derives from new circumstances in the economically advanced countries where an industrial power structure sometimes walls off attention to people's needs and long term interests. Examples abound, whether patenting human gene cells for financial gain without benefiting the contributors, threatening allergy-prone people's health by making snack foods out of genetically altered corn (without full disclosure), or, introducing to unknowing consumers a newly engineered strain of monster fish.

In the mid-1980s researchers began efforts to create a sterile salmon that is not genetically predisposed to spawn in the upstream places where its ancestors were born but instead can be farmed and commercially harvested. Michigan State University scientists sought by genetic engineering to break the reproduction cycle of the chinook salmon so as to produce fish of over seventy pounds compared to the fifteen-pound salmon that normally lose weight struggling under genetic mandate to return to their original spawning waters.[32]

In 2000, when the successfully cultivated giant salmon became a reality, its scientist-developer belittled scepticism aimed at the new "Frankenfish."[33] In the same vein, the spokespersons for the food trade association that stood to gain financially bluntly admonished the U.S. Food and Drug Administration not to "dawdle" in approving the new genetically engineered fish. "This is not rocket science," they insisted. "It's a straightforward question of risk assessment." But food protection specialist Christopher Klose, a sharp critic of the "industry knows best" bias, argued to the contrary that the issues are more tangled than rocket science because public confidence is involved. "Feeding the world's billions is a deadly serious business," he asserted. "If you can create a salmon that can grow as big as Moby Dick, then it should not be a surprise that people will care about what you are up to in the laboratory. Nor should it come as a surprise that you're likely to face greater than normal scientific and public scrutiny." Public participation on issues such as the right to food is feasible and appropriate.[34] The funny fish issue was closely monitored by the International Center for Technology Assessment, an NGO concerned with the public's right to know about safety testing and health risks of genetically altered food, <www.centerforfoodsafety.org>. It noted that, among the risks involved, the transgenic fish could potentially outcompete native species, with the possible effect of depleting the indigenous fish population.[35]

Among those demanding enhanced and enlarged grassroots participation in issues of science policy are people like Christopher Klose, consumer groups sensitive to possible adverse effects of genetically altered foods, the American Federation of Scientists, the Union of Concerned Scientists, and many other NGOs devoted to socioeconomic rights and environmental issues. Their view is that the benefits of biotechnology and other areas of science can be fully realized only if the public has confidence in the process of invention, approval, and use. To win that confidence, industry and its paid scientists must transcend their "trust us" attitude and accept the public as a full partner.[36] This includes recognizing the public's legitimate concerns by opening up access points for popular participation in scientific and technological decision making. Without a system of checks and balances to counter institutional self-interest, the odds are heavily against grassroots initiatives challenging corporate decision-makers.

This scenario is laid out in *The Biotech Century*, in which Jeremy Rifkind argues that the computer revolution is merely a prelude to our more significant transition into the "age of biotechnology." Long associated with the Federation of American Scientists, Rifkind's wide-ranging analysis of genetic engineering prompts him to question, not whether genetic engineering as such is good or bad, but what kind of biotechnologies we should choose, and who should decide. "Will we use our insights into the workings of plant and animal genomes to create genetically engineered 'super crops' and transgenic animals, or new techniques for advancing ecological agriculture and more humane animal husbandry practices?"[37] If not in the market, where will we find the wisdom to guide such decisions?

Enter Catherine Larrère, a thoughtful French philosopher not afraid to answer difficult questions. In *Les Philosophies de l'environnement* (Philosophies of the Environment), she registers deep concern for careless decisions about genetic engineering, arguing that as society faces complex choices regarding the subject it must take into account "the intrinsic ethical value of biodiversity." By that she means to emphasize that nature has its own worth. Moreover, humans, as a part of nature, have responsibilities to preserve it. The underlying empirical basis for her philosophical assertion of the "intrinsic ethical value of biodiversity" centers on recognition that all living organisms, through their existence and their use of complex, non-mechanical strategies to survive and reproduce, have their own value rooted in biological variation. Such variation has intrinsic value because it is the product of evolution over eons of past history and, most important, supplies the condition for its continuation in the future.

Larrère's philosophical perspective applied to the funny fish debate yields several conclusions. First, our pre-engineered unaltered salmon, as a part of evolutionary nature, have an intrinsic worth, and second, we have a duty to help preserve them against the threat of extinction. Third, genetic engineering undertaken simply for the instrumentalist reason of making profits, while not necessarily wrong, nevertheless should be viewed as suspect because instrumental values are less weighty than intrinsic values. To overcome the burden of suspicion we need mechanisms for public criticism, regulations to preserve existing species, and public fora in which to assess risks, taking into account the long term consequences of genetically engineered interventions. We need watchdog groups and public environmental interest networks who understand the intrinsic value of biodiversity. As part of nature, humans have a right to speak up in its defense, alert to the fact that irreparable mistakes can too easily be made. If profit is the sole reason for generating a new strain of salmon, then who are the advocates opposing extinction of indigenous species when overwhelmed by "new salmon"? In Larrère's analysis, the rise of genetic engineering treats genes as raw material, viewing them as an enormous pool of resources to be speedily tapped. "As such, genetic biodiversity is no longer about wise management of nature. It becomes a source of profit and of conflict among those seeking to control it."[38] Alternative voices must be heard, including those of activist scientists who can see beyond the "bottom line" of their paymasters. The challenge is to find ways through education and an enlightened populous to foster the values needed to make wise decisions in the sensitive field of genetic engineering.

Any serious expectation that people will enjoy the benefits of science through participation presupposes education. The need for a public educated on science issues was recognized in 1997 when 186 Member States of UNESCO adopted the Universal Declaration on the Human Genome and Human Rights (see Appendix D). The document says that the international community recognizes its responsibilities generated by the extraordinary advances in the life sciences and their applications. It addresses states' responsibilities to promote knowledge and to "take appropriate measures to foster the material and intellectual conditions favorable" to the free exercise of research activities.[39] During debates on drafting the Genome Declaration, most representatives argued in favor of a balanced approach between ethical concerns and the needs of scientific research. Such balance is sought, for example, in affirming the freedom of research in Article 12 as "necessary for the progress of knowledge," but placed in the context of essential protections: research on the human genome must not prevail over respect for human rights (Article 10); and reproductive cloning of human beings shall not be permitted because it is contrary to human dignity (Article 11). It says the international community recognizes its responsibilities generated by the extraordinary advances in the life sciences and their applications. The document addresses states' responsibilities to promote knowledge and to "take appropriate measures to foster the intellectual and material conditions favorable" to the free exercise of research activities.[40] Article 20 says the principles it sets out should be promoted worldwide through education in bioethics "at all levels."

New prospects for cloning human beings have set off alarm bells and made public education on the matter imperative since the events of 1997. In February of that year, Ian Wilmut, a Scottish scientist, announced that he and colleagues at the Roslin Institute had successfully cloned or nonsexually reproduced a sheep by somatic cell nuclear transfer methods. Soon thereafter, several European countries and others as diverse as Argentina, China, and Japan announced plans to discourage or deter efforts to clone human beings using the Scottish method. In the United States the National Bioethics Advisory Commission addressed the ethical and legal issues that surround the subject. In 1997 the commission recommended continuation of the ban for up to five years. In a significant step recognizing the importance of public education to facilitate participatory decision-making based on informed public opinion, the group recommended that

Federal departments and agencies concerned with science should cooperate in seeking out and supporting opportunities to provide information and education to the public in the area of genetics, and other developments in the biomedical sciences, especially where they affect important cultural practices, values and beliefs.[41]

The mechanics of cloning can be simply described. Take a donor egg, suck out the nucleus with its DNA, and fuse it with a cell, for instance, a human skin cell for a human copy. But the health hazards attendant to cloning cannot be simply described. They are unknown, according to the commission, which also noted that ethical and religious perspectives are divided on many of the moral issues related to creating a child using somatic cell nuclear transfer techniques. For these reasons, they said that the federal government should take responsibility to encourage public discussion and understanding of the issues surrounding cloning "to enable society to produce appropriate long-term policies regarding this technology should the time come when the present concerns about safety have been addressed."

Conclusion

Has politics entered the house of science, and if so, what is it doing there? In a dynamic society, it is impossible to draw a strict line between science and the tides of social change. They overlap, and if it is argued that science is value-free the same cannot be said of scientists. If scientific freedom is half the operative equation, responsibility is the other half. Where trouble comes is in identifying the issues on which scientists should take a stand and in defending the legitimacy of such interventions. Perhaps the only rules to go by are the well-formed conscience and the informed expression of convictions protected by free speech and robust debate. Therein lies the importance, indeed the necessity, for scientists occasionally to take on the mantle of the activist.

Conscience and collegiality have prompted science academies in democratic countries to reject indifference toward police state practices that violate the human rights of fellow scientists. Nor is it beneath scientists to borrow textbook political methods in the defense of basic research against statutory regulation. When state governments dictate what is to be taught in the schools about the origins of life, scientists have little hesitation in taking up the fight. If these responses are legitimate, scientists should also go to the mat for the physically handicapped in science, for the rights of other minority groups, on behalf of equal educational chances for women in science, and in defense of the intrinsic value of biodiversity.

The intersection points between science and human rights are becoming increasingly evident in modern society, no longer dismissed as contaminating science with politics. The four examples above — the use of forensic pathology, psychiatric treatment, statistical expertise on behalf of human rights victims, and educational outreach to promote popular participation in science policy — are components of a much larger phenomenon currently underway: the forging of a working partnership between scientists, health professionals, engineers, and educators putting their expertise in the service of human rights. As a mature partnership, those involved continue, through dialogue and debate, to delineate the boundary lines between science and politics. In 1978, speaking approvingly of the first signs of this partnership developing, AAAS official William D. Carey predicted that in the future "the advancement of science will not be measured entirely by the growth of research budgets or the per capita share of Nobel Prizes."[42]

Chapter 8
NGO Activism in Science, Technology, and Health

> It is not possible to have democracy without NGOs, and in Russia in 2000 it is not possible for NGOs to use technical expertise to focus on human rights, the environment and nuclear safety without running into trouble with the oligarches and the security services.
>
> —Alexandr Nikitin

This chapter is concerned with human rights nongovernmental organizations (NGOs). They provide much of the driving force in the global human rights movement. As human rights expertise among NGOs is often dominated by lawyers, I am eager to show alternatively the importance for such groups of expertise drawn from scientific, health professional, and other areas of competence. I rely on conventional political science analysis to identify the various functions such groups perform in international politics, supplying an example for each of seven types of activities. One NGO is profiled for each function, but among them their work varies widely. Some are devoted to science-linked rights including medicine; others are concerned with civil and political rights of everyone, including health and science professionals; and others use technical methodologies drawn from one of the applied sciences. Among NGOs worldwide, most work on civil and political rights; fewer on economic, social, and cultural rights; and some on the full menu of human rights. Because responding to human rights problems and remedying violations often calls for multidisciplinary approaches, there are ample opportunities for every discipline to make useful contributions.

Figure 7. Nobel laureate Jody Williams speaking at an anti-landmine rally in Washington, D.C. The founding coordinator of the International Campaign to Ban Landmines, she led a coalition of more than 1,000 NGOs in sixty countries. That year she spoke to the lobbying project assembled by Physicians for Human Rights, demanding American ratification of the Landmine Treaty and calling on the United States to stop military reliance on a "cruel and insane weapon daily dismembering people and taking its greatest toll on civilians." Courtesy of Physicians for Human Rights USA.

Global Communications and NGOs

On any given day, the news media may carry a story about individual heroics on behalf of human rights—by Muslims protesting the military shelling of innocent civilians in Bosnian health clinics treating the sick and wounded; by anti-war Salvadoran "co-madres" anguished over the disappearances of their loved ones but quietly contributing to an NGO database of victims; by Kurdish victims cooperating with Physicians for Human Rights to videotape the medical evidence of civilian injuries of Iraqi chemical bombing.

Occasionally, given adequate publicity and fanfare, such actions gain the attention of groups supporting the struggle for human rights by conferring accolades and honors, including the Commission on Global Psychiatry's Human Rights Award (American Psychiatric Association), the Human Rights Prize of the Robert F. Kennedy Memorial Foundation, the Sierra Club's Earthcare Award, or the UNESCO Award for Human

Rights Teaching. The public symbolism involved in these awards lends credibility and strength to individual initiatives. When Soviet physicist Andrei Sakharov, Argentine humanist Adolfo Pérez Esquivel, and Quiché Mayan Indian Rigoberta Menchú speak up against government abuses, their voices are enhanced by their status as Nobel laureates. It is unique to our era that prestigious awards have been conferred on effective internal critics of regimes seen as human rights delinquents. Among the most conspicuous human rights NGOs is, of course, Amnesty International, recipient of the Nobel Peace Prize in 1977.

NGOs such as Amnesty International fill a gap in world affairs because, as states and the UN fall short in the defense of human rights, it is the advocacy groups who are steadily forming a global if not yet systematized movement of investigation, protest and reform. These NGOs, such as Human Rights Watch, Global Lawyers and Physicians, the World Organization Against Torture—SOS Torture, and others, unfettered by the restrictive norms applicable to states, maximize the free flow of information across borders, spreading the word on human rights violations. While governments dally with "quiet diplomacy," the NGOs' daunting task is to turn up the volume on complaints to mobilize shame and enlist world public opinion condemning egregious rights violations. By framing complaints in the language of universal human rights, domestic groups engage the concern of receptive groups overseas. A successful international media-based campaign can bring embarrassment to the offending regime. For example, awarding the Nobel Peace Prize to the Burmese opposition leader Aung San Suu Kyi was a public relations disaster for the junta led by General U Sein Lwin who held her under house arrest. In 1989 her supporters denounced the regime's legitimacy, calling for the dissolution of military government with the rallying cry, "We want Democracy. We want human rights. That means no more U Sein Lwin." Certainly, the direct action demonstration failed to bring down the government, but it helped to render the dictatorship a pariah in the eyes of the world community.

Empowered by modern technological and communications wonders, NGOs have become increasingly effective in countering the overbearing forces of economic markets, military alliances, and entrenched elites when they run roughshod over people's human rights. For example, the American Association for the Advancement of Science has devised a system to document reports on human rights abuses suffered by scientists, engineers and health professionals <shr.aaas.org/aaashran.htm>. Other affinity groups have followed this model. For example, the Canadian Journalists for Free Expression created an electronic mail system for an Action Alert Network linking scores of organizations from more than twenty countries. The goal is to monitor human rights and freedom of expression abuses of journalists, writers, and academics around the world. Visiting their website, one finds a description of current actions and model protest letters <www.ccpj.ca/brknews.html>. The speed and coordination of the crisis-oriented network has saved numerous people from imprisonment and death.

Human Rights Politics

Scholars such as Louis Henkin who follow United Nations developments emphasize that the founders of the UN intended that states not only be prepared to scrutinize other states, but be scrutinized by them as well.[1] In the decades since 1945, the cold war, nationalism, and power politics have largely undermined their optimistic expectation that member states would police each other, and that the United Nations would somehow enforce and protect internationally defined human rights. But NGOs have made a promising beginning in filling the gap. David Forsythe says in *Human Rights in International Relations* that in 2000 there were about 250 private organizations with worldwide operations devoted to full-time advocacy of human rights.[2] The Human Rights Internet (Ottawa) files indicate that, counting part-time and strictly national groups, for example, the Cambodian Health and Human Rights Network or the Ethiopian Professionals Action Group, human rights NGOs number over 5,000, many of which are local and regional <www.hri.ca>. Dean Joseph Nye of the Kennedy School of Government estimates the number of public interest groups (not just those concerned with human rights) at over 26,000 worldwide.[3] They all use the politics of information gathering and advocacy and those that specialize in human rights are able to maximize the free flow of information across borders, spreading the word on human rights violations around the globe.

NGOs Have a Good Reputation

According to StrategyOne, the international public opinion division of the Daniel J. Edelman Company, many people have come to rely on NGOs. An international survey in 2000 found that NGOs are widely trusted, particularly on issues concerning human rights, health, and the environment.[4] The survey reveals that NGOs such as Amnesty International and Greenpeace command far greater trust among the public in industrialized countries than do governments, corporations, and the media. In Europe, almost a third of respondents trust NGOs to do the right thing "in shaping a better world," compared to only a fifth who trusted government, 15 percent business and 11 percent the media. In the U.S., 70 percent of those surveyed were positive about the role NGOs play in shaping a better world, compared to 11 percent so trusting government and business. In France, Amnesty International and the World Wildlife Fund were held in higher esteem (73 percent and 60 percent favorability respectively) than Air France and Microsoft (37 percent and 34 percent respectively). In Australia, 22 times as many respondents as those trusting corporations said they turn to NGOs for information on human rights issues; 13 times more for information on the environment. The survey was conducted in the United States, United Kingdom, Australia, France, and Germany canvassing 1,100 opinion leaders in each country about their attitudes on the reliability of information from NGOs.

NGO Functions

Human rights NGOs are private associations devoted to promoting and protecting universal human rights. There are international, regional, national, and strictly local NGOs. They come from a wide range of political, social, cultural, and financial environments. Some operate in relative freedom and enjoy high prestige; others are brutally repressed. All are independent of the state and do not seek political power themselves. They play an important role in the growth of civil society in virtually every country in the world. The myriad functions they undertake become clear when we answer the question: what do NGOs do?

- They gather and disseminate information on human right violations.
- They organize advocacy campaigns and even lobby, trying to influence public policy at the state, regional and UN levels.
- They work to build solidarity with other domestic and international NGOs.
- They perform service functions and provide humanitarian support.
- They protect and vindicate human rights in litigation.
- They engage in training and educational activities.

Illustrations are set out below for each of these functions, drawing on examples bearing on science, technology and health.

Monitoring and Information Processing

The tragic case of Joelito Filártiga, the seventeen-year-old son of a noted physician in Paraguay, shows the importance of the work of Amnesty International (AI) in monitoring human rights violations.[5] In that small landlocked country in South America, Dr. Joel Filártiga runs a clinic for the 50,000 impoverished people in the Ybycuí Valley. He publicly spoke with admiration of Article 25 of the UDHR, that "Everyone has the right to a standard of living adequate for the health and well-being of himself and of his family, including food, clothing, housing and medical care."

In a devastating incident involving the entire Filártiga family, and a famous case taken up by Amnesty International, ironically it was the doctor's innocent teenage son who suffered most at the hands of General Alfredo Stroessner's dictatorship. Because Dr. Filártiga was an outspoken critic of the government's derelict public health policy and gave free medical care to the campesinos, the right-wing dictatorship's police suspected him of subversive activities. In 1976, young Joelito was abducted by police Inspector Américo Peña, who assumed the boy could be forced to betray his father. Instead, he died of cardiac arrest during the hideous torture interrogation. Thereafter, Dr. Filártiga and his family cooperated with Amnesty International human rights workers in Paraguay. Dr. Richard Alan White, a historian then visiting from the University of California, Los Angeles, documented the case in Asunción, and he in turn transmitted information about the politically motivated torture-murder to AI's research headquarters in London. The Amnesty Secretariat and its medical officer, Dr. James Welch, took an interest in the murdered boy's case because AI is dedicated to acting on behalf of those prisoners of conscience who suffer torture in violation of the Universal Declaration of Human Rights.

As in all cases, Amnesty International doublechecked the facts, making sure that the Filártigas were not advocates of violence, that the boy was taken as a prisoner of conscience and tortured for political reasons. They then organized a worldwide campaign, issuing reports and urgent action memos calling on members to pressure the Paraguayan and other governments to take action. Soon afterward, the dictator buckled under the intense international outcry and suspended Peña. While visiting the United States, Dr. Filártiga and his daughter Dolly traced the policeman responsible for the murder of his son to New York, where he was apprehended by U.S. Immigration authorities. Thereafter, Dolly Filártiga and her father filed a wrongful death action in federal district court under the "Alien Tort" Statute (1789), alleging that in 1976 Peña-Irala kidnaped and tortured to death Joelito Filártiga, the physician's seventeen-year-old son. The district court dismissed the Filártigas' complaint for lack of subject matter jurisdiction.

The court of appeals reversed, however, recognizing the emergence of a universal consensus that international law affords substantive rights to individuals and places limits on a state's treatment of its citizens. From these circumstances, the landmark case of *Filártiga v. Peña* emerged, marking for the first time a U.S. federal court accepting jurisdiction in a civil suit against torture committed in a foreign country. Peña's responsibility for the human rights offense supplied the basis on which the court ruled that officially sanctioned torture is a violation of international law.[6] The court said: "Like the pirate and slave trader before him, the torturer has become the enemy of all mankind." In considering the award of damages in the Filártiga's civil suit against Peña, four medical specialists—physicians and psychiatrists—presented expert testimony on the effects of torture on family survivors. In 1984, Judge Eugene Nickerson announced a total judgment against the defendant amounting to $10,385 million.[7] The *Filártiga* case has become important as a precedent, having many progeny cases, including some directed at corporations for human rights violations[8] (see Chapter 10).

Advocacy

While lobbying by NGOs is normally thought of as advocacy directed toward governmental agencies, persuasion and pressure directed at private groups and corporations is also important. It has become a routine concern of ever more public interest groups, some concerned with human rights issues linked to science, technology and health. An example is Human Rights Watch, a New York based NGO, which regularly reports on problems associated with corporate responsibility, including the role of pharmaceutical companies and whether they place narrow proprietary interests over the life-and-death concerns of people with the human immune deficiency virus, HIV. Another NGO monitoring and reporting on pharmaceutical companies and their response to the AIDS pandemic is Médecins sans frontières/Doctors Without Borders. This group has undertaken heroic work in Africa and played an important role in raising international attention to the need there for HIV/AIDS treatment.

By 2001, nearly two-thirds of the 26 million people afflicted with HIV live in sub-Saharan Africa, five million in the Republic of South Africa. South African health professionals have been most vocal in international fora, complaining that very few can afford the drugs that have enabled richer countries to convert the malady from a killer into a manageable illness. In the United States, sympathetic NGOs, including gay and lesbian organizations and other human rights groups, have sought to pressure pharmaceutical companies to cease all efforts to block access to generic drugs where branded medications are not available or are priced out of reach of people with HIV/AIDS.

In a remarkable article titled "The Scientist's Story," William Prusoff explained that in the Yale University pharmacology laboratory he and his late colleague Dr. Tai-shun Lin developed d4t, an antiretroviral drug.[9] The compound was first synthesized by Dr. J. P. Horwitz, who also produced AZT, a significant inhibitor of HIV-1. It forms a critical part of a "cocktail" used beneficially by people with HIV and AIDS. As the patent holder, Yale University leased usage to the Bristol-Myers Squibb drug company for clinical trials, development, and marketing. Prusoff said that the prompting of a physician advocacy group made all the difference.

Médecins sans Frontières works with HIV patients on a daily basis in South Africa. Dealing with AIDS patients, it directly knows the baleful results of shortages of useful and reliable drugs. Professor Prusoff credits the French based NGO for its critical role in convincing Bristol-Myers Squibb to cut the cost of an antiretroviral drug. The NGO's demands on the drug company prompted Yale University, pressured by law students and the school newspaper, to join the cause. Forgoing substantial profits, the company's vice president announced cooperation "to energize a groundswell of action" to fight AIDS in Africa. Bristol-Myers Squibb reduced the cost of the Yale patented drug Zerit to 15 cents for a daily dose, or 1.5 percent of the cost to an American patient. Professor Prusoff said, "Something has to be done, the African problem is so acute." On the basis of his experience, he suggests, "It would be good if the major industrial countries donated money to the World Health Organization who would buy the drug from the pharmaceutical firms at a reduced price, and then an organization like Doctors Without Borders would be responsible for distributing the drug in Africa, with the clear understanding that in no way is it to get out to be imported here, thereby undercutting sales."[10] Prusoff concluded whimsically, "I find it hard to see any pattern in all this, except perhaps that there is a moral urge among people that, however coincidentally, can sometimes bring results" (regarding UNAIDS, see Chapter 5).

Lobbying

Sometimes, human rights NGOs influence public policy through the standard methods of political lobbying. An example of such work under the sponsorship of Physicians for Human Rights (USA) took place in July 2000, when over seventy-five activists from twenty-six states gathered in Washington, D.C., to participate in the first U.S. Campaign to Ban Landmines (USCBL).[11] As a grassroots and legislative action coalition, they met with hundreds of members of Congress or their aides, gaining the immediate support of over 40 percent. The activists, including medical professionals, teachers, peace advocates, members of the clergy, and others, lobbied Congress, actively urging the president to join the Ottawa Convention, that is, the Convention Banning Land Mines. The international agreement—which calls for a total ban on the use, manufacture, stockpiling, and transfer of antipersonnel landmines—entered into force on March 1, 1999. By then, 137 countries including all NATO nations except the United States and Turkey had signed the treaty and 99 nations had ratified it. The treaty seeks to reduce needless human suffering by increasing resources for mine clearance, mine awareness, and mine assistance.

In 2000, U.S. Representative Jim McGovern from Maine and others circulated a "Dear Colleague" sign-on letter in the House that urged the president to take steps toward joining the treaty. Physicians for Human Rights, the coordinator of the U.S. Campaign to Ban Landmines, also organized an action- and information-packed conference with more than 200 participants. In turn, growing out of the USCBL, the young people who attended launched their own initiative, "Students Against Landmines."

To motivate the participants, Nobel Laureate Jody Williams spoke at the event, and USCBL distributed a new Human Rights Watch report, "Clintons' Landmines Legacy" along with the Watch Committee's website address: <www.hrw.org>. Further solidarity came from representatives of the Buddhist, Catholic, Jewish, Lutheran, Methodist, Muslim, and Bahá'í communities who participated in an interfaith prayer service to remind everyone that the heart and soul behind the ban betokened the tens of thousands of innocent civilians killed and maimed by landmines. Additionally over 250 participants—including ambassadors and representatives from a dozen nations that had signed the treaty—also attended a reception that paid tribute to mines activists and survivors. The efforts of Belgian activists together with members of Handicap International added to the international scope of the campaign by delivering over twenty-five thousand postcards calling on the United States to sign the Landmine Ban Treaty. The world's electronic and print media, Disability Radio Worldwide, Agence France Presse, and stories in the United States, Canada, and the European press enthusiastically reported on the revitalization of the landmine ban movement in the United States.

Building Solidarity

In our global society, building solidarity becomes an ever more important function for nongovernmental organizations. It centers on mobilizing transnational political support among NGOs across national boundaries to achieve human rights for the oppressed.

Consider the case of Alexandr Nikitin, a nuclear safety inspector, former Soviet navy submarine captain, and an environmental activist. In February 1996, he was arrested by Russian authorities and charged with divulging "state secrets" to the Bellona Foundation, a Norwegian environmental organization. That group exposed dangers of nuclear waste disposal practices posed by deteriorating nuclear submarines of the Russian Navy in the White Sea region. Captain Nikitin was held in pretrial detention for ten months, and then released only under the condition that he not leave St. Petersburg. In 1998, after several attempts by the St. Petersburg Procuracy and the Russian security services to produce a viable indictment, Nikitin's first trial ended inconclusively, with the judge sending the case back for further investigation. He was finally acquitted in December 1999, and that decision was upheld in April 2000 by the Russian Supreme Court, which noted that the Russian Constitution clearly states that "everyone has the right to a favorable environment, reliable information about its state, and compensation for damages inflicted on his health and property by ecological violations." Further, the Constitution prohibits employing unpublished laws in prosecuting citizens, a tactic that the Russian Federal Security Service tried to use against Nikitin. The Supreme Court Presidium of the Russian Federation finally closed the case by rejecting the General Prosecutors' protest against the St. Petersburg verdict.[12]

These developments were monitored by the Commission on Security and Cooperation in Europe (the Helsinki Commission). In 1976, Congress set up the U.S. Helsinki Commission to monitor the acts of the signatories to the Helsinki Agreement, with particular attention to its "human dimension" provisions encompassing human rights and humanitarian affairs. Captain Nikitin testified before a Helsinki Commission meeting in 2000 that, as the Russian people have increasingly become aware of their rights, environmental NGOs have emerged as among the strongest and most popular organized groups. Their activism, however, incurred the disapproval of President Vladimir Putin who ominously singled out environmental groups as fronts for international espionage. Nikitin is the founder of the Environmental Rights Center in St. Petersburg, which addresses issues at the intersection of the environmental and human rights, and in turn, it works with the Coalition for Environment and Human Rights, which consists of over forty grassroots NGOs in Russia. Nikitin freely acknowledges that, as a defensive measure, the groups with which he is linked work cooperatively, networking their efforts at national and international levels to enhance their efficacy. Moreover, the Norwegian Bellona Foundation enjoys international solidarity links fostered by the Sierra Club, Amnesty International, and Union of Councils for Soviet Jews. In July 2000, the Sierra Club invited Nikitin to Washington, D.C., and awarded him and the Bellona Foundation its highest international honor, the Earthcare Award in defense of the survival of a livable global environment.

Service and Humanitarian Relief

Human rights violations, especially "gross violations," often impose harsh legal and medical burdens on their victims. Hence, legal aid and medical assistance, commonly uncertain or unavailable in countries accused of violations, become important NGO functions.

By the start of the millennium, nearly 39 million people worldwide have been uprooted from their homes by war, including seven million displaced in 1999 alone. Medical assistance frequently is critically important to persons victimized by armed conflict, torture, cruel, and inhumane treatment and punishment, and other egregious human rights deprivations. The International Committee of the Red Cross is well known for its humanitarian assistance to victims of civil and international hostilities as well as natural disasters, giving medical supplies, blankets, clothing, food, and shelter to countless thousands. Its work is paralleled by that of the World Council of Churches, CARE, Catholic Relief Services, Caritas, and many other organizations concerned with human rights and humanitarian assistance on a global scale.

The Balkan Wars of the 1990s brought terrible suffering to East Central Europe, causing enormous human carnage and dislocations. With the sudden exodus in 1999 of more than 800,000 Kosovars to neighboring regions and countries, Médicins sans frontières/Doctors Without Borders focused on caring for the refugees and displaced persons in Albania, Macedonia, and Montenegro, providing both medical and mental health care in the refugee camps and building housing as well as water and sanitation systems.[13] The French doctors' group also helped refugees as they returned home by initiating mental health training programs, disinfecting thousands of contaminated wells, and bringing mobile clinics to the Roma (Gypsies) and the villages of isolated Serbs.

Medical work done to assist legal investigation, that is, forensic medicine, is a uniquely pertinent humanitarian service proving valuable in human rights cases. In the aftermath of hostilities in the former Yugoslavia, forensic work was critically important. War, ethnic cleansing, persecution of minorities, indiscriminate attacks on civilians, lack of respect for humanitarian principles, and deliberate targeting of aid workers were some of the trademarks of the conflict in Bosnia in the early 1990s. That catastrophe exacted a substantial cost in lives and human health, and the Muslim enclave of Srebenica was perhaps its most tragic example. For almost the entire month of April 1993, Serbian forces surrounding Srebenica obstructed all convoys of humanitarian supplies. Serbian forces also kept out doctors, including physicians from Médicins sans frontières. As a result, Srebenica was left with a single doctor for over 40,000 people, of whom some 30,000 were refugees.

Figure 8. Forensic anthropologist Bill Hagland using a Sokia electronic survey device at a large mass grave site in Bosnia. In 1996 the International Criminal Court in the Hague announced the transfer of hundreds of body bags with human remains to Tuzla, Bosnia for one of the most extensive forensic investigations of war crimes in history. Courtesy of Gilles Peress Studio, photo by Gilles Peress.

During the siege of Srebenica, denial of humanitarian assistance meant the death of thousands of civilians. As Dr. Majkanovic said, "At least half of the wounded brought to the hospital would have survived if we had the medicines and supplies we needed."[14] In the years that followed, the surviving women of Srebrenica joined together to find out what happened to their families. In 2000, at a new morgue facility in the northern Bosnian town of Tuzla, investigators tried to uncover the answer.[15] Dozens of international experts worked for months, digging up 2,028 bodies and finding another 2,500, spread over more than a score of sites. In their cold storage facilities, they assembled the disinterred remains. The International Commission for Missing Persons in coordination with Physicians for Human Rights (USA) provided state of the art technology for the forensic pathologists identifying the remains. The mitochondrial DNA sequencers donated by the California-based PE Biosystems, in fact, made possible matching DNA from the victims' bones with blood samples from a relative. Appropriately, the fit served two purposes. Through this process, the surviving families learned the fate of their missing loved ones. Further, the process built evidence useful in proceedings at the International Criminal Tribunal for the former Yugoslavia at The Hague. That court crossed a historic threshold, because such evidence was not produced during the trials in Tokyo and Nuremberg following World War II but was used to a lesser extent in the trials in Rwanda dealing with massacres there in 1994.

On August 2, 2001, the tribunal at The Hague found former general Radislav Krstic guilty of genocide for his role in the systematic execution of more than 7,000 unarmed Muslim men and boys near Srebrenica in 1995. He was sentenced to 46 years imprisonment. Prosecutors said that the Krstic's trial was the first international trial where forensic evidence played such a crucial role. Presiding Judge Almiro Rodriques said: "By deciding to kill all the men of fighting age, a decision was taken to make it impossible for the Muslim people of Srebrenica to survive." He concluded, "what was ethnic cleansing became genocide."[16] Bringing humanitarian aid as well as some promise of justice to the victims of Srebrenica encompassed the work of many organizations.

Litigation

NGOs in the United States lead the world in reliance on litigation for the protection of and vindication of human rights. Such groups include the Center for Constitutional Rights (New York), the International Human Rights Law Group (Washington, D.C.), the Lawyers Committee for Human Rights (New York), and the Southern Center for Human Rights (SCHR, Atlanta). The SCHR's director Stephen Bright believes that because prison inmates have no political power, lawsuits on their behalf are necessary. He asserts that in all too many cases in the United States, "the human rights of prisoners are dependent upon the order of federal judges."

An NGO such as the SCHR, which operates like a law firm, must wait to receive grievances from potential plaintiffs because, under traditional standards of legal ethics, they cannot initiate lawsuits on their own. In 1999, the Southern Center acted on serious complaints they received by suing the Fulton County jail on behalf of HIV-positive jail inmates.[17] Many of these unfortunate people in Georgia's largest jail were awaiting trial on minor charges and had not been convicted of any crime. They alleged that in the preceding two years twenty-three inmates died in the Fulton County jail for lack of proper medical care. Defendants in the suit included Correctional Healthcare Solutions, Inc., the contractor responsible for inmates' health and medical care. Filed in Federal District Court in Atlanta in early 2000, the suit alleged that the contractor withheld timely medication and was otherwise careless, causing hundreds of inmates infected with HIV and AIDS to suffer excruciating and unnecessary pain, develop resistance to life-saving medication, and risking premature death. The Southern Center reports their case docket on their Internet website, <www.schr.org>.

In the Fulton County case, Judge Marvin Shoob ordered that inmates should be screened for HIV, TB, and other diseases on admission to the jail. Also, a new health care contractor provides an HIV specialist at the jail to diagnose, prescribe, and provide medication for and monitor those who are HIV positive. The judge appointed Dr. Robert Greifinger, MD, the former chief medical officer of the New York Department of Corrections to evaluate improvements over time. On the occasion of his first visit, he found dental equipment dumped in a sink and hardly cleaned before being used on the next patient. His general conclusion was that "the medical staff at the County Jail had not learned the basic hygienic lessons of the nineteenth century." Under Judge Shoob's orders, however, Greifinger soon found conditions "remarkably better," but he insisted after ten months that "they're still not at a point yet where these new systems will continue without, quite frankly, the supervision of the court."

Georgians for Equal Justice, an advocacy group founded by the Southern Center for Human Rights and other community groups, has worked with county leaders to comply with the court's order by reducing the jail's population and expanding alternatives to incarceration. Given their objectives, the group recognizes the need to bring about change with the support of the community, and accordingly, it also undertakes public relations and educational projects on the rights of the incarcerated.

Education and Training

Increasingly, NGOs and transnational organizations are making available international support services for human rights education and training. Human Rights Education Associates, a Dutch-funded NGO, has one of many Internet websites providing multiple human rights education resources: curriculum materials for formal as well as popular education.[18] Their research reports and evaluation studies can be found at <www: http//hrea.org>.

The American Association for the Advancement of Science has offered technical training services and fellowships for forensic anthropologists, pathologists, and other health professionals focusing on the scientific identification of physical torture. The work of the AAAS has had a "multiplier effect" because, through their impetus, training regarding the medical consequences of human rights violations has been shared in Argentina, Bolivia, Guatemala, the Philippines, and the Balkan states. In fact, South/South technology transfer ultimately resulted in Argentine forensic specialists participating as trainers in Guatemala.

Data Analysis for Monitoring Human Rights, by Herbert F. Spirer and Louise Spirer, offers another valuable resource especially appropriate for self-directed training.[19] It is a major contribution to the needs of human rights NGOs whose activist members, staff, and documentalists are seldom trained in statistics. The authors have lovingly and meticulously put together a remarkable manual to help human rights workers overcome their phobia of statistics. Their uniquely user friendly presentation makes it easy for NGO activists to access enough statistics to bolster the quality of their monitoring activities and enhance the accuracy of their reports. The AAAS has published editions in multiple languages, including French, Spanish, and Russian.

The Spirers' training manual achieves its objectives in several ways. First, it constitutes an almost entirely nonmathematical course on data analysis based on statistics. Second, it does not emphasize complex research methodology, but rather procedures suited to practical human rights field work, legal advocacy, and the presentation of evidence. Third, the writing style is uniformly clear and informal, employing many examples that relate directly to health professionals, and all of which cover the full range of human rights—civil and political rights as well as social, economic, and cultural rights. The book's rich array of examples will be familiar to anyone who reads or follows world news. And there are no sacred cows; the manual takes on some of the faulty analysis found in the U.S. Department of State *Human Rights Country Reports* as well as the ideologically motivated repression of the Cuban government. The Spirers' volume is the "little bit of sugar helps the medicine go down."

Conclusions

Increasingly, nongovernmental organizations serve as catalysts in the promotion and protection of internationally recognized human rights. As their numbers proliferate and a global division of labor sets in, science- and health-connected NGOs have built a coalition of international cooperation, particularly in the mutually reinforcing work of monitoring, lobbying, litigating, networking, servicing, training, and educating.

These NGOs have themselves gone through stages of development and growth, moving from passive response to active outreach. In their initial stage of activism, professional affinity groups often start cautiously, relying on polite letter writing, reflecting a collegial, nonpolitical, and formalistic response in solidarity with overseas counterparts facing persecution. Such experience is consciousness-raising, leading to more proactive strategies, until finally developing mature programs that mobilize their professional expertise to alleviate the suffering of humanity everywhere. In this advanced phase, societies of scientists, engineers, and health professionals reach their deepest commitment to humanitarian assistance and human rights consistent with standards of scientific freedom and responsibility.

Jerome J. Shestack compares the NGOs' dedication to the uphill struggle and the mythical Sisyphus, never faltering in his seemingly futile labor of pushing a weighty stone up a steep mountain, saying, "the pinnacle may never be reached. Still, while traveling the upward road, obstructions are overcome, the path is made smoother for others." Like Sisyphus, the NGOs do what they must. The struggle becomes a symbolic end in itself because it enhances human dignity, and "when all is said and done, there is no other human course."[20]

Chapter 9
Grassroots Activism in Science, Technology, and Health

Human rights can and should be declared universal, but the risk of having one's rights violated is not universal.
—Paul Farmer

International political life is energized by social movements, including those focusing on peace, human rights, the environment, and the emerging global economy. Grassroots movements have sprung up everywhere, here challenging the status quo, there demonstrating against specific policies, and often giving birth to constructive fresh ideas.[1] In the field of science and human rights, grassroots initiatives by groups and individuals have been innovative. Examples discussed here include whistle-blowers complaining of technology gone awry and corporate wrongdoing, citizen activists trying to influence science policy and effect social change with short-term popular research projects, and "science shops" linking communities to long-term programs of technical assistance. These novel and promising developments reflect discontent with some of the negative consequences of globalization whereby the concentration of information is exponentially controlled by fewer and fewer people. Grassroots science gives people command of the information that affects them locally. Community-based science also counters some of the alienating features of technological decision making, ever more driven by financial considerations based on formal cost-benefit analysis, risk indicators, and other quantitative markers dictated by competitive market forces. This kind of decision-making often leaves people out, rendering hollow the promise that as a matter of human rights, everyone should enjoy the benefits of the advancements of science. Grassroots science puts the "everyone" back into the promise of Article 27 of the Universal Declaration of Human Rights.

In focusing on science at the grassroots level, this chapter deals with those who, but for their organizing skills and tenacity, would fall beyond the pale of the beneficiaries of scientific advancement. Sometimes these people are whistle-blowers who are outside that circle and want others to know it. They act heroically to expose government and corporate wrongdoing, often putting their own jobs, health, and lives at risk, and thereby entailing human rights issues. Many such cases involve the misuse of science, technology, and public health programs that ignore the public. The motion picture *Erin Brockovitch* dramatically shows and tells the true story of someone who investigates and reports corporate misconduct by Pacific Gas and Electric Company, which is trying to cover up toxic waste dumping (lethal levels of hexavalent chromium). In addition to her risky initiative portrayed in the film, other forms of citizen activism bearing on science, technology, and health are daily generating a new "Who's Who" of individual heros and heroines.

For example, Wendy Watson is showcased here as a person joining with others to influence science policy despite numerous obstacles, not the least of which is the "commodification" of intellectual property such as genetic patenting. Also explored is "social learning," that is, specialized teaching of community folks who lack technical skills. The examples are disparate: one involves a group of Massachusetts citizens vindicating their concerns about pollution by participating in epidemiological research; the another involves ethnocartography in the Bolivian Gran Chaco. Finally, the new grassroots phenomenon of "popular research" is explored in terms of technically trained people conscientiously cooperating locally in "science shops." These novel institutions first proved their worth in the Netherlands and are now proliferating in Europe and North America. Whereas "social learning" involves short-term partnering initiated by citizens in need of technical support, "science shops" reflect a long-term commitment by scientists and university students to make themselves available for work at the grassroots level, often on a pro bono basis, effectively ensuring that everyone enjoys the benefits of the advancements of science and its applications.

Citizen Action "Against the Odds"

In a memorable statement, the anthropologist Margaret Mead once affirmed, "A small group of thoughtful people can change the world; indeed, it's the only thing that ever has."[2] Moral support for such individual citizen action on behalf of responsible social change comes from many local and international sources. Nevertheless, whistle-blowers often find themselves in painful isolation when they report instances of fraud in research, misuse of technology, and industrial corruption, and the like.

Whistle-Blowers in Australia and the United States

Whistleblowers Australia (WBA) is a private organization set up to help promote social conditions in which committed citizens can speak out about corruption, dangers to the public, and other vital social issues and can do so without reprisal. This form of citizen action often entails great personal risk because in industrialized countries, the law does not always protect workers who "blow the whistle" by reporting fraud or corruption to authorities.[3] For example, in 1996, WBA received credible complaints alleging that certain government officials manipulated medical advisory services to diagnose whistle-blowers as having a "psychiatric illness" or "personality disorder" so as to discredit them and dismiss them on medical grounds.[4] WBA emphasizes that more than waste and corruption is involved because inhibiting workers from making embarrassing disclosures thereby violates their rights of free speech. Criticizing Australian state laws for only providing compensation, but not protecting whistle-blowers against attacks in the first place, WBA lobbies for legislation to protect public and private sector employees who speak out on issues of social importance.

In the United States, by contrast, a nineteenth-century law has taken on new life both to protect and compensate whistle-blowers. The False Claims Act has become useful in defense, health care, and environmental cases where a contractor defrauds the government.[5] Under its terms, a whistle-blower, called a "relator," can file a lawsuit "under seal," meaning their complaints are not available to the public and not even to the defendant. While the complaint is sealed for as much as one year, the government investigates and decides whether it wants to join the lawsuit. If they do, and if the defendant is found liable, the defendant must pay for the government's losses plus penalty fees, and the whistle-blower is entitled to share in the recovery.

An example of a successful whistle-blower's lawsuit arose in Paducah, Kentucky, and was initiated by three employees of the Lockheed Martin Corporation.[6] They feared not only that their health was endangered but that the government was being cheated as well. The U.S. Department of Energy responded to their sealed complaint by launching a massive investigation into the company's practices at a uranium enrichment plant. Joining the suit, the Department of Energy satisfied a court that the company bilked the federal government of hundreds of millions of dollars

related to several improprieties. These included inadequately controlling radioactive materials and waste at the plant, exposing employees
to radioactive materials, recycling contaminated metals, and dumping
harmful wastes into landfills.

To address such problems with internationally defined standards, the
Sierra Club Legal Defense Fund joined with others in 1994 to promote
the formulation of the Draft Declaration of Principles on Human Rights
and the Environment (see Appendix E). Among its provisions, Article 9
says, "All persons have the right to a safe and healthy working environment." Moreover, Article 22 says, "All States shall respect and ensure the
right to a secure, healthy and ecologically sound environment. Accordingly, they shall adopt the administrative, legislative and other measures
necessary to effectively implement the rights in this Declaration." The
Paducah case shows that the U.S. False Claims Act provides an effective
procedure both to protect the whistle-blower from employer reprisal and
to compensate them, as well as to hold corporations financially liable for
violations of environmental laws.

Wendy Watson Challenges Biogenetic Patenting

Linking human rights to science, technology, and health sometimes depends on committed citizens. If people are truly to enjoy the benefits of
the advancements of science, heroic individuals must sometimes lead the
way. One such person is British health activist Wendy Watson. Beset by a
genetic predisposition to breast cancer, she came to recognize she has a
personal stake in human rights. Watson's activities illustrate the tenacity
and organizing skills needed when an individual is up against the opposition of corporate and political institutions denying her human rights.[7]

Watson learned from experience that microbiology and biogenetic
science have made great medical strides. Through genetic testing, she
grasped the fact that gene activity inside cells can give up important secrets concerning which type of breast cancer a woman has. This technology enables doctors to choose the most promising treatment with the
fewest side effects, and to determine which women face a high risk of
recurrence and need close follow-up. For example, examining the activity of 51 genes—to determine whether they are turned on, and thus
making proteins, or turned off—enables doctors to distinguish among
three types of breast cancer: the noninherited forms or the inherited
forms caused by either the *BRAC1* or the *BRAC2* gene. Fewer than one in
ten women with breast cancer have the hereditary form, but those with
a mutation on the *BRAC1* or *BRAC2* gene have a four out of five times
greater lifetime risk than others of contracting breast cancer. Uncovering

this critically important medical information has not been easy—scientifically, politically, or legally.[8]

Research on breast cancer took on political salience in Great Britain in the late 1990s when Watson participated in a worldwide research project that helped to identify the "*BRAC1* predisposition gene." The work leading to the discovery was largely publicly funded. When Watson learned that the Myriad Genetics Company (USA) was attempting to patent two genes, she organized with other British women to establish the Hereditary Breast Cancer Foundation (HBCF). The patent would cover diagnostic tests and therapeutic treatments, which are estimated to cost minimally $2,500. Watson lobbied for protective international guidelines, arguing before the European Parliament that "They cannot patent a gene which was only found with the help of people like me where there was evidence of hereditary cancer—nine people in my case. No company should benefit commercially from that kind of research." She asserted, "We will take all the action we can to stop the patenting of this gene."[9]

Watson's arguments and those of her NGO touched off vigorous debate over the "commodification" of genetic research in the European Parliament. Bolstering the HBCF's representations is the Universal Declaration on the Human Genome and Human Rights (1995), which states in Article 4 that, "The human genome in its natural state shall not give rise to financial gains" (see Appendix C). Watson's claims point up the tension sometimes seen in such cases and for which the World Intellectual Property Organization (WIPO) provides a forum to discuss needed new remedial standards and procedures. Watson's case is difficult, raising, on one hand, the competing intellectual property claims of the Myriad Genetics Company and, on the other, the needs of British women who contributed the genetic material that made possible the gene patented by the corporation.

Watson's group insisted that human rights claims favoring the women tissue donors should prevail over patent rights of the Myriad Genetics Company. Their view was that the claims on behalf of intellectual property are becoming more and more commercial, thereby linking them with the powerful forces of pharmaceutical corporations and placing them on uneven par with the human rights claims of isolated individuals.[10] HBCF sympathizers asserted that to grant monopoly patents would be to discourage the open exchange of vital information and impede cooperation in advancing scientific research in developing genetic diagnostic tools, in finding cures for diseases, and in developing new medical treatments. The women tested along with Watson said that, but for their contribution, the diagnostic tests would not have been developed. This kind of innovation is protected by the first part of Article 15 of the International Covenant on Economic, Social and Cultural Rights saying: "The State Parties to the present Covenant recognize the right of everyone . . . to enjoy the benefits of scientific progress and its applications."

The patent holders relied on the second part of Article 15 saying everyone has a right to "benefit from the protection of the moral and material interests resulting from any scientific, literary or artistic production of which [s]he is the author." An American corporate spokesman said, "The gene would probably not have been discovered but for the potential of patenting. Without the protection that the patent affords, a company could not invest hundreds of millions of dollars in getting it to the market place."[11] Undergirding their argument was the fact that the commercialization of genetics has become a multi-billion-dollar industry, which many governments see as a vital part of the economy. Broad human rights norms lacking the precision of regulatory standards can easily prove fragile under the attack of corporate lawyers.

The *Cancer Journal* editorialized that the conflict could be described as "gene hunters" at play in a field of "wild west law." And like a game with confusing rules, the campaign by the HBCF had mixed results—the UN called for more study, the Europeans said limited human rights standards should apply, and Americans issued a patent by the very group to which Watson contributed live tissue. More precisely:

- The WIPO Working Group on Biotechnology resolved to study "the relationship between the grant of patent exclusivity in a biotechnological invention and societal concerns about commercialization of biotechnology."[12]
- The European Parliament passed a "Life Patents Directive" recognizing proprietary claims for life patents provided that gene and life-tissue donors give informed consent.[13] Soon thereafter, the new Charter of Fundamental Rights of the European Union (2000) prohibited "making the human body and its parts as such a source of financial gain."[14]
- The U.S. Patent Office awarded patent number 5,837,492, entitled, "Chromosome 13-Linked Breast Cancer Susceptibility Gene" to Myriad Genetics for use in diagnostic and therapeutic applications (see <genewatch.org>).

The impacts of genetic patenting are multiple, and at least three perspectives are negative, reflecting concern that human rights may be overshadowed by market considerations. *Science* magazine opened its pages to the argument that, where scientists are concerned, if their research agendas become increasingly commercialized—a process enriched by patents —funds will likely be channeled into marketably attractive projects rather than research for the common good.[15] From the point of view of poor developing countries, "A fence is being built around biotechnological knowhow, which can only be opened from the inside." According to Piet Bukman in the Dutch Ministry of Foreign Affairs, "it is the developed countries that hold the key."[16] As for Wendy Watson, she is also pessimistic. She noted that Myriad's breast cancer test in the United States cost more than double the price in Britain, "a statistic which speaks volumes about future trends if patenting takes off here in the UK." These ominous prognostications fly in the face of everyone's human right to enjoy the benefits of the advancement of science.

Social Learning with Technical Help

Watson was on her own in gathering technical information and organizing her lobbying efforts. Sometimes technical support is accessible on a more friendly and supportive basis. That is the goal of "social learning," a process whereby people with little or no technical training but with serious local problems in need of technical remedies successfully call on the resources of science to assist them on a cooperative basis of popular research. When the plumber, the exterminator, or the health safety engineer are not available, people beset by problems sometimes turn elsewhere, including to do-it-yourself technical projects involving "social learning." Examples can be cited from the developed world as well as the less developed world. The first case reviewed here, set in Woburn, Massachusetts, helped community members in a life-saving epidemiological study to track down the sources of environmental pollution. The second entails the help of cartographers with support from civil engineers and others in assisting Bolivian Indians with instruction and social learning to undertake their own local "mapping" projects.

Woburn Epidemiology

In the 1980s, children in Woburn, Massachusetts, contracted leukemia at alarming rates. While other ailments, such as miscarriages, urinary tract disorders, and respiratory diseases were also unusually common, it was the families of the children with leukemia that first perceived a geographical pattern in the spread of disease. Chance meetings with other victims' families prompted one resident to begin gathering information about sick children in the community.[17] Anne Anderson, whose son had leukemia, theorized that the proliferation of the disease had something to do with the towns' water supply. She asked state officials to test the water, but she was rebuffed. The government knew better.

Woburn families responded by initiating their own epidemiological research with the help of scientists at the Harvard School of Public Health. Eventually, they located a cluster of leukemia cases and then tied the area to industrial carcinogens in the water supply. For years, W. R. Grace and Beatrice Foods had been dumping a cancer-causing industrial solvent into the water table of Woburn. The families of eight of the leukemia victims sued. The civil suit in *Anderson v. Cryovac* resulted in an $8 million out-of-court settlement and spurred additional federal funding for cleaning up other toxic waste sites in the United States.[18]

The Woburn case is a high-profile example of what community-based scientific research can accomplish. It caught the popular imagination when Jonathan Harr seared the incident onto the American's conscience with his prize-winning and best-selling 1996 novel, *A Civil Action*, and the 1998 movie starring John Travolta.[19] Recognizing the story's educational value, its rich lessons in science, human rights, and the environment, Lewis A. Grossman and Robert G. Vaughn compiled *A Documentary Companion to a Civil Action*.[20] It includes photographs, maps, and excerpts from Woburn's epidemiological studies as well as from other scientific reports that discredit corporate slurs on "junk science."

Community Mapping in Bolivia

Throughout history, maps have been used in areas of imperial penetration by the politically powerful to dictate their jurisdictional boundaries, undermine cultural rights, and impose their land-holding ambitions on native communities. Indigenous peoples have rarely had the opportunity to make their own maps, much less to enlist professionals to provide technical help backing up their traditional territorial claims. A nonprofit conservation group, the Center for the Support of Native Lands, works in Central and South America, facilitating community mapping that empowers indigenous and peasant groups to create their own maps. Native Lands responds to initiatives by the indigenous peoples themselves seeking to gain social and political advantage from detailed and long-standing knowledge of their environmental heritage, <www.nativelands.org> Professional ethnocartographers recruited by Native Lands lend a technical helping hand to train Indian community workers. As a result, the Bolivian indigenous "people of the Izozog" have learned mapping techniques that they effectively used in an area encompassing over 19,000 square kilometers.

The huge Gran Chaco alluvial plains cover parts of Argentina, Paraguay and Bolivia. In the small Bolivian corner of the Chaco, more than 7,500 Izoceño Guarani live in twenty-two communities straddling the Parapeti River. The Izoceños constitute a single cohesive ethnic community. They have a well-organized political structure topped by a General

Figure 9. Susaño Padilla (right) points out the shortcomings of existing government maps of Bolivia for the traditional lands of his people. He is the "captain" of
his local community of the Lower Izozog near the Paraguay border. With him are
Marcellino Apurani, another member of the Isozeño community, Andrew Tabor
of the Wildlife Conservation Society, and Mac Chapin, Director of the Center for
the Support of Native Lands. The center supplied ethnocartographic assistance
in the mid-1990s for the Indian initiative to map their native lands. Courtesy of
the Center for the Support of Native Lands.

Assembly and a Capitan Grande, and they have traditionally enjoyed a
positive and constructive relation with Bolivian authorities.

   With the support of the Ministry of Sustainable Development and with
training by Native Lands ethnocartographers, surveyors, and draftsmen,
Indian leaders enthusiastically took on responsibility to handle the mapping project, managing all the field activities. Meticulously, the "para-
cartographers" documented the locations of their traditional homeland,
settlements, temporary structures, soils, trees, water, forests, and trea-
sured natural resources such as sites where honey and medicinal plants
can be found. Displacing official maps that showed enormous swaths of
land as "uninhabited," the new map resulted in the naming of many physical features and renaming some landmarks from Spanish back to the
original Guarani names.

   The Bolivian model is described by Native Lands in their book *Indige-*

nous Landscapes, along with comparable examples from Honduras and Panama, and is used for teaching purposes in other less developed areas.[21] One of the lessons learned through experience is that prospects for success of indigenous management are enhanced when, from the beginning, the beneficiaries actually conduct the popular research themselves. The cultural self-affirmation by the Bolivian mapping campaign helped "the people of the Izozog" to reclaim their traditional heritage. This important objective is recognized in the UN Principles and Guidelines for the Protection of the Heritage of Indigenous People, because as Principle 6 states:

The discovery, use and teaching of indigenous peoples' heritage is inextricably connected with the traditional lands and territories of each people. Control over traditional territories and resources is essential to the continued transmission of indigenous peoples' heritage to future generations, and its full protection.

In addition to the empowerment objectives of the project, a major outcome was the national development of a plan to establish the Gran Chaco National Park and Integrated Management Area, a 3.4-million-hectare tract extending to the Paraguayan border. A major part of it is designed to be administered by the Izoceños and when fully implemented will be the largest territorial protected area in Tropical America. In September 1995, the area was legally established by presidential decree, and a year later an agreement was signed giving the Indian Assembly and Captain Grande administrative control over the protected area where they live.

Conservationists see the protected area as a way to conserve the last relatively intact remnant of the Gran Chaco and its unique biodiversity, relying on indigenous management as the key to maintaining biodiversity. Biodiversity is necessary for all human survival. The safeguarding and maintenance of the diverse range of species of plants and animals and their habitats is the aim of the United Nations Convention on Biological Diversity (1992). Under its terms, states agree to conserve biodiversity, ensure its sustainable development, and provide for the fair and equitable sharing of benefits from the use of genetic resources. One of the 1992 Treaty's provisions reads like an international endorsement of the Bolivian plan to entrust sustainable biodiversity to the people of the Izozog. It says: "States should enact legislation designed to respect, preserve and maintain knowledge, innovations and practices of indigenous and local communities embodying traditional lifestyles relevant for the conservation and sustainable use of biological diversity" (Article 8 (j)).

Community-Based Research

Cooperation between community members and people with technical training—whether in social organizing, law, business, or technology—can forge new connections that go beyond ad hoc social learning with its "project partnerships." Instead of one-time tasks with popular participation as described above, community-based research is an on-going process to produce sustainable change. Popular research for the common good pays social dividends over time to the general citizenry and local communities, nonprofits, educational institutions, businesses, and government. At least that is the philosophy of the Loka Institute.

Popular Research with Loka

Countless creative examples of grassroots activities drawing on science and technology do not fly under the banner of human rights, but in fact involve professional activities whereby scientists, concerned citizens, and policy-makers cooperate for mutually beneficial objectives.

Leadership in advancing community-based research comes from diverse sources. Some of the most fascinating manifestations of popular research are found in the "science shops" proliferating in Europe and North America.[22] Their work is documented by the Loka Institute, a nonprofit organization dedicated to promoting the "democratic politics of science and technology." In his prize-winning book *Democracy and Technology*, Richard Sclove focuses critically on whether the public is the beneficiary of science and its applications.[23] "Loka" is derived from the ancient Sanskrit word *lokasamgraha*, which means unity of the world, interconnectedness of society, and the duty to perform action for the benefit of the world.

Founded in 1987, the Loka Institute is both a research and advocacy organization concerned with the social, political, and environmental impact of science and technology. Loka works to make science and technology more responsive to social and environmental concerns by expanding opportunities for grassroots public-interest groups and everyday citizens, promoting their involvement in various facets of science and technology decision making. The Loka methodology uses "democratic questions" and the popular education methods of Paulo Freire within "scenario workshops."[24] In contrast to the prevailing undemocratic model of top-down decision-making on science policy, grassroots science for the common good selects tasks as they arise from the community. The Institute acknowledges that many valuable approaches are conceivable under the rubric of democratic science; thus one aspiration of the Loka Institute's project on "Identifying Democratic Technologies" is to stimulate others to design novel ways to serve the community's interests and encourage citizen participation at all levels. The goal is to seek innovative methods for empowering people to understand the social significance of the technologies that seem almost daily to make, unmake, and remake their lives.

In 1995, Loka's Community Research Network began to promote the organization of community-based research by creating an international searchable Internet discussion forum on popular research, inspiring such efforts in the United States, Canada, Israel and South Korea (see <www. loka.org>). To promote its objectives, it also relies on conferences and publications, in which Loka often hold out the European science shops as a tested and workable model.[25]

Dutch and Danish Science Shops

Loka has taken a particular interest in community-based research initiated with the first Wetenshaps Winkel (science shops). Their clinical approach to community service was a "town-gown" accommodation—a Dutch offshoot of the European democratization of universities in the late 1960s.[26] In the last quarter of the twentieth century, thirteen universities in the Netherlands established a network of multiple science shops. By design, they conduct research on social and technological issues in response to specific questions posed by community groups, public interest organizations, provincial governments, and individual citizens. The inquiries come from people concerned with environmental and energy issues, housing movements, consumer organizations, handicap organizations, and local trade unions.

Democratic and human rights values supply the guiding theory behind the science shops and their emphasis on popular research. To increase the ability for communities to make informed decisions, and not abdicate the control of information to outside agencies, the locus of control remains with those who generate the knowledge to be used in their best interests. In order for popular research to work, science shop trainers instruct community researchers in their participatory methodology, requiring shared responsibilities between the local people and the technical specialists. Participatory researchers are taught to be an integral part of any given project. Likewise, community people must be directly involved in the popular research process, beginning with their articulation of the problems that concern them, followed by the construction of questions in need of answers, and the collection and analysis of data. Through a back-and-forth process of planning, observation, reflection, and evaluation, a course of action emerges. Typical grassroots inquiries and requests have engaged participants with urban ecology, organic food production, handicap equipment, city and traffic planning, sustainable energy, external environment management, and designing programs in association with developing countries.

By 2000 the shops were providing answers to about 170 inquiries per month. In one of the world's most extensive systems for conducting popular research, graduate and undergraduate students interact with the community, cooperatively performing much of the research under faculty supervision. As with college internships and clinical law programs, students frequently receive university credit for their work and sometimes turn their investigations into theses. Because both students and faculty are doing what they would be doing as part of their regular academic workloads, the extra costs and time are minimal. The difference is that project results are not simply filed away; instead, they help people in the real world address important social problems. Moreover, the science students involved are socialized through experience to a stronger sense of community-based scientific responsibility, which may later incline them to apply their respective skills in the service of the community and of human rights.

The Dutch program of participatory and popular research has been emulated elsewhere. For example, the first Danish science shop was established at the Technical University of Denmark in 1985. In the Danish practice, science shops have resulted not only in on-going consulting relations with the community, but also in inaugurating interdisciplinary courses and research based on the problems brought to them. Traditionally, the university-centered projects are undertaken with community members on a free-of-charge basis. Like the Dutch participants, Danish science shop supervisors expect the impact on student participants will be to prepare them to fulfill their future role as experts in a way that, to a larger degree than is the tradition, includes the users' experience and an expanded sense of scientific responsibility.

Community-based research has taken hold in the United States as well. Examples include the Cornell Project in Harlem, the Chicago Center for Neighborhood Technology, the Worcester, Massachusetts, Childhood Cancer Research Institute, and the Oakland, California, Applied Research Center. Reports by the Loka Institute on the activities of these and other groups found that U.S. community research centers conduct more participatory research than do their Dutch counterparts. That is, they try to involve community members in all stages of the research process. By contrast, in the Netherlands, the community group that poses a question plays a lesser role, frequently being involved in the research process only as a member of an ad hoc research oversight group. The research itself is usually conducted by university students.

The Institute for Health and Social Justice

Some community-based research is organized in the North but carried out in the South, on site in less developed countries. An outstanding example was initiated by Paul Farmer, a Harvard professor in the Department of Social Medicine. Farmer has been a social activist since the early 1980s, when as a medical student doing elective course work in Haiti, he began a long-term project to improve the health of rural Haitians—the Clinique Bon Sauveur, which now sees more than 30,000 patients per year and trains hundreds of Haitian health care workers.

Partners in Health, the group Farmer helped to found, takes the practice of popular research one step beyond the science shops with their microscale community-based projects. They try to surpass traditional human rights research involving monitoring, description, and analysis in favor of research in quest of strategies and operational responses to the question: what is to be done? To Partners in Health, the answer is often to provide pragmatic services to the afflicted, but always in a carefully researched context of the causes of human rights violations. Partners in Health places its research priorities on issues of strategy, linking academe to new agendas in health and human rights and prompting higher education toward thoughtful programs in the service of community needs. In "Pathologies of Power: Rethinking Health and Human Rights," Farmer demonstrates the broad scope of his group's thinking:

> We need to make room in the academy for serious scholarly work on the multiple dynamics of health and human rights, on the health effects of war and political-economic disruption, and on the pathogenic effects of social inequalities, including racism, gender inequality, and the growing gap between rich and poor. By what mechanisms, precisely, do such noxious events and processes become embodied as adverse health outcomes? Why are some at risk and others spared?[27]

Set up to deal with such weighty questions, the Institute for Health and Social Justice acts as the research and educational arm of Partners in Health. A visit to their website at <www.pih.org> demonstrates how they function on the principle that human rights research should be operationally linked to service. Their internships in places like Haiti and Peru testify to their goal of examining the impact of poverty and inequality on health by linking scholarly analysis with community-based service bringing local participation into the mix. Farmer argues that such bottom-up research in the field of public health and human rights holds promise for many reasons, not least of which is that traditional approaches relying overmuch on appeals to government have often failed. In many countries, the reason is not far to find: top-down approaches are suspect because state power is responsible for most human rights violations embedded in social and economic inequities. Under these circumstances, health and human rights research directed toward improving government service too often simply helps entrenched powers shore up failing public health systems.

Certainly, this analysis was applicable in the Chiapas province of Mexico at the turn of the century. There government at odds with its own people was epitomized by the hopelessness of official public health programs where the massacre of Tzotzil Indians was the response to citizen demands for basic human needs. In 1999, Physicians for Human Rights(USA) reported on conditions in Chiapas, then beset by armed hostility and rebellion:

At best, Government health and other services are subordinate to Government counterinsurgency efforts. At worst, these services are themselves components of repression, manipulated to reward supporters and to penalize and demoralize dissenters. In either case, Government health services in the zone are discriminatory, exacerbated political divisions, and fail utterly to address the real health needs of the population.[28]

Conclusions

If popular research, science shops and health clinics initiate projects responding to needs expressed at the grassroots level, and if these developments are seen as new and unusual, then we must ask: for whom are most scientific and public health projects undertaken? The answers are well known: for-profit corporations, economically motivated interest groups, security and military institutions, government bureaucracies, and the scientific community's intellectual interests. There is nothing surprising about this situation, common in postindustrial democratic societies. Indeed, there is much to celebrate in the medical innovations, material wonders, and technological conveniences this system of self-interest has contributed to our lives, especially for those of us who live in the post-industrial North. Yet there is something fundamentally unjust when elite institutional giants set research agendas to the exclusion of most others, whether North or South. In bypassing the concerns of people in need, corporate- and defense-driven science, technology, and public health often cannot meet the test of the human rights framework, because, by definition, that approach must ask: who decides, who benefits, who is left out, and what is lost? Frequently, what is lost is technology for the common good, especially when science policy in our globalized world consistently favors elite decision-makers to the exclusion of grassroots input.

These decision-makers who employ methods bypassing popular participation routinely shape marketing strategies and public policy. Such positivist research conducted on their behalf, sometimes represented as "value free," is central to our market system and to government policy-making, and it is the research hallmark of top-down decision-making. Because this is the prevailing standard, captains of industry and elite power brokers are dismayed when people show resistence because they are excluded from participation. Consequently protests take many other forms: consumer boycotts of genetically engineered foods; rallies and demonstrations directed at pharmaceutical companies who challenge generic production of AIDS fighting drugs; and protests of architectural failings to include handicapped-access for public facilities.

Participation as dissent will unavoidably remain with us, at least so long as popular activism is needed to serve as a counter force to top-down decision-making. Citizen activism, popular research, and science shops are among the components of a culture of human rights organized by people who, wittingly or not, seek to implement everyone's right to share in scientific advancement and its benefits. The projects described in this chapter illustrate the fact that many human rights are implemented, not by official programs of centralized authorities and enforcement, but by people conscientiously responding to the values of human rights. That such value-based behavior can be projected on a larger global scale is the topic of the next chapter on governance.

Chapter 10
Emerging Governance Among Transnational Organizations

Good governance requires that legislation be the last step in regulating human affairs.
— Davinder Lamba, Mazingira Institute, Nairobi

At the dawn of our new millennium we should focus on social possibilities struggling to be born rather than clinging to the traditions that are dying before our eyes. On a grand level, the term "globalization" summarizes these possibilities. Globalization refers to our shrinking world, reduced in size by advances in travel and communications technologies and ever more interdependent environmentally, economically, and socially. These effects of globalization may take on negative or positive connotations depending on what we make of them. Impoverishing the South by enriching the North is one nightmare scenario; another is the specter of centralized control of the levers of technology by self-serving and irresponsible elites; and a world order warped by merchants of weaponry and war is one more. Of course, there are alternative futures, some that can be beneficial. In his year 2000 presidential address to the American Political Science Association, Robert O. Keohane observed that globalization can be good or bad, depending on the cultivation of appropriate and effective governance; this means that to make a globalized world benign, we need to think in ethical terms about our future.[1] "Governance arrangements to promote cooperation and help resolve conflict must be developed if globalization is not to stall or go into reverse."

Governance is not the same as government. When we think of legislation, law enforcement, and adjudication, we usually think of governments that perform these functions backed by the coercive police powers of the state. Governance is a broader term. Political scientists define governance as a network of shared goals that may or may not issue from legal and formally constituted state power.[2] Governance is a system of rule that relies on consent, widespread understanding, and agreement and is thus inconsistent with coercion. Governance is a more embracing phenomenon than government because it includes state institutions but also embodies informal, nongovernmental entities such as professional associations, corporations, and intergovernmental organizations. In this chapter we take a critical look at the governance of such transnational groups in terms of human rights values—both those agreed on and those being promoted. And we look at them as these communities self-consciously focus on issues of science and technology while also incorporating human rights norms into their own guiding standards. Two communities are examined: multinational corporations involved in the "Global Compact" to align themselves with environmental and human rights standards in cooperation with the United Nations, and science and technology professional societies revising their codes of ethics regarding human rights. Their respective developments are only beginning to emerge, each step a frail but salutary marker in the evolution of international human rights. Taken together, they raise as yet untested hopes for a benign globalization directing technology for the common good.

Multinational Corporations

Human rights standards are increasingly directed at the activities of business enterprises and multinational corporations that are not treaty-bound by human rights standards applicable to states. Sometimes they do respond to grassroots criticism for engaging in irresponsible and inhumane practices so as to maximize "the bottom line." When faced with such negative publicity, some multinational corporations accede to international compacts of good behavior, including standards linking human rights norms with science and technology. It is good corporate citizenship that matters, whether in fact cooperative behavior is prompted by enlightened leadership or pressured by boycotts, street demonstrations, stockholder caucuses, and public criticism.

In 2000, the British government commissioned a "white paper" on globalization and development published by the Department for International Development.[3] In recent years, the policy study noted, public interest in corporate social responsibility had exposed problems of child labor, corruption, human rights, labor standards, and the environment. The corporate interests of global businesses sometimes entail trading in technology that subjects people to harm to health and life. British courts have begun to respond favorably to complaints about UK-based multinationals, enabling South African and Namibian victims of mercury poi-

Figure 10. UN Secretary General Kofi Annan addressing the World Economic Forum, January 1999. He challenged major international corporation executives and labor, human rights, environmental, and development leaders to make economic globalization work for everyone. It makes good business sense for firms to internalize human and environmental rights as integral elements of corporate strategies. Courtesy of the United Nations, UN 196971C, UN/DPI photo by Milton Grant.

soning, uranium ore radiation, and asbestos exposure to file indemnification suits against Thor Chemicals, Rio Tino, and Cape Industries.[4] The report called for corporate self-reform, noting that by applying "best practices" in the areas complained of, business can play an increased role in reducing poverty, sustaining development, and avoiding litigation. The United Kingdom report concluded that "Many companies have also realized important commercial benefits in terms of reputation, risk-management and enhanced productivity" by respecting internationally defined human rights, labor, and environmental standards.

The British study precisely paralleled views gaining strength in the Office of the Secretary General of the United Nations. In January 1999, at the World Economic Forum in Davos, Switzerland, Secretary General Kofi Annan challenged business leaders to join a "global compact of shared values and principles" and give globalization a human face.[5] He argued that unless the global market, like national markets, was held together by shared values, it would be exposed to backlashes from protectionism, populism, nationalism, ethnic chauvinism, fanaticism, and terrorism. Calling for a proactive approach, Annan asserted that in addition to the efforts of the United Nations and other international agencies to promote human rights, the corporate sector must directly tackle issues linking enterprise with internationally defined human rights. He urged them to "use these universal values as the cement binding together your global corporations, since they are values people all over the world will recognize as their own." He also cautioned business executives to "make sure that in your own corporate practices you uphold and respect human rights, and that you are not yourselves complicit in human rights abuses."

Over the next two years, Mr. Annan's warning to international business leaders that globalization was more fragile than they realized became prophetic as serious rioting disrupted meetings of trade organizations and international financial institutions. The demonstrators are demanding that international financial institutions and multinational corporations clean up the dehumanizing face of globalization.

Showcasing Best Practices: The Global Compact Office

These popular pressures have given rise to a constructive UN initiative. To enlist the help of the private sector and to give institutional shape to the secretary general's proposal, a Global Compact Office has been established in the United Nations, working with other agencies such as the Office of the High Commissioner for Human Rights and the International Labor Organization. As a first step toward full participation, the Office requires a letter of support from a company's chief executive officer which is taken as a declaration of intent at the highest corporate

Global Compact Principles:
Human Rights, Labor and Environment*
In the field of human rights, the Secretary General asked world
business to:

(1) support and respect the protection of international human
rights within their sphere of influence; and
(2) make sure their own corporations are not complicit in human
rights abuses.

In the field of labor, the Secretary-General asked world business to
uphold:

(3) freedom of association and the effective recognition of the
right to collective bargaining;
(4) the elimination of all forms of forced and compulsory labor;
(5) the effective abolition of child labor; and
(6) the elimination of discrimination in respect of employment
and occupation.

In the field of the environment, the Secretary-General asked world
business to:

(7) support a precautionary approach to environmental challenges;
(8) undertake initiatives to promote greater environmental responsibility; and
(9) encourage the development and diffusion of environmentally
friendly technologies.

*UN Website: <www.unglobalcompact.org./gc/UNWeb.nsf/
content/thenine.htm>.

level. One of the attractions of the Global Compact—initially endorsed
by companies including British Petroleum, Daimler Chrysler, Unilever,
Deutsche Bank, Ericsson, and Novartis—is that it operates from a baseline of clear international standards. These companies have announced
their intentions to accept the compact's nine principles, and they unquestionably open themselves thereby to sharp criticism if they fall short.
    Putting the secretary general's nine principles into practice through

a "learning forum" and using a "soft" educational approach, the Global Compact Office does not assess performance but seeks to identify and promote good practices.[6] One way it does this is by developing and disseminating individual case studies to provide the basis for sharing experiences among participants, promoting complementary research findings resulting in an information bank of "good practices." Thus, companies supporting the Compact will post specific examples of progress on the Global Compact web site, <www.unglobalcompact.org>. The Global Compact Office also encourages the growing trend for companies to publish social reports—in which they account for their social, ethical, and environmental activities as well as their financial ones—enabling the reports to be verified externally.

Disseminating the results of any external review has become easier in light of new efforts to define standards for judgment. For example, Amnesty International's business unit has drafted proposed human rights standards for corporations.[7] As the Internet has moved to the center of the social responsibility arena, issues are quickly engaged. For example, Christopher L. Avery's "Business and Human Rights in a Time of Change," an important manifesto on corporate responsibility, first appeared as an Internet publication sponsored by British Amnesty International in 1999, <www.Amnesty.org.uk>. In our global age of instant communication, monitors scrutinizing large corporations use websites to present critical assessments and performance evaluations and even to mount attacks on corporate behavior, calling for boycotts and demonstrations, while companies have begun using their own sites to promote examples of responsible corporate citizenship.

Of course, not only have businesses sometimes been judged harshly, but the Compact itself has come under significant scrutiny. For example, the Director of the International Center for Law in Development Clarence J. Dias complains that the Global Compact is no substitute for "the binding code of conduct which was so painstakingly negotiated and so abruptly and prematurely abandoned when the UN Center on Transnational Corporations received the diplomatic equivalent of the death penalty!" Dias said that, in view of insistent pressures from the North and absent a binding Code of Conduct, "the strategy for now must be to apply existing international legal standards on human rights, on workers rights, on the environment, etc., as binding—even if only on the basis of consent."[8] Consistent with this view, Corporation Watch announced the formulation of a new "Citizens' Compact" with nine points that go further than Annan's Global Compact and call for regulation and enforcement.[9] For instance, it would provide a legal framework for the United Nations to monitor companies' activities worldwide and would prevent association with companies with destructive practices, <www.corpwatch.org>.

When the Global Compact was announced, Human Rights Watch (HRW) notified the secretary general of its approval of the initiative as constructive governance, but hopefully only a first step toward eventually establishing binding legal standards of corporate conduct. Binding legal standards require institutional oversight or external monitoring. Expressing fear that NGOs do not have the resources to be the sole monitors of compliance, HRW's Executive Director Kenneth Roth asserted:

Human Rights Watch has devoted substantial resources to promoting corporate respect for human rights, but our efforts are just a drop in the bucket. Neither we nor other NGOs begin to have sufficient resources to assume an enforcement role that should be the province of governments and the UN.[10]

Investigating corporate and government irresponsibility certainly requires more than the showcasing of "best practices"; critical reports based on careful monitoring are also essential in uncovering the complexities of corporate mischief. While the Global Compact Office highlights "best practices" without spotlighting transgressions, NGOs will need to do a great deal more, reporting on broken corporate promises. Of course, such monitoring is limited by the capacities and resources of NGOs. HRW's report on a Taiwanese company's toxic waste dumping in Cambodia in 1998 shows how difficult and intricate monitoring in this technical area can be. It also illustrates the ways in which human rights and environmental issues can be inextricably interwoven.

Monitoring Worst Cases

In November 1998 the Formosa Plastics Group of Taiwan shipped nearly 3,000 tons of Taiwanese toxic waste to the southern port of Sihanoukville, Cambodia.[11] Even though at the time there existed no Cambodian law on the subject, Minister of Environment Mok Mareth said publicly and repeatedly that national policy prohibited toxic waste dumping in the country. Nevertheless, mercury-laden refuse was deposited in an open field where impoverished villagers scavenged the poisonous cargo. Soon many of them complained of sickness, and one quickly died.

The Royal Cambodian government, expressing concern, promised a thorough investigation. Thousands of local people panicked and fled the city. Others in Sihanoukville exercised their constitutional rights and, through two days of demonstrations, blamed government corruption for the disaster. The demonstrators had failed to obtain permission to protest publicly, and when some of them grew violent, ransacking buildings, police made several arrests. The local authorities sought to blame incitement of the riots on two human rights defenders, Kim Sen and Meas

Minear, staff members of the Cambodian human rights group Licadho—the Cambodian League for the Promotion and Defense of Human Rights. Arrested in December 1998, the two were held for a month and charged with committing robbery and property damage. No convincing evidence was presented against them, but the arrests of the Licadho activists served to divert attention from corruption and the cause of the demonstrations, sending a chilling message to environmentalists and other nongovernmental groups.

HRW concluded that importation and environmental regulations in Cambodia are inadequate, as are scientific technology and expertise to cope with issues such as toxic waste. Moreover, there was no law that clearly defined, restricted, or prohibited hazardous waste imports.[12] Nevertheless, HRW said the importation of toxic garbage was almost certainly approved by senior government officials who were accused of having accepted bribes.

The discarding of deadly refuse in Cambodia illustrates the linkage between social and economic rights and political and civil rights, between science, technology, health, and human rights. To defend their right to health, Cambodians must be able to press their claims for restitution for violations of that right, both through reliance on freedom of assembly and expression, and through a functioning legal system free of political influence. In that context, human rights defenders need to be able to monitor possible rights violations without harassment or intimidation. The authorities frustrated the legitimate work of human rights defenders in this case by detaining them arbitrarily and also by not allowing pretrial release until after their month-long detention, thereby treating them more harshly than the officials finally arrested for permitting the importation and dumping of the toxic waste in the first place.

HRW identified not only corporate and government shortcomings, but also recommended long-term remedial responses, including the following:

- The government, in consultation with independent experts and organizations, should ensure periodic medical surveillance of persons exposed to the toxic waste in Sihanoukville.
- The Cambodian government and Formosa Plastics should consult with the communities most exposed to the waste in order to provide restitution.
- The Ministry of Environment should launch an urgent investigation to identify and investigate other possible industrial waste sites in Cambodia that may pose health risks.[13]

Linking Environmental and Human Rights

Human rights NGOs and other groups mandated to defend environmental integrity have begun to cooperate constructively in recent years, formulating new international standards. In *Activists Beyond Borders,* Margaret E. Keck and Kathryn Sikkink ably analyze the development of networks of environmental NGOs.[14] They say the very process of networking promotes the search for common ground. "A common advocacy position," as they describe it, is more likely to produce concrete results. An example is the Draft Universal Declaration of Human Rights and the Environment, drawn up under UN auspices and with NGOs playing a central role; it makes an important start linking science, technology, health, and human rights provisions (see Appendix E).

Beginning in 1989 at the United Nations in Geneva, Special Rapporteur on Human Rights and the Environment Madam Fatma Zohra Ksentini presided over a study of the connections between human rights and the environment. The Geneva meeting of experts drafted the first-ever declaration of principles on human rights and the environment. The group assembled at the invitation of the Sierra Club Legal Defense Fund in cooperation with the Swiss group, Association mondiale pour l'École instrument de paix, and the Société suisse pour la protection de l'environnement.[15] In 1994, Ksentini's report to the UN subcommission included their final work product.[16]

The Draft Declaration comprehensively demonstrates that accepted environmental and human rights principles embody the right of everyone to a secure, healthy, and ecologically sound environment. The document describes the environmental dimensions of established human rights, such as the rights to life, health, and culture, and also underscores procedural rights, such as the right to participation necessary for realization of the substantive rights. Further, the document is innovative for additionally prescribing the duties assigned to individuals, government, international organization, and transnational corporations.

These freshly drafted international norms put us in a position to return to the toxic dumping fields in Cambodia for several provisions of the new document obviously apply. Announcing the imperative to save our fragile planet, the Declaration calls on us to recognize the connections among its many issues: human rights, an ecologically sound environment, sustainable development, and peace. Moreover, we must apprehend these goals and standards as interdependent and indivisible. In provisions clearly applicable to the Cambodia case, it says all persons:

• have the right to a secure, healthy, and ecologically sound environment.

- have the right to freedom from pollution, environmental degradation and activities that adversely affect the environment, threaten
life, health, livelihood, well-being, or sustainable development within,
across, or outside national boundaries.
- have the right to timely assistance in the event of natural or technological or other human-caused catastrophes.
- have the right to hold and express opinions and to disseminate ideas
and information regarding the environment.
- have the right to associate freely and peacefully with others for purposes of protecting the environment or the rights of persons affected
by environmental harm.
- have the right to effective remedies and redress in administrative or
judicial proceedings for environmental harm or the threat of such
harm.

Irresponsible dumping of toxic waste is but one problem among many
increasingly drawing international public attention. Other corporate
abuses linked to globalization have also been subjected to the spotlight
of publicity. The anti-sweatshop movement insistently calls on the public to pay attention to the impact on human rights of labor policies and
free-trade pacts such as NAFTA. Activist company stockholders such as
those linked to the Interfaith Center on Corporate Responsibility have
facilitated shareholder resolutions demanding codes of conduct and the
avoidance of certain countries with poor human rights records.[17] The
legal departments of multinational corporations increasingly issue warnings to clients about the willingness of courts in Australia, the United
States, and elsewhere to scrutinize human rights issues including those
initiated by plaintiffs from overseas.[18]

The Unocal Corporation learned this lesson through experience. In
2001 shareholders of the multinational natural gas company lobbied with
members of the board of directors to adopt a code of conduct discourag-
ing involvement in countries that used forced labor. For the previous six
years the company had been involved in the Yadana natural gas project
off the coast of Myanmar (Burma). Human rights advocacy groups reported that the Burmese military employed forced labor in constructing
a pipeline that connects the gas field to Thailand. The line was completed
in 1998, but in 2000 a federal judge in California dismissed two lawsuits
against Unocal saying there was no evidence that the company conspired
with the military in human rights abuses.[19] The plaintiffs sought to hold
Unocal accountable for complicity in a construction project using slave
labor. Having lost in the courts, shareholders took up the cause to change
corporate policy. The California Public Employees' Retirement System—
the largest pension fund in the United States—voted its 1.5 million shares

of Unocal in favor of a resolution to tie executive compensation with the company's ethical and social performance. Heidi Quante, coordinator of the Unocal Campaign, said their strategy, if not successful at first, will continue because shareholder activism is increasing, and the task is to educate shareholders that "the cost of doing business in Burma is not worth the revenues."[20] That is why, by 2002, scores of Western businesses had left Burma.

Having focused a critical eye on corporate and environmental house-keeping, it is time to scrutinize the science, engineering and technology professions. Do members take human rights and environmental standards seriously, or leave them at the door when they enter the inner sanctum of their own governance?

Professional Science Societies

In the seventeenth-century utopian treatise *New Atlantis*, Francis Bacon envisioned an ethical code for scientists to promote their responsible social interaction.[21] But in 1955, remarking on Bacon's ancient suggestion, Albert Einstein and Bertrand Russell announced a dystopian vision of a world at risk of thermonuclear war. As the Pugwash founders noted, their fears were heightened by virtue of the fact that professional associations in the sciences and engineering fields were slow to formalize and draft detailed codes of ethics encouraging their members not only to protect their interests, but potentially to voice cautionary advice about the misuse of the fruits of their own labors. Nevertheless, in recent years, some science, technology, and health societies have actively moved to formulate standards of professional responsibility with explicit or implicit human rights norms.

Making these connections between how professionals behave in their daily work and whether human rights standards should apply is a lesson sometimes learned through painful experience. Certainly that was the case for the Colegeo Médico de Chile, the Medical Association of Chile. Shortly after the 1973 military coup that overthrew Chile's democratically elected government, Amnesty International issued a startling report implicating leading members of the medical profession in the torture of political prisoners taking place within the military hospital itself.[22] Ariel Dorfman's famous play and motion picture *Death and the Maiden*, based on Amnesty's evidence, showed a doctor actually monitoring torture sessions to ensure victims could take punishment short of dying. As the Chilean Medical Association was preparing to investigate physicians alleged to have taken part in torture, the dictatorship revoked their authority to set professional standards. Nevertheless, in 1983, they publically called on the Pinochet regime to end torture, warning that the

Chilean Medical Association "would not be turned into a bastion for people who transgress professional ethics."[23]

In an effort to strengthen the backbone of professional societies in Chile and elsewhere, in 1975 the World Medical Association unanimously adopted the Declaration of Tokyo. The document's first paragraph began by proclaiming that doctors shall not "countenance, condone or participate in the practice of torture or other forms of cruel, inhuman or degrading procedures," in any situations, whether armed conflict or civil strife. The Declaration justifies this unqualified imperative in terms of the "higher purpose" of every doctor's professional ethics (see box, paragraph 4).

The Chilean case points up the fact that a professional group's code of ethics is not only its pledge to do good and avoid evil, it is also a badge of the profession's autonomy, signifying its capacity to engage in humane self-governance. It is intended both to inspire people's trust in professionals and to supply the foundation for the group's self-regulating structure.

Typical of police state tactics, the Pinochet regime thwarted disciplinary action by the medical association through clumsy political interference in the form of dictatorial fiat. Nevertheless the World Medical Association's declaration made clear the responsibility of all physicians to comply with the common understanding of the norms and expectations within the world community of health professionals. Thus, even without disciplinary actions, a professional group is still able to use its standards to hold members accountable for their conduct, encouraging collegial inquiries about professional shortcomings and calling for explanations of possible wrongdoing. Avoiding strong sanctions and disciplinary measures, some societies simply rely on their ethics codes for educational purposes. For those who think unprofessional behavior deserves expulsion or suspension, the absence of formal sanctioning mechanisms is troubling. Thus, the Declaration of Tokyo has been criticized because it does not demand that national medical societies discipline doctors who "countenance, condone or participate in the practice of torture."[24]

In programs of governance, it is not unusual for norms to be promulgated and promoted without coercive mechanisms, relying instead on informal sanctions of consent and collegial support. The community, as a visible and enduring entity, undertakes the collective responsibility to educate their colleagues and protégées in the values, expectations, and roles appropriate for professional membership. Achieving this lofty goal is a work in progress for each autonomous and self-governing professional society.

In 1980 the American Association for the Advancement of Science conducted the first major survey of the use of codes among its affiliate soci-

The Declaration of Tokyo (World Medical Association, 1975)

It is the privilege of the medical doctor to practice medicine in the service of humanity, to preserve and restore bodily and mental health without distinction as to persons, to comfort and to ease the suffering of his or her patients. The utmost respect for human life is to be maintained even under threat, and no use made of any medical knowledge contrary to the laws of humanity.

For the purpose of this Declaration, torture is defined as the deliberate, systematic or wanton infliction of physical or mental suffering by one or more persons acting alone or on the orders of any authority, to force another person to yield information, to make a confession, or for any other reason.

1. The doctor shall not countenance, condone or participate in the practice of torture or other forms of cruel, inhuman or degrading procedures, whatever the offense of which the victim of such procedures is suspected, accused or guilty, and whatever the victim's beliefs or motives, and in all situations, including armed conflict and civil strife.
2. The doctor shall not provide any premises, instruments, substances or knowledge to facilitate the practice of torture or other forms of cruel, inhuman or degrading treatment or to diminish the ability of the victim to resist such treatment.
3. The doctor shall not be present during any procedure during which torture or other forms of cruel, inhuman, or degrading treatment is used or threatened.
4. A doctor must have complete clinical independence in deciding upon the care of a person for whom he or she is medically responsible. The doctor's fundamental role is to alleviate the distress of his or her fellow men, and no motive whether personal, collective or political shall prevail against this higher purpose.
5. Where a prisoner refuses nourishment and is considered by the doctor as capable of forming an unimpaired and rational judgment concerning the consequences of such a voluntary refusal of nourishment, he or she shall not be fed artificially. The decision as to the capacity of the prisoner to form such a judgment should be confirmed by at least one other independent doctor. The consequences of the refusal of nourishment shall be explained by the doctor to the prisoner.

6. The World Medical Association will support, and should encourage the international community, the national medical associations and fellow doctors to support the doctor and his or her family in the face of threats or reprisals resulting from a refusal to condone the use of torture or other forms of cruel, inhuman or degrading treatment.

eties yielding disappointing results.[25] They found that the objectives and underlying principles defining their standards were poorly explained. Having polled 240 scientific and technical organizations, the AAAS found "little attention and only minimal resources have been directed toward professional ethics matters." Similarly, conclusions reached in 1992 by the U.S. National Academy of Sciences, the National Academy of Engineering, and the Institute of Medicine confirmed the need to clarify and strengthen codes of professional ethics.[26] There is no science counterpart to the Hippocratic Oath.

The Toronto Principles and the Berlin Pledge

By 1991, work was underway to update standards of self-governance of professional societies. The Toronto Resolution, formulated in Canada at a Workshop on "Ethical Considerations in Scholarship and Science" and attended by scientists and scholars from Africa, Asia, Europe, and the Americas, provides a checklist for norms governing the professions.[27] All such codes, the resolution concluded, should contain certain key elements important for contemporary science professionals:

- the articulation of guiding principles;
- measures for adherence to those principles;
- anticipation of consequences;
- promotion of peer review;
- general availability of research methods and results;
- procedures to identify and report code violations;
- respect for individual and collective human rights;
- broad educational and informal dissemination of a code.

Included among these Toronto Principles are two precepts specifically relating to human rights. The codes of ethics should: "oppose prejudice with respect to sex, religion, national or ethnic origin, age, sexual preference, color, or physical or mental disability" and "forbid research directed towards developing or using methods of torture, or other devices and techniques that threaten or violate individual or collective human rights."

Also in 1991, these principles and other standards of ethics were taken up by the newly founded International Network of Engineers and Scientists for Global Responsibility (INES).[28] The seventeen hundred people from around the world who attended the NGO's inaugural meeting in Berlin voted to promote a universal code of science ethics. Rather than drafting model legislation that would call on professional societies to rewrite their charters and rules, the INES used a plebiscite strategy. It called on individual professionals in all the engineering and science disciplines, plus health professionals engaged in research, to endorse an eight-point set of pledges. Scientists and others are encouraged to register their support with the Centre for Research Ethics in Goteborg, Sweden.

The full terms of the pledge are accessible on the INES Internet website, <www.inesglobal.org/ines3.htm>. They include provisions commonly found in most codes of ethics, including (1) honesty in conducting and reporting research; (2) integrity in intellectual ownership and authorship; (3) avoiding deception and honoring informed consent, privacy, and confidentiality; and (4) respect and humane treatment of living subjects. On the last topic, the pledge makes explicit references to human rights, saying:

- I pledge to use my knowledge and abilities for the protection and enrichment of life. I will respect human rights, and the dignity and importance of all forms of life in their interconnectedness.
- I pledge to support research projects, whether in basic or applied science, that contribute to the solution of vital problems of humankind, including poverty, violations of human rights, armed conflicts and environmental degradation.

At the turn of the millennium, what transpired in the Toronto and Berlin initiatives demonstrates the healthy ferment yielding new regard for codes of ethics among professional societies. Certainly the INES efforts to promote internationally defined human rights standards among scientists pushes forward the cause of humane governance taking global perspectives into account. With the end of the paralyzing ideological rivalries of the Cold War and with advances in international communication and travel, communities of scholars and professionals everywhere should recognize the opportunity to tie the inexorable trends in globalization to the more humane goals of human rights and environmental protection.

The New Zealand Engineers Code

Skeptics may scoff at these expressions of lofty intentions and nonbinding declarations, seeing them as little more than the "feel good" musings of cosmopolitan elites enjoying junkets to world capitals such as Toronto and Berlin. To the contrary, recognition is globally widespread for everyone's responsibilities on behalf of human rights and environmental integrity. Indeed, the trend is even evident at the grassroots level of hard hat professionals setting calipers, directing fleets of backhoes, interpreting oscilloscope readings or fitting steam release values.

The New Zealand Institution of Professional Engineers revised their code of ethics moving to a broader perspective from an earlier set of norms saying the engineer's primary responsibilities are first to the client and second to the profession.[29] In consulting widely on proposed revisions, they heard the argument voiced by a theologian that the engineer's first responsibility is to the planet! Avoiding that cosmic formulation, they nevertheless adopted a new code in 1998 recognizing five fundamental ethical values expressed as follows. Members shall:

- take all reasonable steps to protect life and to safeguard people.
- use the planet's resources in a sustainable manner and minimize any adverse environmental impact of their engineering works or applications of technology for both present and future generations, while at the same time giving due consideration to the social and economic benefits associated with the work.
- undertake their professional duties with professionalism, competence, integrity and in good faith
- continue the development of their own and other people's knowledge, skill and expertise in the art and science of engineering and technology throughout their careers.

With professional codes of ethics undergoing revision all over the world and in many disciplines, and because such codes for the first time promote global perspectives on human rights and the environment, education becomes critically important. Institutional knowledge is not always effectively transmitted from one generation to the next, or for that matter, even to the current members of a professional society. Thus, education on these matters is the essential method for promotion and dissemination.[30] To ensure globalization with a human face, educational curricula in the various disciplines must include an ethics component reflecting life-affirming human rights norms and global-friendly environmental standards. These canons are and should become prominent in professional society governance.

Conclusions

Globalization presents the most daunting challenge to international co-operation in the twenty-first century. Heretofore, we have lived in a world in which international relations were conducted by multiple states in a framework of international law. Now we are rapidly moving toward a new world of multilayered relations among various forms of authority (government, citizens, and markets) and assorted kinds of rules and principles (laws, conventions, and social norms) working together in pursuit of common objectives and new modes of governance and working out new accommodations to conflicting interests.[31]

Governance depends on respect for principles and the voluntary adherence to guiding norms, rules, and decision-making procedures. As globalization takes on a bad name but inexorably proceeds anyway, new fields of governance are hesitantly moving to alleviate worldwide harm. The adoption of corporate compacts, newly defined human and environmental rights, and codes of professional ethics testify to the acceptance of interrelated principles and the emergence of a holistic vision for human and world survival. Of course, formal acceptance of a new ethos is not enough. Such norms must really influence attitudes and behavior for the better. At least that is the utopian vision.

We might benefit by the fresh utopian views of a modern-day Francis Bacon. Imagine compact-respecting corporations; human and environmental rights NGOs; and science, engineering and health professional societies all reading from the same book—all voluntarily bound to internationally defined human rights—acknowledging that nonstate actors do not have the responsibilities borne by governments. If the values of such transnational organizations converge, the cultures of nonstate actors align with the same expectations that are applied to governments under treaties and declarations. Can we reasonably hope that under such a visionary scenario the world might pull together in the framework of a global human rights culture that is both seen as legitimate and in which its norms effectively influence behavior?

The idealist will argue that support for the legitimacy of human rights governance will depend on many diverse strategies, including human rights education. That is the strategic perspective of the Draft Declaration of Principles on Human Rights and the Environment which says, "All persons have the right to environmental and human rights education" (Article 17). And that is why the Universal Declaration of Human Rights announced that "teaching and education" are not simply state functions but are also the obligations of "every individual and every organ of society." Of course, education is strengthened by appeals to conscience and culture, but certainly, enlightenment is not enough. While it fosters belief in the legitimacy of human rights governance, effectiveness is quite another matter. It requires action, and conventionally, action flows from enlightened self-interest.

The realist will argue that prospects for effective human rights governance among corporations and professional societies are slim unless codes, compacts and declarations grow in strength based on enlightened self-interest whether

- by consumers pressuring corporations to see that to do well they must do good;
- by all of us waking up to our responsibilities to preserve the integrity of the global environment; or
- by self-governing science societies intent on preserving their autonomy in the context of scientific freedom and responsibility linked to human rights standards.

Chief Oren Lyons, Faithkeeper of the Turtle Clan, Onondaga Nation, cut to the core of self-interest, human rights, and respect for our planet earth. He said people have rights but the planet must be seen differently. Trying to apply rights to Mother Earth is arrogant. She has her own rules and regulations and laws. There is no negotiation with this law. The only thing you can do is learn it and understand it and follow it, because if you don't you will be subject to very strong reprisal. He concluded "There are no appeals courts for these laws."[32]

Even as the negative forces of globalization threaten our fragile blue planet, nevertheless, an international culture that truly respects human rights can take us one step closer to globalization with a human face. And humanity could not have a more vital stake in taking the next step on the trail the framers of the Universal Declaration of Human Rights said led to international peace. For in the words of the poet Schiller's aphorism: "What is left undone one minute is restored by no eternity."

Appendix A. International Covenant on Economic, Social and Cultural Rights (selected provisions)

Opened for signature on 19 December 1966; entered into force on 3 January 1976. U.N.G.A. Resolution 2200 (XXI), 21 U.N. GAOR, Supp. (No.16) 49, U.N. Doc. A/6316 (1967)

Preamble

The States Parties to the Present Covenant,

Considering that, in accordance with the principles proclaimed in the Charter of the United Nations, recognition of the inherent dignity and of the equal and inalienable rights of all members of the human family is the foundation of freedom, justice and peace in the world,

Recognizing that these rights derive from the inherent dignity of the human person,

Recognizing that, in accordance with the Universal Declaration of Human Rights, the ideal of free human beings enjoying freedom from fear and want can only be achieved if conditions are created whereby everyone may enjoy his economic, social and cultural rights, as well as his civil and political rights,

Considering the obligation of States under the Charter of the United Nations to promote universal respect for, and observance of, human rights and freedoms,

Realizing that the individual, having duties to other individuals and the community to which he belongs, is under a responsibility to strive for the promotion and observance of the rights recognized in the present Covenant,

Agree upon the following articles:

Part I

Article 1

(1) All peoples have the right of self-determination. By virtue of that right they freely determine their political status and freely pursue their economic, social and cultural development.

(2) All people may, for their own ends, freely dispose of their natural wealth and resources without prejudice to any obligations arising out of international economic co-operation, based upon the principle of mutual benefit, and international law. In no case may a people be deprived of its own means of subsistence.

(3) The States Parties to the present Covenant, including those having responsibility for the administration of Non-Self-Governing and Trust Territories, shall promote the realization of the right to self-determination, and shall respect that right, in conformity with the provisions of the Charter of the United Nations.

Part II

Article 2

(1) Each State Party to the present Covenant undertakes to take steps, individually and through international assistance and cooperation, especially economic and technical, to the maximum of its available resources, with a view to achieving progressively the full realization of the rights recognized in the present Covenant by all appropriate means, including in particular the adoption of legislative measures.

(2) The States Parties to the present Covenant undertake to guarantee that the rights enunciated in the present Covenant will be exercised without discrimination of any kind as to race, colour, sex, language, religion, political or other opinion, national or social origin, property, birth or other status.   (3) Developing countries, with due regard to human rights and their national economy, may determine to what extent they would guarantee the economic rights recognized in the present Covenant to non-nationals.

Article 3

The States Parties to the present Covenant undertake to ensure the equal right of men and women to the enjoyment of all economic, social and cultural rights set forth in the present Covenant.

Article 4

The States Parties to the present Covenant recognize that, in the enjoyment of those rights provided by the State in conformity with the present Covenant, the State may subject such rights only to such limitations as are determined by law only in so far as this may be compatible with the nature of these rights and solely for the purpose of promoting the general welfare in a democratic society.

Article 5

(1) Nothing in the present Covenant may be interpreted as implying for any State, group or person any right to engage in any activity or to perform any act aimed at the destruction of any of the rights and freedoms recognized herein, or at their limitation to a greater extent than is provided for in the present Covenant.

(2) No restriction upon or derogation from any of the fundamental human rights recognized or existing in any country in virtue of law, conventions, regulations or custom shall be admitted on the pretext that the present Covenant does not recognize such rights or that it recognizes them to a lesser extent.

Part III

Article 6

(1) The States Parties to the present Covenant recognize the right to work, which includes the right of everyone to the opportunity to gain his living by work which he freely chooses or accepts, and will take appropriate steps to safeguard this right.

(2) The steps to be taken by a State Party to the present Covenant to achieve the full realization of this right shall include technical and vocational guidance and training programmes, policies and techniques to achieve steady economic, social and cultural development and full and productive employment under conditions safe-guarding fundamental political and economic freedoms to the individual.

Article 7

The States Parties to the present Covenant recognize the right of everyone to the enjoyment of just and favourable conditions of work which ensure, in particular: (a) Remuneration which provides all workers, as a minimum, with: (i) Fair wages and equal remuneration for work of equal value without distinction of any kind, in particular women being guaranteed conditions of work not inferior to those enjoyed by men, with equal pay for equal work; (ii) A decent living for themselves and their families in accordance with the provisions of the present Covenant; (b) Safe and healthy working conditions; (c) Equal opportunity for everyone to be promoted in his employment to an appropriate higher level, subject to no considerations other than those of seniority and competence; (d) Rest, leisure and reasonable limitation of working hours and periodic holidays with pay, as well as remuneration for public holidays.

Article 8

The right to form trade unions and to strike . . .

Article 9

The States Parties to the present Covenant recognize the right of everyone to social security, including social insurance.

Article 10

The States Parties to the present Covenant recognize that:

(1) The widest possible protection and assistance should be accorded to the family, which is the natural and fundamental group unit of society, particularly for its establishment and while it is responsible for the care and education of dependent children. Marriage must be entered into with the free consent of the intending spouses.

(2) Special protection should be accorded to mothers during a reasonable period before and after childbirth. During such period working mothers should be accorded paid leave or leave with adequate social security benefits.

(3) Special measures of protection and assistance should be taken on behalf of all children and young persons without discrimination for reasons of parentage or other conditions. Children and young persons should be protected from economic and social exploitation. Their employment in work harmful to their morals or health or dangerous to life or likely to hamper their normal development should be punishable by law. States should also set age limits below which the paid employment of child labour should be prohibited and punishable by law.

Article 11

(1) The States Parties to the present Covenant recognize the right of everyone to an adequate standard of living for himself and his family, including adequate food, clothing and housing, and to the continuous improvement of living conditions. The States Parties will take appropriate steps to ensure the realization of this right, recognizing to this effect the essential importance of international cooperation based on free consent.

(2) The States Parties to the present Covenant, recognizing the fundamental right of everyone to be free from hunger, shall take, individually and through international co-operation, the measures, including specific programmes, which are needed: (a) To improve methods of production, conservation and distribution of food by making full use of technical and scientific knowledge, by disseminating knowledge of the principles of nutrition and by developing or reforming agrarian systems in such a way as to achieve the most efficient development and utilization of natural resources; (b) Taking into account the problems of both food-importing and food-exporting countries, to ensure the equitable distribution of world food supplies in relation to need.

Article 12

(1) The States Parties to the present Covenant recognize the right of everyone to the enjoyment of the highest attainable standard of physical and mental health.

(2) The steps to be taken by the States Parties to the present Covenant to achieve the full realization of this right shall include those necessary for: (a) The provision for the reduction of the stillbirth-rate and of infant mortality and for the healthy development of the child; (b) The improvement of all aspects of environmental and industrial hygiene; (c) The prevention, treatment and control of epidemic, endemic, occupational and other diseases; (d) The creation of conditions which would assure to all medical service and medical attention in the event of sickness.

Article 13

(1) The States Parties to the present Covenant recognize the right of everyone to education. They agree that education shall be directed to the full development of the human personality and the sense of its dignity, and shall strengthen the respect for human rights and fundamental freedoms. They further agree that education shall enable all persons to participate effectively in a free society, promote understanding, tolerance and friendship among all nations and all racial, ethnic or religious

groups, and further the activities of the United Nations for the maintenance of peace.

(2) The States Parties to the present Covenant recognize that, with a view to achieving the full realization of this right: (a) Primary education shall be compulsory and available free to all; (b) Secondary education in its different forms, including technical and vocational secondary education, shall be made generally available and accessible to all by every appropriate means, and in particular by the progressive introduction of free education; (c) Higher education shall be make equally accessible to all, on the basis of capacity, by every appropriate means, and in particular by the progressive introduction of free education; (d) Fundamental education shall be encouraged or intensified as far as possible for those persons who have not received or completed the whole period of their primary education; (e) The development of a system of schools at all levels shall be actively pursued, an adequate fellowship system shall be established, and the material conditions of teaching staff shall be continuously improved.

(3) The States Parties to the present Covenant undertake to have respect for the liberty of parents and, when applicable, legal guardians to choose for their children schools, other than those established by the public authorities, which conform to such minimum educational standards as may be laid down or approved by the State and to ensure the religious and moral education of their children in conformity with their own convictions.

(4) No part of this article shall be construed so as to interfere with the liberty of individuals and bodies to establish and direct educational institutions, subject always to the observance of the principles set forth in paragraph 1 of this article and to the requirement that the education given in such institutions shall conform to such minimum standards as may be laid down by the State.

Article 14

Right to compulsory primary education . . .

Article 15

(1) The States Parties to the present Covenant recognize the right of everyone: (a) To take part in cultural life; (b) To enjoy the benefits of scientific progress and its applications; (c) To benefit from the protection of the moral and material interests resulting from any scientific, literary or artistic production of which he is the author.

(2) The steps to be taken by the States Parties to the present Covenant to achieve the full realization of this right shall include those necessary

for the conservation, the development and diffusion of science and culture.

(3) The States Parties to the present Covenant undertake to respect the freedom indispensable for scientific research and creative activity.

(4) The States Parties to the present Covenant recognize the benefits to be derived from the encouragement and development of international contacts and co-operation in the scientific and cultural fields.

Part IV

Article 16

(1) The States Parties to the present Covenant undertake to submit in conformity with this part of the Covenant reports on the measures which they have adopted and the progress made in achieving the observance of the rights recognized herein.

(2) (a) All reports shall be submitted to the Secretary-General of the United Nations, who shall transmit copies to the Economic and Social Council for consideration in accordance with the provisions of the present Covenant. (b) The Secretary-General of the United Nations shall also transmit to the specialized agencies copies of the reports, or any relevant parts therefrom, from States Parties to the present Covenant which are also members of these specialized agencies in so far as these reports, or parts therefrom, relate to any matters which fall within the responsibilities of the said agencies in accordance with their constitutional instruments.

Article 17

(1) The States Parties to the present Covenant shall furnish their reports in stages, in accordance with a programme to be established by the Economic and Social Council within one year of the entry into force of the present Covenant after consultation with the States Parties and the specialized agencies concerned.

(2) Reports may indicate factors and difficulties affecting the degree of fulfillment of obligations under the present Covenant.

(3) Where relevant information has previously been furnished to the United Nations or to any specialized agency by any State Party to the present Covenant, it will not be necessary to reproduce that information, but a precise reference to the information so furnished will suffice.

Articles 18–25

Relation to UN Specialized Agencies . . .

Part V

Articles 26–31

Terms for entry into force, accession and amendment . . .

Appendix B. Reporting Objectives of the Treaty Committee, General Comment Number 1

Introduction

At its second session, in 1988, the Committee [on Economic, Social and Cultural Rights] decided (E/1988/14, paras. 366 and 367), pursuant to an invitation addressed to it by the Economic and Social Council (resolution 1987/5) and endorsed by the General Assembly (resolution 42/102), to begin, as from its third session, the preparation of general comments based on the various articles and provisions of the International Covenant on Economic, Social and Cultural Rights with a view to assisting the States parties in fulfilling their reporting obligations. . . .

The Committee endeavours, through its general comments, to make the experience gained so far through the examination of these reports available for the benefit of all States parties in order to assist and promote their further implementation of the Covenant. . . .

General Comment Number 1, Reporting by States Parties

The Reporting obligations . . . contained in part IV of the Covenant [on Economic, Social and Cultural Rights] . . . serve to achieve a variety of objectives.

A *first objective*, which is of particular relevance to the initial report required to be submitted within two years of the Covenant's entry into force for the State party concerned, is to ensure that a comprehensive review is undertaken with respect to national legislation, administrative rules and procedures, and practices in an effort to ensure the fullest possible conformity with the Covenant. . . .

A *second objective* is to ensure that the State party monitors the actual situation with respect to each of the rights on a regular basis and is thus aware of the extent to which the various rights are, or are not, being enjoyed by all individuals within its territory or under its jurisdiction. From the Committee's experience to date, it is clear that the fulfilment of this objective cannot be achieved only by the preparation of aggregate national statistics or estimates, but also requires that special attention be given to any worse-off regions or areas and to any specific groups or subgroups which appear to be particularly vulnerable or disadvantaged. Thus, the essential first step towards promoting the realization of economic, social and cultural rights is diagnosis and knowledge of the existing situation. The Committee is aware that this process of monitoring and gathering information is a potentially time-consuming and costly one and that international assistance and cooperation, as provided for in article 2, paragraph 1 and articles 22 and 23 of the Covenant, may well be required in order to enable some States parties to fulfil the relevant obligations. . . .

While monitoring is designed to give a detailed overview of the existing situation, the principal value of such an overview is to provide the basis for the elaboration of clearly stated and carefully targeted policies, including the establishment of priorities which reflect the provisions of the Covenant. Therefore, a *third objective* of the reporting process is to enable the Government to demonstrate that such principled policy-making has in fact been undertaken. . . .

A *fourth objective* of the reporting process is to facilitate public scrutiny of government policies with respect to economic, social and cultural rights and to encourage the involvement of the various economic, social and cultural sectors of society in the formulation, implementation and review of the relevant policies. In examining reports submitted to it to date, the Committee has welcomed the fact that a number of States parties, reflecting different political and economic systems, have encouraged inputs by such non-governmental groups into the preparation of their reports under the Covenant. Other States have ensured the widespread dissemination of their reports with a view to enabling comments to be made by the public at large. In these ways, the preparation of the report, and its consideration at the national level can come to be of at least as much value as the constructive dialogue conducted at the international level between the Committee and representatives of the reporting State.

A *fifth objective* is to provide a basis on which the State party itself, as well as the Committee, can effectively evaluate the extent to which progress has been made towards the realization of the obligations contained in the Covenant. For this purpose, it may be useful for States to identify specific benchmarks or goals against which their performance in a given area can be assessed. Thus, for example, it is generally agreed that it is important to set specific goals with respect to the reduction of infant mortality, the extent of vaccination of children, the intake of calories per person, the number of persons per health-care provider, etc. In many of these areas, global benchmarks are of limited use, whereas national or other more specific benchmarks can provide an extremely valuable indication of progress.

In this regard, the Committee wishes to note that the Covenant attaches particular importance to the concept of "progressive realization" of the relevant rights and, for that reason, the Committee urges States parties to include in their periodic reports information which shows the progress over time, with respect to the effective realization of the relevant rights. By the same token, it is clear that qualitative, as well as quantitative, data are required in order for an adequate assessment of the situation to be made.

A *sixth objective* is to enable the State party itself to develop a better understanding of the problems and shortcomings encountered in efforts to realize progressively the full range of economic, social and cultural rights. For this reason, it is essential that States parties report in detail on the "factors and difficulties" inhibiting such realization. This process of identification and recognition of the relevant difficulties then provides the framework within which more appropriate policies can be devised.

A *seventh objective* is to enable the Committee, and the States parties as a whole, to facilitate the exchange of information among States and to develop a better understanding of the common problems faced by States and a fuller appreciation of the type of measures which might be taken to promote effective realization of each of the rights contained in the Covenant. This part of the process also enables the Committee to identify the most appropriate means by which the international community might assist States, in accordance with articles 22 and 23 of the Covenant.

Appendix C. Universal Declaration on the Human Genome and Human Rights (International Bioethics Committee of UNESCO, 1999)

A. Human Dignity and the Human Genome

Article 1

The human genome underlies the fundamental unity of all members of the human family, as well as the recognition of their inherent dignity and diversity. In a symbolic sense, it is the heritage of humanity.

Article 2

(a) Everyone has a right to respect for their dignity and for their rights regardless of their genetic characteristics. (b) That dignity makes it imperative not to reduce individuals to their genetic characteristics and to respect their uniqueness and diversity.

Article 3

The human genome, which by its nature evolves, is subject to mutations. It contains potentialities that are expressed differently according to each individual's natural and social environment including the individual's state of health, living conditions, nutrition and education.

Article 4

The human genome in its natural state shall not give rise to financial gains.

B. Rights of the Persons Concerned

Article 5

(a) Research, treatment or diagnosis affecting an individual's genome shall be undertaken only after rigorous and prior assessment of the potential risks and benefits pertaining thereto and, in accordance with any other requirement of national law. (b) In all cases, the prior, free and informed consent of the person concerned shall be obtained. If the latter is not in a position to consent, consent or authorization shall be obtained in the manner prescribed by law, guided by the person's best interest. (c) The right of each individual to decide whether or not to be informed of the results of genetic examination and the resulting consequences should be respected. (d) In the case of research, protocols shall, in addition, be submitted for prior review in accordance with relevant national and international research standards or guidelines. (e) If according to the law a person does not have the capacity to consent, research affecting his or her genome may only be carried out for his or her direct health benefit, subject to the authorization and the protective conditions prescribed by law. Research which does not have an expected direct health benefit may only be undertaken by way of exception, with the utmost restraint, exposing the person only to a minimal risk and minimal burden and if the research is intended to contribute to the health benefit of other persons in the same age category or with the same genetic condition, subject to the conditions prescribed by law, and provided such research is compatible with the protection of the individual's human rights.

Article 6

No one shall be subjected to discrimination based on genetic characteristics that is intended to infringe or has the effect of infringing human rights, fundamental freedoms and human dignity.

Article 7

Genetic data associated with an identifiable person and stored or processed for the purposes of research or any other purpose must be held confidential in the conditions set by law.

Article 8

Every individual shall have the right, according to international and national law, to just reparation for any damage sustained as a direct and determining result of an intervention affecting his or her genome.

Article 9

In order to protect human rights and fundamental freedoms, limitations to the principles of consent and confidentiality may only be prescribed by law, for compelling reasons within the bounds of public international law and the international law of human rights.

C. Research on the Human Genome

Article 10

No research or research applications concerning the human genome, in particular in the fields of biology, genetics and medicine, should prevail over respect for the human rights, fundamental freedoms and human dignity of individuals or, where applicable, of groups of people.

Article 11

Practices which are contrary to human dignity, such as reproductive cloning of human beings, shall not be permitted. States and competent international organizations are invited to co-operate in identifying such practices and in taking, at national or international level, the measures necessary to ensure that the principles set out in this Declaration are respected.

Article 12

(a) Benefits from advances in biology, genetics and medicine, concerning the human genome, shall be made available to all, with due regard for the dignity and human rights of each individual. (b) Freedom of research, which is necessary for the progress of knowledge, is part of freedom of thought. The applications of research, including applications in biology, genetics and medicine, concerning the human genome, shall seek to offer relief from suffering and improve the health of individuals and humankind as a whole.

D. Conditions for the Exercise of Scientific Activity

Article 13

The responsibilities inherent in the activities of researchers, including meticulousness, caution, intellectual honesty and integrity in carrying out their research as well as in the presentation and utilization of their findings, should be the subject of particular attention in the framework of research on the human genome, because of its ethical and social implications. Public and private science policy-makers also have particular responsibilities in this respect.

Article 14

States should take appropriate measures to foster the intellectual and material conditions favourable to freedom in the conduct of research on the human genome and to consider the ethical, legal, social and economic implications of such research, on the basis of the principles set out in this Declaration.

Article 15

States should take appropriate steps to provide the framework for the free exercise of research on the human genome with due regard for the principles set out in this Declaration, in order to safeguard respect for human rights, fundamental freedoms and human dignity and to protect public health. They should seek to ensure that research results are not used for non-peaceful purposes.

Article 16

States should recognize the value of promoting, at various levels as appropriate, the establishment of independent, multidisciplinary and pluralist ethics committees to assess the ethical, legal and social issues raised by research on the human genome and its applications.

E. Solidarity and International Co-operation

Article 17

States should respect and promote the practice of solidarity towards individuals, families and population groups who are particularly vulnerable to or affected by disease or disability of a genetic character. They should foster, inter alia, research on the identification, prevention and treatment of genetically-based and genetically-influenced diseases, in particular rare as well as endemic diseases which affect large numbers of the world's population.

Article 18

States should make every effort, with due and appropriate regard for the principles set out in this Declaration, to continue fostering the international dissemination of scientific knowledge concerning the human genome, human diversity and genetic research and, in that regard, to foster scientific and cultural co-operation, particularly between industrialized and developing countries.

Article 19

(a) In the framework of international co-operation with developing countries, States should seek to encourage measures enabling: assessment of the risks and benefits pertaining to research on the human genome to be carried out and abuse to be prevented; the capacity of developing countries to carry out research on human biology and genetics, taking into consideration their specific problems, to be developed and strengthened; developing countries to benefit from the achievements of scientific and technological research so that their use in favour of economic and social progress can be to the benefit of all; the free exchange of scientific knowledge and information in the areas of biology, genetics and medicine to be promoted.

(b) Relevant international organizations should support and promote the initiatives taken by States for the abovementioned purposes.

F. Promotion of the Principles Set out in the Declaration

Article 20

States should take appropriate measures to promote the principles set out in the Declaration, through education and relevant means, inter alia through the conduct of research and training in interdisciplinary fields and through the promotion of education in bioethics, at all levels, in particular for those responsible for science policies.

Article 21

States should take appropriate measures to encourage other forms of research, training and information dissemination conducive to raising the awareness of society and all of its members of their responsibilities regarding the fundamental issues relating to the defence of human dignity which may be raised by research in biology, in genetics and in medicine, and its applications. They should also undertake to facilitate on this subject an open international discussion, ensuring the free expression of various socio-cultural, religious and philosophical opinions.

G. Implementation of the Declaration

Article 22

States should make every effort to promote the principles set out in this Declaration and should, by means of all appropriate measures, promote their implementation.

Article 23

States should take appropriate measures to promote, through education, training and information dissemination, respect for the abovementioned principles and to foster their recognition and effective application. States should also encourage exchanges and networks among independent ethics committees, as they are established, to foster full collaboration.

Article 24

The International Bioethics Committee of UNESCO should contribute to the dissemination of the principles set out in this Declaration and to the further examination of issues raised by their applications and by the evolution of the technologies in question. It should organize appropriate consultations with parties concerned, such as vulnerable groups. It should make recommendations, in accordance with UNESCO's statutory procedures, addressed to the General Conference and give advice concerning the follow-up of this Declaration, in particular regarding the identification of practices that could be contrary to human dignity, such as germ-line interventions.

Article 25

Nothing in this Declaration may be interpreted as implying for any State, group or person any claim to engage in any activity or to perform any act contrary to human rights and fundamental freedoms, including the principles set out in this Declaration.
<www.unesco.org/ibc/uk/genome/projet/index.html>

Appendix D. International Code of Medical Ethics of the World Medical Association (1949, 1968, 1983)

Duties of Physicians in General

A Physician Shall

always maintain the highest standards of professional conduct.

A Physician Shall

not permit motives of profit to influence the free and independent exercise of professional judgement on behalf of patients.

A Physician Shall

in all types of medical practice, be dedicated to providing competent medical service in full technical and moral independence, with compassion and respect for human dignity.

A Physician Shall

deal honestly with patients and colleagues, and strive to expose those physicians deficient in character or competence, or who engage in fraud or deception.

The following practices are deemed to be unethical conduct:

a) Self advertising by physicians, unless permitted by the laws of the country and the Code of Ethics of the National Medical Association.

b) Paying or receiving any fee or any other consideration solely to procure the referral of a patient or for prescribing or referring a patient to any source.

A Physician Shall

respect the rights of patients, of colleagues, and of other health professionals and shall safeguard patient confidences.

A Physician Shall

act only in the patient's interest when providing medical care which might have the effect of weakening the physical and mental condition of the patient.

A Physician Shall

use great caution in divulging discoveries or new techniques or treatment through non-professional channels.

A Physician Shall

certify only that which he has personally verified.

Duties of Physicians to the Sick

A Physician Shall

always bear in mind the obligation of preserving human life.

A Physician Shall

owe his patients complete loyalty and all the resources of his science. Whenever an examination or treatment is beyond the physician's capacity he should summon another physician who has the necessary ability.

A Physician Shall

preserve absolute confidentiality on all he knows about his patient even after the patient has died.

A Physician Shall

give emergency care as a humanitarian duty unless he is assured that others are willing and able to give such care.

Duties of Physicians to Each Other

A Physician Shall

behave towards his colleagues as he would have them behave towards him.

A Physician Shall Not

entice patients from his colleagues.

A Physician Shall

observe the principles of the "Declaration of Geneva" approved by the World Medical Association.

Appendix E. Draft Declaration of Principles on Human Rights and the Environment (1994)

Preamble

Guided by the United Nations Charter, the Universal Declaration of Human Rights, the International Covenant on Economic, Social and Cultural Rights, the International Covenant on Civil and Political Rights, the Vienna Declaration and Program of Action of the World Conference of Human Rights, and other relevant international human rights instruments,

Guided also by the Stockholm Declaration of the United Nations Conference on the Human Environment, the World Charter for Nature, the Rio Declaration on Environment and Development, Agenda 21: Programme of Action for Sustainable Development, and other relevant instruments of international environmental law,

Guided also by the Declaration on the Right to Development, which recognizes that the right to development is an essential human right and that the human person is the central subject of development,

Guided further by fundamental principles of international humanitarian law,

Reaffirming the universality, indivisibility and interdependence of all human rights,

Recognizing that sustainable development links the right to development and the right to a secure, healthy and ecologically sound environment,

Recalling the right of peoples to self-determination by virtue of which they have the right freely to determine their political status and to pursue their economic, social and cultural development,

Deeply concerned by the severe human rights consequences of envi-

ronmental harm caused by poverty, structural adjustment and debt programmes and by international trade and intellectual property regimes,

Convinced that the potential irreversibility of environmental harm
gives rise to special responsibility to prevent such harm,

Concerned that human rights violations lead to environmental degradation and that environmental degradation leads to human rights violations,

The Following Principles Are Declared:
Part I

1. Human rights, an ecologically sound environment, sustainable development and peace are interdependent and indivisible.
2. All persons have the right to a secure, healthy and ecologically sound
environment. This right and other human rights, including civil, cultural,
economic, political and social rights, are universal, interdependent and
indivisible.
3. All persons shall be free from any form of discrimination in regard to
actions and decisions that affect the environment.
4. All persons have the right to an environment adequate to meet equitably the needs of present generations and that does not impair the rights
of future generations to meet equitably their needs.

Part II

5. All persons have the right to freedom from pollution, environmental
degradation and activities that adversely affect the environment, threaten
life, health, livelihood, well-being or sustainable development within,
across or outside national boundaries.
6. All persons have the right to protection and preservation of the air,
soil, water, sea-ice, flora and fauna, and the essential processes and areas
necessary to maintain biological diversity and ecosystems.
7. All persons have the right to the highest attainable standard of health
free from environmental harm.
8. All persons have the right to safe and healthy food and water adequate
to their well-being.
9. All persons have the right to a safe and healthy working environment.
10. All persons have the right to adequate housing, land tenure and living
conditions in a secure, healthy and ecologically sound environment.
11. All persons have the right not to be evicted from their homes or land
for the purpose of, or as a consequence of, decisions or actions affecting
the environment, except in emergencies or due to a compelling purpose

benefiting society as a whole and not attainable by other means. All persons have the right to participate effectively in decisions and to negotiate concerning their eviction and the right, if evicted, to timely and adequate restitution, compensation and/or appropriate and sufficient accommodation or land.

12. All persons have the right to timely assistance in the event of natural or technological or other human-caused catastrophes.

13. Everyone has the right to benefit equitably from the conservation and sustainable use of nature and natural resources for cultural, ecological, educational, health, livelihood, recreational, spiritual or other purposes. This includes ecologically sound access to nature. Everyone has the right to preservation of unique sites, consistent with the fundamental rights of persons or groups living in the area.

14. Indigenous peoples have the right to control their lands, territories and natural resources and to maintain their traditional way of life. This includes the right to security in the enjoyment of their means of subsistence. Indigenous peoples have the right to protection against any action or course of conduct that may result in the destruction or degradation of their territories, including land, air, water, sea-ice, wildlife or other resources.

Part III

15. All persons have the right to information concerning the environment. This includes information, howsoever compiled, on actions and courses of conduct that may affect the environment and information necessary to enable effective public participation in environmental decision-making. The information shall be timely, clear, understandable and available without undue financial burden to the applicant.

16. All persons have the right to hold and express opinions and to disseminate ideas and information regarding the environment.

17. All persons have the right to environmental and human rights education.

18. All persons have the right to active, free, and meaningful participation in planning and decision-making activities and processes that may have an impact on the environment and development. This includes the right to a prior assessment of the environmental, developmental and human rights consequences of proposed actions.

19. All persons have the right to associate freely and peacefully with others for purposes of protecting the environment or the rights of persons affected by environmental harm.

20. All persons have the right to effective remedies and redress in admin-

istrative or judicial proceedings for environmental harm or the threat of such harm.

Part IV

21. All persons, individually and in association with others, have a duty to protect and preserve the environment.
22. All States shall respect and ensure the right to a secure, healthy and ecologically sound environment. Accordingly, they shall adopt the administrative, legislative and other measures necessary to effectively implement the rights in this Declaration.

These measures shall aim at the prevention of environmental harm, at the provision of adequate remedies, and at the sustainable use of natural resources and shall include, inter alia,

- collection and dissemination of information concerning the environment;
- prior assessment and control, licensing, regulation or prohibition of activities and substances potentially harmful to the environment;
- public participation in environmental decision-making;
- effective administrative and judicial remedies and redress for environmental harm and the threat of such harm;
- monitoring, management and equitable sharing of natural resources;
- measures to reduce wasteful processes of production and patterns of consumption;
- measures aimed at ensuring that transnational corporations, wherever they operate, carry out their duties of environmental protection, sustainable development and respect for human rights; and
- measures aimed at ensuring that the international organizations and agencies to which they belong observe the rights and duties in this Declaration.

23. States and all other parties shall avoid using the environment as a means of war or inflicting significant, long-term or widespread harm on the environment, and shall respect international law providing protection for the environment in times of armed conflict and cooperate in its further development.
24. All international organizations and agencies shall observe the rights and duties in this Declaration.

Part V

25. In implementing the rights and duties in this Declaration, special attention shall be given to vulnerable persons and groups.

26. The rights in this Declaration may be subject only to restrictions provided by law and which are necessary to protect public order, health and the fundamental rights and freedoms of others.

27. All persons are entitled to a social and international order in which the rights in this Declaration can be fully realized.

Notes

Introit

1. Steven Mufson, "Chinese Doctor Tells of Organ Removals After Executions," *Washington Post*, 20 June 2001, pp. A1, 22.

2. Karen DeYoung, "U.N. Pledges Support in Fight Against AIDS," *Washington Post*, 28 June 2001, pp. A1, 10.

3. Alastair T. Iles and Morton H. Sklar, *The Right to Travel: An Essential Freedom for Scientists and Academics* (Washington, D.C.: American Association for the Advancement of Science, 1996), 4.

4. Audrey R. Chapman, "A 'Violations Approach' for Monitoring the International Covenant on Economic, Social and Cultural Rights," *Human Rights Quarterly* 18, 1 (February 1996): 23–66.

5. C. G. Weeramantry, *Justice Without Frontiers: Protecting Human Rights in the Age of Technology*, 2 vols. (The Hague: Kluwer Law International, 1998), 2: 551–59, 631.

6. "Recommendation on the Status of Scientific Researchers," 18 C/Res.40, adopted 20 November 1974, *UNESCO Standard-Setting Instruments*, Section II.B.1.

Part I Introduction

1. Sadako Ogata, "United Nations Approaches to Human Rights and Scientific and Technological Developments," in *Human Rights and Scientific and Technological Development*, ed. C. G. Weeramantry (Tokyo: United Nations University Press, 1990), 1–10 at 4.

2. UN Commission on Human Rights, 1998/36, "Human Rights and Forensic Science," 51st Meeting, 17 April 1998, adopted without a vote. The scientific dimensions of this field are explored in a symposium issue on "Human Rights and the Forensic Scientist," *American Journal of Forensic Medicine and Pathology* 5, 4 (1984): 293–372.

3. UN Commission on Human Rights, 1998/12, "Adverse Effects of the Illicit Movement and Dumping of Toxic and Dangerous Products and Wastes on the Enjoyment of Human Rights," 38th Meeting, 9 April 1998, adopted by a roll-call vote of 33 to 14 with 6 abstentions.

Chapter 1

1. Paul R. Josephson, "Aryan Science and the Führer Principle," in *Totalitarian Science and Technology* (Atlantic Highlands, N.J.: Humanities Press, 1996), 9–14.

2. Robert N. Proctor, "Nazi Doctors, Racial Medicine, and Human Experimentation," in *The Nazi Doctors and the Nuremberg Code: Human Rights in Human Experimentation*, ed. George J. Annas and Michael A. Grodin (New York: Oxford University Press, 1992), 17–31.

3. "Unit 731 Tried to Hide Atrocities," *Japan Times*, 8 January 1997, p. 1; "Germ War Evidence Ordered Covered up," *Japan Times*, 5 July 1994, p. 2; "Unit 731 Immunity Papers Revealed," *Japan Times*, 18 December 1994, p. 1.

4. Dexter Masters and Katherine Way, eds., *One World or None: A Report to the Public on the Full Meaning of the Atomic Bomb* (New York: McGraw-Hill, 1946).

5. Joseph Turner, "Between Two Extremes," Editorial, *Science* 131 (1960): 1013.

6. C. P. Snow, "The Moral Un-Neutrality of Science," *Science* 133 (1961): 255–59.

7. Inter-American Conference on the Problems of War and Peace, Mexico City, 21 February 21–8 March, 1945. See also Johannes Morsink, "The Latin American Connection," in *The Universal Declaration of Human Rights: Origins, Drafting, and Intent* (Philadelphia: University of Pennsylvania Press, 1999), 130–34.

8. Preamble, United Nations Charter, signed at San Francisco 26 June 1945; entered into force 24 October 1945.

9. "Statement on Human Rights," *American Anthropologist* n.s. 49 (1947): 539–43; "Comment on Statement on Human Rights, n.s. 50 (1948): 351–55.

10. "Memorandum and Questionnaire Circulated by UNESCO on the Theoretical Bases of Human Rights," Appendix I, UNESCO, *Human Rights: Comments and Interpretations* (New York: Columbia University Press, 1949; reprint Westport, Conn.: Greenwood Press, 1973), 251–57.

11. Julian Huxley, *Freedom and Culture*, United Nations Educational, Scientific and Cultural Organization (Freeport, N.Y.: Books for Libraries, 1971), 7.

12. R. W. Gerard, "The Rights of Man: A Biological Approach," UNESCO, *Human Rights: Comments*, 205–9 at 205.

13. W. A. Noyes, "Science and the Rights of Man," *UNESCO, Human Rights: Comments*, 215–17 at 215.

14. J. M. Burgers, "Rights and Duties Concerning Creative Expression, in Particular in Science," UNESCO, *Human Rights: Comments*, 210–14 at 214.

15. F. S. C. Northrop, *The Logic of the Sciences and the Humanities* (New York: Macmillan, 1947).

16. Northrop, "Toward a Bill of Rights for the United Nations," *Logic of the Sciences*, 182–85.

17. Consistent with Northrop's "critical scientific study of human rights," the Gallup International Millennium Survey (2000) reports global views on respect for human rights by country, region, and rights. The greatest dissatisfaction with human rights performance was found in Latin America and the least pronounced dissatisfaction in Western Europe. Gallup International, "Universal Human Rights?" <www.gallup-international.com/survey6.htm>.

18. Universal Declaration of Human Rights, United Nations General Assembly Resolution 217A (III) 3(1) U.N. GAOR Res.71, U.N.Doc. A/810 (1948).

19. René Cassin, "Historique de la Déclaration Universelle de 1948," in *La Pensée et l'action* (Paris, Éditions du Centre National de la Recherche Scientifique, 1981), 114.

20. United Nations Commission on Human Rights, 3rd Session, *Summary Record of the Sixty-Fifth Meeting*, U.N.Doc.E/CN.4/SR.65, p. 15, note 2.

21. Henry W. Kendall, "World Scientists Warning to Humanity," (1992), reprinted in *A Distant Light: Scientists in the Policy Process* (New York: Springer-Verlag, 1999), 198–201.

22. Committee for Human Rights of the American Anthropological Association, Declaration on Anthropology and Human Rights, adopted by the AAA membership June 1999 (Arlington, Va.: American Anthropology Association, 1999), <www.aaanet.org/stmts/humanrts.htm> For a comprehensive history of change in the AAA, see Karen Engle, "From Skepticism to Embrace: Human Rights and the American Anthropological Association from 1947–1999," *Human Rights Quarterly* 23, 2 (August 2001): 536–59.

Chapter 2

1. United Nations, ECOSOC Resolution 1/5 of 16 February 1946.

2. United Nations, *These Rights and Freedoms* (New York: United Nations Department of Public Information, 1950), 4–5.

3. Ibid.,10.

4. Ibid., 15.

5. Ibid., 13.

6. *Report of the Third Session of the Commission on Human Rights* (E/800, 28 June 1948). *Summary Records of Meetings* (E/CN.4/SR. 46–81.

7. United Nations, *These Rights*, 7.

8. John P. Humphrey, *Human Rights and the United Nations: A Great Adventure* (Dobbs Ferry, N.Y.: Transnational Publishers, 1984), 37.

9. Mary Ann Glendon, *A World Made New: Eleanor Roosevelt and the Universal Declaration of Human Rights* (New York: Random House, 2001), 57.

10. This text is found at E/CN.4/95 (p. 11) in combination with alternative texts suggested by France and by the United States. For various drafts of Article 25 presented in sequence, see also United Nations, *These Rights*, 65–57 and *Yearbook on Human Rights* 1948 (Lake Success, N.Y.: United Nations, 1950), 460.

11. The Third Committee spent 84 meetings in considering and discussing the draft prepared by the Commission on Human Rights. As they voted, Representatives indicated the meaning they attached to certain expressions and noted reservations. The summary records of these meetings report such statements and reservations in documents A/C.3/SR.88–116; A/C.3/SR.119–170; and A/C.3/SR.174–178.

12. *Official Records of the Third Session of the General Assembly*, Part I, "Social, Humanitarian, and Cultural Questions," Third Committee, *Summary Records of Meetings*, 21 September–8 December. See also Vladimir Kartashkin, "Economic, Social and Cultural Rights," in *The International Dimensions of Human Rights*, ed. Karel Vasak and Philip Alston (Paris: UNESCO; Westport Conn.: Greenwood Press, 1982), 1: chap. 6; Johannes Morsink, *The Universal Declaration of Human Rights: Origins, Drafting, and Intent* (Philadelphia,: University of Pennsylvania Press, 1999), 30–31, 217–22; Glendon, *A World Made New*.

13. Eleanor Roosevelt, *On My Own* (New York: Harper, 1958), 83.

14. *Official Records*, 632.

15. Ibid., 622.

16. Ibid., 630.

17. Ibid., 634.

18. Ibid., 627.

19. Ibid.

20. See Morsink, "The Right to Full Development," in *Universal Declaration*, 210–12.

21. The American Declaration of the Rights and Duties of Man antedates the UDHR by several months. OAS Res. XXX, adopted by the Ninth International Conference of American States (30 March–2 May 1948), Bogotá.

22. *Official Records*, 629–30.

23. United Nations, *These Rights*,10.

24. Ibid., 15–16.

25. Ibid., 21.

Chapter 3

1. Audrey R. Chapman, "A 'Violations Approach' for Monitoring the International Covenant on Economic, Social and Cultural Rights," *Human Rights Quarterly* 18, 1 (February 1996): 23–66.

2. United Nations General Assembly, 12th Session, Third Committee, Agenda Item 33, "Article 16 [later renumbered 15] of the Draft Covenant on Economic, Social and Cultural Rights (E/2573, Annex I A), A/C.3/SR.795, pp. 169–91. Useful accounts of the origins of Article 15 may be found in Stephen P. Marks, "Education, Science, Culture and Information," in *United Nations Legal Order*, ed. Oscar Schachter and Christopher C. Joyner (London: Cambridge University Press, 1991), 2: chap. 12; and Stephen P. Marks with the assistance of Sofia Gruskin, "Article 15—Rights Relating to Culture and Science," in *U.S. Ratification of the International Covenants on Human Rights*, ed. Hurst Hannum and Dana D. Fischer (Irvington-on-Hudson, N.Y.: Transnational Publishers, 1993).

3. United Nations Commission on Human Rights, *Report on the 8th Session*, 14 April-14 June 1952; (E/2256 E/CN.4/669) ECOSOC Records; 14th Sess., Supplement No. 4, p. 19.

4. UNGA, 12th Session, Third Committee, 173.

5. Ibid., 172.

6. Committee on Economic, Social and Cultural Rights, *General Comment No. 3*, 5th Sess., 1990, UN Doc. E/1991/23, Annex III, sec. 10

7. Physicians for Human Rights, "Malaysian Women's Group Stifled by Criminal Prosecution," *Urgent Action Report* (Boston: Physicians for Human Rights, October 1996); Richard Pierre Claude, "Human Rights Activist on Trial Criminalizing Criticism in Malaysia," *Human Rights Tribune* (Ottawa) 4, 3 (September 1997): 30.

8. David Dembo, Clarence J. Dias, Ayesha Kadwani, and Ward Morehouse, eds., *Nothing to Lose But Our Lives: Empowerment to Oppose Industrial Hazards in a Transnational World* (New York: New Horizons Press, 1988). See also Bhopal Gas Peedit Sangharsh Sahayog Samiti and Bhopal Group for Information and Action, *Bhopal Lives, 1984–94* (New Delhi: Other Media, 1994).

9. *In re Union Carbide Corporation Gas Plan Disaster at Bhopal, India in December 1984*, 634 F. Supp. 842 (S.D. New York), upheld on appeal 800 F 2d 195 (2d Cir.1987).

10. Editorial, "Has the World Forgotten Bhopal?" *The Lancet* 356 (2 December 2000): 1863.

11. "The Maastricht Guidelines on Violations of Economic, Social and Cultural Rights," *Human Rights Quarterly* 20, 3 (1998): 691–705, at 697. See also Scott Leckie, "The Maastricht Guidelines on Violations of Economic, Social and Cultural Rights," *Human Rights Tribune* 4, 2–3 (June 1997): 38–39.

12. Associated Press Tokyo, "Japan Says Yes to Viagra, Swift Approval of Drug Angers Pill Advocates," *International Herald Tribune*, Asia Pacific Edition, Friday, 12 February 1999, p. 1.

13. Joel L. Swerdlow, "The Promise of Plants," *Washington Post*, 19 September 2000, Health Section, pp. 12–17.

14. Vanada Shiva, *Biopiracy: The Plunder of Nature and Knowledge* (Boston: South End Press, 1997).

15. Jeremy Rifkin, *The Biotech Century: Harnessing the Gene and Remaking the World* (New York: Jeremy P. Tarcher/Putnam, 1998), 49–58.

16. UN Commission on Human Rights, *Report on the 8th Session*, 188.

17. Ibid., 184.

18. Ibid., Costa Rica and Uruguay Amendment, A/C.3/L.636/Rev.1.

19. Article XIII of the Bogatá Declaration says: "Every person . . . has the right to the protection of his moral and material interests as regards his inventions or any literary, scientific or artistic works of which he is the author."

20. In human rights terms relating to science, Marie Curié the discoverer of radium was cited. United Nations, *Official Records of the Third Session of the General Assembly*, 629–30.

21. UNGA, 12th Session, Third Committee, 189–90. By virtue of the 1970 Patent Cooperation Treaty, making possible simultaneous applications for patents in over 100 countries, patenting is now more globally uniform than ever before.

22. Ibid., 190.

23. United Nations, *United Nations Human Development Report, 2001* (New York: Oxford University Press for the United Nations Human Development Programme, 2001), 103–4. The report also offers a preliminary analysis of the new treaty on Trade Related Intellectual Property Rights, but indicates that it is too early to assess its impact, especially as an instrument to create "a level playing field" between conflicting claims, some with human rights components. See Chapter 5, "Global Initiatives to Create Technologies for Human Development," 95–117.

24. Questions associated with copyright are complex and have been dealt with in many different international agreements from the Berne Conference of 1886 to the Universal Copyright Convention of 1952. Adopted in Geneva on 6 September 1952 by the Inter-governmental Copyright Conference Convened by UNESCO; 6 U.S.T. 2731, T.I.A.S. No. 3324, 216 U.N.T.S. 132. Article I of the Universal Copyright Convention provides for the protection of copyright proprietors and takes into account the special conditions of different countries and diverse legal systems, including socialist systems.

25. The break-up of the Soviet Union and allied states has resulted in increasing reliance on WIPO for technical assistance and training in the areas of patents, copyrights and trademarks. Gerald J. Mossinghoff and Ralph Oman, "The World Intellectual Property Organization," *World Affairs* 160, 2 (Fall 1997): 104–8.

26. World Intellectual Property Organization, *Roundtable on Intellectual Prop-*

erty and Indigenous Peoples (Geneva: World Intellectual Property Organization, 1998); Antonio Jacanimijoy, "Initiatives for Protection of Rights of Holders of Traditional Knowledge, Indigenous Peoples and Local Communities," citing the ILO Convention 169 "Concerning Indigenous and Tribal Peoples in Independent Countries," the Draft UN "Declaration on the Rights of Indigenous Peoples," and the "Convention on Biological Diversity" (Geneva: WIPO/INDIP/RT/98/4E. 15 July 1998). Legal arguments on behalf of Indigenous claims were made by the Center for International Environmental Law (Washington, D.C.) <www.econet. apc.org/ciel/>.

27. United Nations, *Principles and Guidelines for the Protection of the Heritage of Indigenous Peoples* (Geneva: United Nations, 1994).

28. Philip Alston, "The International Covenant on Economic, Social and Cultural Rights," in *Manual on Human Rights Reporting Under Six Major International Human Rights Instruments* (New York: United Nations, 1991), 39–78, at 70.

Chapter 4

1. "Status of Major International Human Rights Instruments," in *Human Development Report 2001: Making New Technologies Work for Human Development* (New York: Oxford University Press, for the United Nations Development Programme, 2001), 233. For current counts on treaty ratifications, see "Universal Instruments" on the UNESCO website: <www.unesco.org/human_rights/index.htm>.

2. "Issues at the UN World Conference on Human Rights," doc. IOR 41/WU/02/93, 29 March 1993, *Vienna Declaration and Programme of Action, World Conference on Human Rights,* U.N. Doc. A/CONF. 157/23 (1993). The Vienna Declaration supplies important commentary on the ESC Covenant, including the provisions of Article 15 on culture and science. See Part 1, para.5, section 4, "Substantive Provisions of the International Covenant on Economic, Social and Cultural Rights."

3. Lenore L. Cahn, ed., *Confronting Injustice: The Edmond Cahn Reader* (Boston: Little, Brown, 1966).

4. "Mexico: Scientific Freedom and Freedom of Expression—Environmental Scientists," American Association for the Advancement of Science *Human Rights Action Network,* 1 November 1993.

5. WUS News, "Mexico Dismissal of Professors Monitoring Environmental Projects," World University Service (Geneva), *Human Rights Bulletin* 11 (December 1993): 7

6. *The Lima Declaration on Academic Freedom and Autonomy of Institutes on Higher Education* (Lima: World University Service, 68th General Assembly of the World University Service, 1988).

7. In the debates on this topic in 1958, Mr. Maheu, representing UNESCO, told the General Assembly that his organization had taken an active part in the drafting of this article. He warned the delegates involved in reviewing the draft Covenant to avoid ideological references because the article on science [and culture] was especially delicate. For example, for science to be developed and conserved, it must be unfettered by limiting statements propounding political objectives. He reasoned the draft article: "dealt with matters in which the State, although playing a considerable part, could act only with great caution, since the very freedom of the human mind was involved. The Third Committee should therefore take care that freedom was respected if it did not wish to destroy what it sought to

protect." UN General Assembly, 12th Session, Third Committee, Agenda Item 33, "Article 16 [later renumbered 15] of the Draft Covenant on Economic, Social and Cultural Rights (E/2573, Annex I A), A/C.3/SR.795, 171.

8. The fanatical former Taliban regime in Afghanistan invoked religious justifications to restrict women to their homes (unless totally covered and accompanied by a close male relative). Without male support they had no resources to support themselves or their families. At the same time, the theocratic regime made a labor exception allowing women's employment in the health sector, but forbidding them to pursue higher education. Lynn Amowitz and Vincent Iacopino, MD, "Women's Health and Human Rights Needs," *Lancet Perspectives* 356 (December 2000): 65.

9. George Campbell, Jr., "Support Them and They Will Come," *Issues in Science and Technology* 15, 4 (Summer 1999): 59–66.

10. "Maintaining Diversity in Science," *Science* 271 (29 March 1996): 1901.

11. Jun Kinoshita, "Women Fight Uphill Battle for Equity," *Science* 274 (4 October 1996): 49–51, at 50.

12. Lynda Richardson, "White Patients More Likely to Use AIDS Drugs, Study Says," *New York Times*, 17 July 1997, p. 2.

13. "Law on Promotion of Human Rights Education and Human Rights Awareness Raising" (Tokyo: Monbu Kagakusho, Japan Ministry of Education, Science, Sports and Culture, 2001). For advice on this issue I am indebted to Dr. Hidetoshi Hashimoto.

14. Audrey Chapman, Herbert Spirer, Louise Spirer, and Caroline Whitbeck, "Science, Scientists, and Human Rights Education," in *Human Rights Education for the Twenty-First Century*, ed. George J. Andreopoulos and Richard P. Claude (Philadelphia: University of Pennsylvania Press, 1997), 359–74.

15. UNGA, 12th Session, Third Committee, 171.

16. Ibid., 185.

17. Ibid., 189.

18. Elisa Muñoz, ed., *Directory of Persecuted Scientists, Engineers, and Health Professionals* (Washington, D.C.: American Association for the Advancement of Science, 1996), 49.

19. UNGA, 12th Session, Third Committee, 183–85.

20. Ibid., 191.

21. Elisa Muñoz, American Association for the Advancement of Science, *AAASHRAN Internet transmission, Case Number US 9702,* "USA—Visa Denial to Cuban Scientists," 5 March 1997; and *Memorandum of 22 December 1993 to AAAS Affiliate Groups Interested in U.S./Cuba Travel Policies.* See also her report, *The Right to Travel: The Effect of Travel Restrictions on Scientific Collaboration Between American and Cuban Scientists* (Washington, D.C.: American Association for the Advancement of Science, 1998).

22. "Recommendation on the Status of Scientific Researchers," 18 C/Res.40, adopted 20 November 1974, *UNESCO Standard-Setting Instruments,* Section II.B.I.(26).

23. For the history of the Pugwash, see Pugwash Online <www.pugwash.org>; Joseph Rotblat, ed., *World Citizenship: Allegiance to Humanity* (Cambridge, Mass.: Palgrave, 1997).

24. Colin Woodard, "Fighting for Scraps, Western Nuclear Companies Are on the Prowl in Eastern Europe," *Bulletin of the Atomic Scientists* 52, 3 (May–June 1996): 56–59.

25. See "Shadow Reports," in Christof Heyns and Frans Viljoen, "The Impact

of the United Nations Treaties on the Domestic Level," *Human Rights Quarterly* 23, 3 (August 2001), 483–535, at 507.

26. UN Committee on Economic, Social and Cultural Rights, "NGO participation in activities of the Committee," Eighth Session. E/C.12/1993/WP.14, 10–28 May 1993. See also Fausto Pocar and Cecil Bernard, "National Reports: Their Submission to Expert Bodies and Follow-up," in *Manual on Human Rights Reporting Under Six Major International Human Rights Instruments* (New York: United Nations, 1991), 25–28.

27. United Nations Commission on Human Rights, Sub-Commission on Prevention of Discrimination and Protection of Minorities, 49th Session, Item 11, "Potentially Adverse Consequences of Scientific Progress and its Applications for the Integrity, Dignity and Human Rights of the Individual," Working paper prepared by Mr. Osman El-Hajjé in conformity with Sub-Commission decision 1996/110.

28. Calestous Juma, "The UN's Role in the New Diplomacy," *Issues in Science and Technology* 17, 1 (Fall 2000): 37–38.

29. C. G. Weeramantry, *Justice Without Frontiers: Protecting Human Rights in the Age of Technology*, 2 vols. (The Hague: Kluwer Law International, 1998), 2: 551–59, 631. For a useful related view focusing on the U.S. "Government Performance and Results Act" of 1993, see Susan E. Cozzens, "Are New Accountability Rules Bad for Science?" *Issues in Science and Technology* 15, 4 (Summer 1999): 59–66.

Part II Introduction

1. United Nations World Conference on Human Rights, Vienna Declaration and Programme of Action, adopted 25 June 1993, Paragraph 6.

2. United Nations Commission on Human Rights, Sub-Commission on Prevention of Discrimination and Protection of Minorities, 49th Session, Item 11, "Potentially Adverse Consequences of Scientific Progress and its Applications for the Integrity, Dignity and Human Rights of the Individual." Working paper prepared by Mr. Osman El-Hajjé in conformity with Sub-Commission decision 1996/110.

3. Working Paper, citing Nicole Lenoir, "Les Etats et le droit de la bioéthique," *Revue de droit sanitaire et social* 31, 2, (1995): 274.

Chapter 5

1. Franklin Delano Roosevelt, "Four Human Freedoms," Address by the President, *Congressional Record* 87 (1941): 46–47.

2. The American Declaration of the Rights and Duties of Man antedates the Universal Declaration of Human Rights by several months. A health provision that parallels that formulated by the UN includes Article XI: "Every person has the right to the preservation of his health through sanitary and social measures relating to food, clothing, housing and medical care, to the extent permitted by public and community resources. OAS Res. XXX, adopted by the Ninth International Conference of American States (30 March–2 May 1948), Bogotá.

3. John P. Humphrey, *Human Rights and the United Nations: A Great Adventure* (Dobbs Ferry, N.Y.: Transnational Publishers, 1984), 37.

4. Johannes Morsink, *The Universal Declaration of Human Rights: Origins, Drafting,*

and Intent (Philadelphia: University of Pennsylvania Press, 1998), "Food, Clothing, Housing, and Medical Care," 192–98.

5. United Nations Commission on Human Rights, 3rd session, U.N. Doc. E/CN.4/85, pp. 6–7.

6. Albert Verdoodt, *Naissance et signification de la Déclaration universelle des droits de l'homme* (Louvain: Editions Nauwelaerts, 1963).

7. The several comments reported here and below are drawn from Commission on Human Rights, 3rd Session, Summary Record of the Seventy-First Meeting held 14 June 1948, U.N. Doc. E/CN.4/SR.71, pp. 2–5.

8. This debate is found in *Official Records of the Third Session of the General Assembly*, Part I, "Social, Humanitarian and Cultural Questions," Third Committee, *Summary Records of Meetings*, 21 September–8 December, 1948, pp. 559–78.

9. Ibid. The vote is recorded at 575; the "Chinese compromise" draft is U.N. Doc. A/C.3/347/Rev.1.

10. The "motherhood debate" is found in *Official Records*, 560–78.

11. United Nations Commission on Human Rights, 3rd Session, Summary Record of the Sixty-Fifth Meeting, U.N. Doc. E/CN.4/SR.65, p. 5.

12. United Nations, Economic and Social Council, Committee on Economic, Social and Cultural Rights, "The Right to the Highest Attainable Standard of Health," 11/08/2000. E/C.12/2000/4, CESCR General Comment 14.

13. World Health Organization, *Declaration of Alma Ata* (Geneva: World Health Organization, 1978).

14. Vincent Iacopino, M.D., "Health, Human Rights, and Bioethics: A Critical Commentary," unpublished paper for Physicians for Human Rights (USA).

15. United Nations, Commission on Human Rights, Resolution 2001/51 "The protection of human rights in the context of human immunodeficiency virus (HIV) and acquired immune deficiency syndrom (AIDS)." E/CN.4RES/2001/51.

16. In November 1947 the War Crimes Commission said its report "was designed to serve the specific purpose of contributing to the task of the Commission on Human Rights in preparing an international bill of human rights." United Nations Commission on Human Rights Drafting Committee, U.N. Doc. E/CN.4/W.20, p. vi. That it was so received is evidenced by René Cassin's statement to fellow members of the UDHR drafting committee considering a prohibition of torture (Article 5) that doctors have no "right to inflict suffering pain other human beings without their consent, even for ends that may appear 'good'." U.N. Doc. E/CN4/AC.1/SR.3, p. 13.

17. *Annotations on the Text of the Draft International Covenants on Human Rights*, UN GAOR, 10th Sess., Annex, Agenda Item 28 (Part II) at 31, U.N. Doc. A/2929 (1955).

18. Robert N. Proctor, "Nazi Doctors, Racial Medicine, and Human Experimentation," in *The Nazi Doctors and the Nuremberg Code: Human Rights in Human Experimentation*, ed. George J. Annas and Michael A. Grodin (New York: Oxford University Press, 1992), 17–31.

19. Ibid., 7.

20. *Tribunals of War Criminals Before the Nuremberg Military Tribunals Under Control Council Law No. 10* (Washington, D.C.: U.S. Government Printing Office, 1949), 2: 181.

21. Ruth Macklin, "Which Way Down the Slippery Slope? Nazi Medical Killing and Euthanasia Today," in *When Medicine Went Mad: Bioethics and the Holocaust*, ed. Arthur L. Caplan (Totowa, N.J.: Humana Press, 1992), 173–200. The two principles that individuals should be treated as autonomous agents and that persons

with diminished autonomy are entitled to protection are incorporated in the U.S. National Commission for the Protection of Human Subjects of Biomedical and Behavioral Research, *The Belmont Report: Ethical Principles and Guidelines for the Protection of Human Subjects of Research* (Washington, D.C.: U.S. Government Printing Office, 1979), 4.

22. Amy L. Fairchild and Ronald Bayer, "Uses and Abuses of Tuskegee," *Science* 284 (7 May 1999): 919–20. White House Press Release, "Remarks by the President in Apology for Study Done in Tuskegee," 16 May 1997. For a more comprehensive view, see Ruth R. Faden, Susan Lederer, and Jonathan D. Moreno, "U.S. Medical Researchers, the Nuremberg Doctors Trial, and the Nuremberg Code: A Review of Findings of the Advisory Committee on Human Radiation Experiments," *Journal of the American Medical Association* 276, 20 (27 November 1996): 1667–71.

23. Michael Day, "How the West Gets Well: The Urgent Need for Solution to Desperate Diseases is Tempting Western Drug Companies and Medical Research into Taking Ethical Short Cuts in Poor Countries," *New Scientist* (17 May 1997: 14–15.

24. Michael W. Adler, "HIV: The Other Dimension," *The Lancet* 349 (15 February 1997): 498–500. For positive recommendations, see Tessa Tan-Torres Edeje, "The Ethics of Drug Trials in Less Developed Countries," *Lancet Perspectives* 356 (December 2000): 38.

25. "Declaration of Helsinki," Recommendations Guiding Physicians in Biomedical Research Involving Human Subjects. Adopted by the 18th World Medical Assembly, Helsinki, June 1964.

26. Paul Blustein and Barton Gellman, "HIV Drug Prices Cut for Poorer Countries," *Washington Post*, 8 March 2001, p. 1. See also "Pharmaceuticals: Drug-induced Dilemma," *Economist*, 21 April 21, 2001, 59–60.

27. United Nations Special Session on HIV/AIDS, "Declaration of Commitment on HIV/AIDS, Global Crisis—Global Action," 27 June 2001, <www.unaids.org>.

28. Henrik Decker, "New Turkish Strategy to Eliminate Charges of Torture," *Torture, Quarterly Journal on Rehabilitation of Torture Victims and Prevention of Torture* 6, 3 (1996): 53; "Turkish Trial Demonstrates Need for CVT Initiative," *Storycloth: A Publication of the Center for Victims of Torture* 7(Spring 1997): 7, 11

29. Eric Stover and Richard Pierre Claude, *Medicine Under Siege in the Former Yugoslavia, 1991–1995: A Report* (Boston: Physicians for Human Rights, 1996).

30. See Theo C. Van Boven, "Converging Tendencies, in "Reliance on Norms of Humanitarian Law by United Nations Organs," in *Humanitarian Law of Armed Conflict: Challenges Ahead, Essays in Honour of Frits Kalshaven,* ed. Astrid J. M. Delissen and Gerard J. Tanja (Dordrecht: Martinus Nijhoff, 1991), 495–513 at 509–13.

31. This classification scheme was devised by James Welch, MD, Eric Stover, and Richard Pierre Claude and is derived in part from two reports by Physicians for Human Rights, *El Salvador, Health Care Under Siege: Violations of Medical Neutrality During the Civil Conflict* (Boston: Physicians for Human Rights, 1990) and Stover and Claude, *Medicine Under Siege in the Former Yugoslavia, 1991–1995: A Report* (Boston: Physicians for Human Rights, 1996), 66–67. See also Julia Devin, "Medical Neutrality in International Law and Practice," in *Violation of Medical Neutrality,* ed. G. L.Wackers and C. T. M.Wennekes (Amsterdam: Thesis Publishers, 1992), 104–23. Full legal citations for each category and annotations in the Yugoslavia report were supplied by Jill Guzman, International Human Rights Law Institute, DePaul University College of Law, and they appear in Appendix C of the

Report, entitled "Comprehensive Set of Legal Citations on the Classifications of Violations of Medical Neutrality."

32. Leslie C. Green, "War Law and the Medical Profession," chap. 6 in *Essays on the Modern Law of War* (Dobbs Ferry, N.Y.: Transnational Publishers, 1999), 492.

33. *Kadic v. Karadžić*, 70 3d 732 (2d Cir. 1995).

34. Paul Farmer, "Pathologies of Power: Rethinking Health and Human Rights," *American Journal of Public Health* 89, 10 (October 1999): 1486–96.

Chapter 6

1. William Haller, ed., *The Leveller Tracts* (New York: Columbia University Press, 1944).

2. *Writings of Thomas Jefferson*, ed. P. L. Ford, 10 vols. (New York: G.P. Putnam, 1892–99), 4: 477.

3. Eric Sottas and Ben Schonveld, "Information Overload: How Increased Information Flows Affect the Work of the Human Rights Movement," in *Human Rights and the Internet*, ed. Steven Hick, Edward F. Halpin, and Eric Hoskins (New York: St. Martin's Press, 2000), 76–88.

4. James N. Rosenau, *Turbulence in World Politics: A Theory of Change and Continuity* (Princeton, N.J.: Princeton University Press, 1990); Marvin S. Soroos, *Beyond Sovereignty: The Challenge of Global Policy* (Columbia: University of South Carolina Press, 1986; John W. Burton, *Global Conflict: The Domestic Sources of International Conflict* (London: Wheatsheaf, 1984). See also Richard P. Claude and David R. Davis, "The Global Society Perspective on International Human Rights," in *Human Rights and Responsibilities for the 21st Century*, ed. Timothy Mack and Kenneth Hunter (Westport, Conn.: Greenwood Press, 1996), 83–90.

5. Samuel A. Cacas, "Countering Cyberhate: More Regulation or More Speech," *Human Rights* (American Bar Association) 25, 3 (Summer 1998): 21–23.

6. Hick, Halpin, and Hoskins, eds., *Human Rights and the Internet*.

7. "Today's Technological Transformation—Creating the Network Age," Chapter 2 in *United Nations Human Development Report, 2001* (New York: Oxford University Press for United Nations Development Programme, 2001), 35.

8. "OneWorld-Hivos Partnership to Help Bring South Online"; <www.oneworld.org/about/ppack/releases/hivospress190600.shtml>.

9. David Banisar and Simon Davies, *Privacy and Human Rights 1998: An International Survey of Privacy Laws and Developments* (Washington, D.C.: Electronic Privacy Information Center, 1998). See also "Electronic Privacy Advocacy," Technology and Human Rights Project, Human Rights Research and Education Centre, University of Ottawa, <www.uottawa.ca/hrrec/techno/techno.html>.

10. Boris Grondahl, "Europe: Net Crime-Stoppers," *Industry Standard* (2 July 2001), <www.thestandard.com/article/0,1902.274000,00html?printer-friendly=>.

11. Richard P. Claude and Thomas B. Jabine, "Exploring Human Rights Issues with Statistics," in *Human Rights and Statistics: Getting the Record Straight*, ed. Jabine and Claude (Philadelphia: University of Pennsylvania Press, 1992), 5–34.

12. Association of Major Religious Superiors in the Philippines, *Political Detainees in the Philippines* (Manila: Task Force Detainees-Philippines, 1977).

13. Bicutan Rehabilitation Center, Prisoners' Newsletter (August 18, 1977), detailed in Richard P. Claude, "The Decline of Human Rights in the Philippines:

A Case Study," in *Essays in Honor of Myres S. McDougal, New York Law School Law Review* 24 (1978): 215–16.

14. U.S. *Congressional Record* H 11211 (daily edition), October 18, 1977, remarks of Representative Burke.

15. *Hilao v. Estate of Marcos*, 910 F. Supp. 1460 (D. Hawaii, 1995).

16. Alien Tort Claims Act, 28 U.S.C. 1350 as construed for purposes of assessing damages in *Filártiga v. Peña*, 577 F. Supp. 860 (E.D.N.Y., 1984). Also *In re Estate of Marcos*, 25 F. ed 1467 (9th Cir., 1994).

17. *Hilao v. Estate of Marcos*, 103 F.3d 767 (9th Cir, 1996).

18. Patrick Ball, Paul Kobrak, and Herbert F. Spirer, *State Violence in Guatemala, 1960–1996: A Quantitative Reflection* (Washington, D.C.: American Association for the Advancement of Science, 1999).

19. I. Richard Savage, "Hard-Soft Problems," Presidential Address, *Journal of the American Statistical Association* 80 (March 1985): 1–7.

20. Jabine and Claude, Introduction, *Human Rights and Statistics*, 12ff.

21. Richard Pierre Claude, "The Philippines," in *International Human Rights Handbook*, ed. Jack Donnelly and Rhoda Howard (Boulder, Colo.: Westview Press, 1987), 279–99.

22. "Vicaría Records Under Legal Siege," *Record, Physicians for Human Rights* 2, 2 (1989): 4.

23. Statement of Warren Christopher, Deputy Secretary of State, Human Rights and U.S. Foreign Policy, *Hearings Before the Subcommittee on International Organizations of the Committee on Foreign Affairs, House of Representatives*, 96th Cong.,1st Sess., 2 May 1979, 15.

24. Whether the U.S. *Country Reports* reflect ideological bias or bias toward trading partners is statistically explored by Steven C. Poe, Sabine C. Carey, and Tanya C. Vazquez, "How Are These Pictures Different? A Quantitative Comparison of the U.S. State Department and Amnesty International Human Rights Reports, 1976–1995," *Human Rights Quarterly* 23, 2 (Fall 2001): 650–77.

25. *Political Killings in Kosova/Kosovo, March-June, 1999*, Cooperative Report by the Central and East European Initiative of the American Bar Association and the Science and Human Rights Program of the American Association for the Advancement of Science (Washington, D.C.: American Association for the Advancement of Science, 2000).

26. Ibid., 2.

27. Judith Dueck, "HURIDOCS Standard Formats as a Tool in the Documentation of Human Rights Violations," in Jabine and Claude, eds., *Human Rights and Statistics*, 127–58.

28. Patrick Ball, Herbert F. Spirer, and Louise Spirer, eds., *Making the Case: Investigating Large Scale Human Rights Violations Using Information Systems and Data Analysis* (Washington, D.C.: American Association for the Advancement of Science, 2000).

29. Thomas B. Jabine and Denis F. Johnston, "Socio-Economic Indicators and Human Rights," American Statistical Association, *Proceedings of the Social Statistics Section* (Washington, D.C.: American Statistical Association, 1993).

30. *UN Human Rights Development Report, 2001* (New York: Oxford University Press for United Nations Development Programme, 2001), 133–264.

31. Kevin Watkins, *The Oxfam Education Report*, (London: Oxfam GB, 2001), App. 1, "The Education Performance Index."

32. Jabine and Johnston, "Socio-Economic Indicators," 23.

33. Stephen A. Hansen, *Thesaurus of Economic, Social, and Cultural Rights: Ter-*

minology and Potential Violations (Washington, D.C.: American Association for the Advancement of Science, 2000).

34. Ibid., 171–73.

35. Ronald Paul Hill, Robert M Peterson, and Kanwalroop Kathy Dhanda, "Global Consumption and Distributive Justice: A Rawlsian Perspective," *Human Rights Quarterly* 23 (2001): 171–87.

Part III Introduction

1. Barbara Crossette, "DNA Test Reunites Salvadoran Mother and Child," *New York Times International*, 21 January 1995, 1, p. 3. DNA refers to deoxyribonucleic acid, a chromosomal constituent of cell nuclei that determines individual hereditary characteristics. It is the genetic material passed from one generation to the next.

Chapter 7

1. James R. Newman, *The World of Mathematics*, 4 vols. (New York: Simon and Schuster, 1956), 1: 103.

2. Ibid., 2: 732–33. See Maurice Finocchiaro, *The Galileo Affair: A Documentary History* (Berkeley: University of California Press, 1989).

3. Pope John Paul II, "Address to the Einstein Session of the Pontifical Academy of Science," 10 November 1979, Vatican City, translated from French and published in *Science* 207 (14 March 1980): 1165–67. The pope said that Galileo "had to suffer much, we cannot deny it, from men and organizations within the Church" (1166).

4. William McGucken, *Scientists, Society, and State: The Social Relations of the Science Movement in Great Britain, 1931–1947* (Columbus: Ohio State University Press, 1984); Peter J. Kuznick, *Beyond the Laboratory: Scientists as Political Activists in 1930s America* (Chicago: University of Chicago Press, 1987).

5. Paul R. Josephson, *Totalitarian Science and Technology* (Atlantic Highlands, N.J.: Humanities Press, 1996), 17–25.

6. J. D. Bernal, *The Social Functions of Science* (London: Routledge and Kegan Paul, 1939; reprint Cambridge, Mass.: MIT Press, 1967). One of Britain's most famous scientists, Bernal sidestepped criticizing Lysenko, saying, "This controversy has been magnified out of all proportion" (237).

7. Joseph Rotblat, "The End," in *Life Stories: World Renowned Scientists Reflect on Their Lives and the Future of Life on Earth*, ed. Heather Newbold (Berkeley: University of California Press, 2000), 183–192 at 184.

8. Interview with National Academy of Sciences President Philip Handler, by E. M. Leeper, *BioScience* 27 (April 1977): 244.

9. José Goldemberg, "Scientists and Human Rights in Latin America," in *Scientific Cooperation, Problems and Opportunities in the Americas*, ed. Eric Stover and Cathie McCleskey, American Association for the Advancement of Science Workshop (Washington, D.C.: AAAS Committee on Scientific Freedom and Responsibility, 1981), 42–51 at 48.

10. Editor's Page, "Andrew Huxley on Science and Politics," Address to the British Association for the Advancement of Science, *Chemical and Engineering News*, 26 September 1977, p. 5.

11. AAAS File Letter from Professor John Edsall to Sir Andrew Huxley (11 October 1977).

12. Andrei Sakharov, *Memoirs*, trans. Richard Lourie (New York: Alfred A. Knopf, 1990), 98–100.

13. Andrei Sakharov, *Moscow and Beyond, 1986–1989* (New York: Knopf, 1991), 36–37.

14. Ibid., 476.

15. Dedication to Lipman Bers, Chair, Committee on Human Rights, 1979–1984, Symposium "Challenges in Science and Human Rights, Past, Present, and Future" (Washington, D.C.: National Academy of Science, 1996), 1–2.

16. Elisa Muñoz, *Directory of Persecuted Scientists, Health Professionals, and Engineers* (Washington, D.C.: American Association for the Advancement of Science, 1995), iv.

17. Frank von Hippel and Joel Primack, "Public Interest Science," *Science* 177 (29 September 1972): 1166–71.

18. Maurice M. Gibbons et al., *The New Production of Knowledge: The Dynamics of Science and Research in Contemporary Societies* (London: Sage, 1994).

19. John Ziman, "Is Science Losing its Objectivity?" *Nature, International Weekly Journal of Science* 382 (29 August 1996): 751–54.

20. Iain Guest, *Behind the Disappearances: Argentina's Dirty War Against Human Rights and the United Nations* (Philadelphia: University of Pennsylvania Press, 1990). From the period when the "Dirty War" began, see also Robert W. Kates, "Human Issues in Human Rights," *Science* 201 (11 August 1978): 502–6.

21. Clyde Collins Snow, Eric Stover, and Kari Hannibal, "Scientists as Detectives: Investigating Human Rights," *Technology Review* 92, 2 (March 1989): 43–51.

22. Clyde Collins Snow and Maria Julia Bihurriet, "An Epidemiology of Homicide: Ningún Nombre Burials in the Province of Buenos Aires from 1970 to 1984," in *Human Rights and Statistics: Getting the Record Straight*, ed. Thomas B. Jabine and Richard P. Claude (Philadelphia: University of Pennsylvania Press, 1992), 328–63.

23. Christopher Joyce and Eric Stover, *Witnesses from the Grave: The Stories Bones Tell* (Boston: Little Brown, 1991), 238–39.

24. Jacobo Timerman, *Prisoner Without a Name, Cell Without a Number* (New York: Knopf, 1981).

25. Roger Gurr and José Quiroga, "Approaches to Torture Rehabilitation: A Desk Study Covering Effects, Cost-Effectiveness, Participation, and Sustainability," *Torture, Quarterly Journal on Rehabilitation of Torture Victims and Prevention of Torture* (International Rehabilitation Council for Torture Victims, Copenhagen) 11, 1a (March 2001).

26. Allen Keller, MD, "Tortured Immigrants Endure a Catch 22," Editorial, *New York Times*, 8 April 1997.

27. Shana Swiss and Joan Giller, "Rape as a Crime of War," *Journal of the American Medical Association* 270, 5 (4 August 1993): 612–15.

28. "The Limburg Principles on the Implementation of the International Covenant on Economic, Social and Cultural Rights," U.N. Doc. E/CN.4/1987/17, Annex. See also *Human Rights Quarterly* 9 (1987): 122–35.

29. *Health and Human Rights: An International Journal* (Harvard School of Public Health, François-Xavier Bagnoud Center for Health and Human Rights).

30. COPUS publishes *Snapshot Review*, a report on how the Committee on the Public Understanding of Science engages the public. Reflecting its mission, its membership is drawn from science, the media, museums, education, govern-

ment, and public life. It is sponsored by the Royal Society, the British Association for the Advancement of Science, and the Royal Institution of Great Britain.

31. John Street, *Politics and Technology* (New York: Guilford Press, 1992), 130–36.

32. Emily T. Smith, Andrea Durham, Edith Terry, Neil Gilbride, Phil Adamsak, and Jo Ellen Davis, "How Genetics May Multiply the Bounty of the Sea," *Business Week*, 16 December, 1985, pp. 94–95.

33. Christopher Klose, "Food Fears," *Washington Post*, 31 October 2000, p. 23.

34. UN standards say: "The formulation and implementation of national strategies for the right to food requires full compliance with the principles of accountability, transparency, people's participation, decentralization, legislative capacity and the independence of the judiciary." *General Comment 12*, "The Right to Adequate Food," Committee on Economic, Social and Cultural Rights," Twentieth Session, Geneva, 26 April-May 14 1999; U.N. Doc. E/C.12/1999/5, CESCR. See also Gene Rowe and Lynn Frewer, "Public Participation Methods: A Framework for Evaluation," *Science, Technology, and Human Values* (Sage Publications) 25, 1 (Winter 2000): 3–29.

35. Sue Mayer, "Environmental Threats of Transgenic Technology," in *Animal Genetic Engineering: Of Pigs, Oncomice, and Men*, ed. Peter Wheale and Ruth McNally (London: Pluto Press, 1995), 128.

36. Edward Groth, III, "The Debate over Food Biotechnology in the United States: Is A Societal Consensus Achievable?" *Science and Engineering Ethics* 7, 3 (2001): 3227–46.

37. Jeremy Rifkind, *The Biotech Century: Harnessing the Gene and Remaking the World* (New York: Jeremy P. Tarcher/Putnam, 1998), 233.

38. Catherine Larrère, "A Necessary Partnership with Nature," *UNESCO Courier*, online edition, <www.unesco.org/courier/courier/2000_05/uk/edito.htm>. The article is derived from her *Les Philosophies de l'environnement* (Paris: Presses Universitaires de France, 1997).

39. *Cloning Human Beings: Report and Recommendations of the National Bioethics Advisory Commission* (Rockville, Md.: U.S. National Bioethics Advisory Commission, 1997), 108.

40. Ibid.

41. Ibid., 110.

42. William D. Carey, "A Very Human Business," Editorial, *Science* 199 (17 March 1978): 1161.

Chapter 8

1. Louis Henkin, *The Rights of Man Today* (Boulder, Colo.: Westview Press, 1980), 94. Cf. Ann Kent, "States Monitoring States: The United States, Australia, and China's Human Rights, 1990–2001," *Human Rights Quarterly* 2, 3 (August, 2001): 583–624.

2. David P. Forsythe, *Human Rights in International Relations* (New York: Cambridge University Press, 2000), 163.

3. Joseph S. Nye, Jr., "Defining National Interests in an Information Age," *Morgenthau Memorial Lecture* (New York: Carnegie Council on Ethics and International Affairs, 1989).

4. Strategy One, *Institutional Trust: A Five Country Survey*, (New York: Edelman Public Relations Worldwide, 2001).

5. Richard P. Claude, "The Case of Joelito Filártiga and the 'Clinic of Hope,'" *Human Rights Quarterly* 5 (1983): 275–95, recounting *Filártiga v. Peña*, 630 F. 2d 876 (2d Cir. 1980). See also Anne-Marie Slaughter and David Bosco, "Plaintiff's Diplomacy," *Foreign Affairs* 79 (September–October 2000): 102–16.

6. *Filártiga*, 630 F.2d at 884.

7. *Filártiga v. Peña*, 577 F.Supp.860 (1984).

8. *Jota v. Texico, Inc.*, 157 F. 3d 153 (2d Cir. 1998) involving an action against the Southern Peru Copper Corporation brought in Texas for harm caused by toxic emissions in Peru. See also *Doe I v. Unocal*, 963 F. Supp.880 (Cent. Dist. Cal., 1997) and 27 F. Supp. 2d 1174 (Cent. Dist. Cal., 1998) involving an action against Unocal for responsibility for an oil pipeline construction project in Burma relying on Burmese recruited slave labor.

9. William Prusoff, "The Scientist's Story," *New York Times*, 6 March 2001, p. 4.

10. Abigail Zuger, "A Molecular Offspring, Off to Join the AIDS Wars," *New York Times*, 21 March, 2001, 4.

11. Physicians for Human Rights (USA), "PHR Steps Up Efforts to Get U.S. to Join Mine Ban Treaty," *Record* 13, 1 (April 2000): 1, 4.

12. *Case Number 476p2000pr. Decision of the Supreme Court Presidium of the Russian Federation, 13 September 2000*, examining the General Prosecutor Deputy's protest against the verdict of the St. Petersburg City Court, 29 December 1999.

13. Doctors Without Borders USA, "Kosovo Report," accessible at <www.doctorswithoutborders.org/reports/kosovo.htm>.

14. Eric Stover and Richard Pierre Claude, *Medicine Under Siege in the Former Yugoslavia, 1991–1995* (Boston: Physicians for Human Rights, 1996), 98.

15. David J. Lynch, "'One of the Worst Places on Earth': DNA Identifies the Victims of Bosnian Slaughter at Srebrenica in July 1995, Europe's Worst Massacre Since the Nazi Era," *USA Today*, 17 November 2000, pp. 19A, 20A.

16. Marlise Simons, "Tribunal in Hague Finds Bosnia Serb Guilty of Genocide," *New York Times*, 3 August 2001, pp. 1, 8.

17. *Ruben Foster et al. v. Fulton County, Georgia et al.*, No.1:99-CV-0900 (MHS), 1999.

18. Frank Elbers, *Human Rights Education Resourcebook* (Cambridge, Mass.: Human Rights Education Associates, 2000). See also Nancy Flowers, *The Human Rights Education Handbook: Effective Practices for Learning, Action and Change* (Minneapolis: Human Rights Resource Center, University of Minnesota, 2000).

19. Herbert F. Spirer and Louise Spirer, *Data Analysis for Monitoring Human Rights* (Washington, D.C.: American Association for the Advancement of Science, 1997).

20. Jerome J. Shestack, "Sisyphus Endures: The International Human Rights NGO," *New York Law School Review* 24 (1978): 89–123 at 90.

Chapter 9

1. Saul H. Mendlovitz and R. B. J. Walker, *Towards a Just World Peace: Perspectives from Social Movements* (London: Butterworths, 1987).

2. Margaret Mead, in *The Utne Reader*, 1992, cited by *New Beacon Book of Quotations by Women* (Boston: Beacon Press, 1996), 7.

3. Martin Curd and Larry May, *Professional Responsibility for Harmful Actions* (Chicago: Center for the Study of Ethics in the Professions Module Series in Applied Ethics, 1984).

4. Jean Lenname, "The Canary Down the Mine: What Whistleblowers' Health Tells Us About Their Environment," *The Whistle* (Newsletter of Whistleblowers Australia, Inc.) (June 1996): 2–4 at 3; Lenname, "Whistleblowing: A Health Issue," *British Medical Journal* 307 (1993): 667–70.

5. Lisa Foster and Eric Havian, "Environment Is New Target for Old Fraud Law," *BNA Toxic Law Reporter* (14 September 2000): 37–41.

6. Ibid., 38.

7. Wendy Watson, "Breast Cancer Awareness: The Gene Carrier's Story," *London Sunday Mirror*, 17 September 2000, Features Section, pp. 16, 17.

8. Nicholas Hildyard and Sarah Sexton, "No Patents on Life," *Forum for Applied Research and Public Policy* (Spring 2000).

9. Roger Dobson, "Women Fight Patent on Cancer Test," *Sunday Times* (London), 20 April 1997, Features Section, pp. 14–15.

10. Roger Dobson, "Women's Anger over Cancer Gene Patents," *Independent* (London), 29 June, 1997, p. 7.

11. Roger Dobson, "Fearless Talk Saves Lives, Breast Cancer Is Not an Easy Conversation Topic," *The Guardian* (London), 12 May 1998, p. 13.

12. World Intellectual Property Organization, *Report of the Working Group on Biotechnology*, Geneva, document E WIPO/BIOT/WG/99/1 (November 8 and 9, 1999).

13. Directive 98/44/EC of the European Parliament, Paragraph 23.

14. Charter of Fundamental Rights of the European Union, Article 3, "Right to the Integrity of the Person." Article 17 simply says, "Intellectual property shall be protected."

15. Michael A. Heller and Rebecca S. Eisenberg, "Can Patents Deter Innovation? The Anticommons in Biomedical Research," *Science* 280 (1 May 1998): 698–701; in the same issue, see also John J. Doll, "The Patenting of DNA," 689.

16. Nick Thorpe, "Where Should the Line Be Drawn on Who Owns Life Itself?" *The Scotsman*, 23 July 1997, p. 15.

17. Richard Sclove and Madeleine Scammell, "Research by the People: Community Picks Up Where Science Leaves Off," *Yes! A Journal of Positive Futures* (Summer 1998): 43–50.

18. *Ann Anderson v. Cryovac*, 862 F. ed 910 (1st Cir., 1988).

19. Jonathan Harr, *A Civil Action* (New York: Vintage Books, 1996).

20. Lewis A. Grossman, Robert G. Vaughn, and Jonathan Harr, eds., *A Documentary Companion to A Civil Action* (New York: Foundation Press, 1999).

21. Mac Chapin and William Threlkeld, *Indigenous Landscapes: A Study in Ethnocartography* (Arlington, Va.: Center for the Support of Native Lands, 2001).

22. Gary Chapman and Joel Yudken, *The 21st Century Project: Setting A New Course of Science and Technology Policy* (Palo Alto, Calif.: Computer Professionals for Social Responsibility, 1993).

23. Richard E. Sclove, *Democracy and Technology* (New York: Guilford Press, 1995).

24. Paulo Freire, *Pedagogy of the Oppressed*, trans. Myra Bergman Ramos (New York: Continuum, 1980).

25. Richard E. Sclove, Madeleine L. Scammell, and Breena Holland, *Community-Based Research in the United States: An Introductory Reconnaissance, Including Twelve Organizational Case Studies and Comparison with the Dutch Science Shops and the Mainstream American Research System—Executive Summary* (Amherst, Mass.: Loka Institute, 1998), vi.

26. Sclove, *Democracy*, 225–26.

27. Paul Farmer, "Pathologies of Power: Rethinking Health and Human Rights," *American Journal of Public Health* 89, 10 (October 1999): 1486–96 at 1492.

28. Physicians for Human Rights (USA), *Health Care Held Hostage: Human Rights Violations and Violations of Medical Neutrality in Chiapas, Mexico*, (Boston: Physicians for Human Rights, 1999), 4.

Chapter 10

1. Robert O. Keohane, "Governance in a Partially Globalized World," Presidential Address, American Political Science Association, 2000, *American Political Science Review* 95, 1 (March 2001): 1–13 at 1.

2. Oran R. Young, *Governance in World Affairs*, (Ithaca, N.Y.: Cornell University Press, 1999); Young, "Rights, Rules and Resources in International Society," in *Rights to Nature: Ecological, Economic, Cultural, and Political Principles of Institutions for the Environment*, ed. Susan Hanna, Carl Folke, and Karl-Göran Möle (Washington, D.C.: Island Press for the Beijer International Institute of Ecological Economics, Royal Swedish Academy of Sciences, 1996), 245–63. See also Michael Edwards, *Future Positive: International Co-operation in the 21st Century* (London: Earthscan Publications, 1999).

3. United Kingdom Government White Paper, *Eliminating World Poverty: Making Globalization Work for the Poor* (London: Her Majesty's Stationery Office, 2000), 50–54.

4. R. Meeran, "Accountability of Transnationals for Human Rights Abuses," *New Law Journal* 148, 6864–65 (13, 20 November 1998): 1686–87, 1706–7.

5. "UN Launches New Effort on Global Business Compact," Press Release, World Economic Forum, <www.weforum.org/pressreleases.nsf/>, 28 January 2001.

6. "Twenty Questions on the UN Global Compact: What Companies Need to Know," UN website, <www.unglobalcompact.org./gc/UNWeb.nsf/content/questions.htm>.

7. Amnesty International, *Human Rights: Is It Any of Your Business?* (London: Amnesty International-UK, 2000).

8. Clarence J. Dias, unpublished memorandum to UN Secretary General, "The Future of the UN and the Future of the UN Secretary-General's Global Compact," International Center for Law in Development, New York, 2001.

9. William New, "UN: NGOs Wary of Corporate Links," 26 May 2000, <www.corpwatch.org>.

10. Letter dated 28 July 2000 from Kenneth Roth, Director of Human Rights Watch, to UN Secretary General Kofi Annan, <www.hrw.org/advocacy/corporations/index.htm>.

11. Khuy Sokhoeun and Jeff Smith, "Families Still Afraid They're Victims of Waste," *Cambodian Daily*,17 February 1999, p. 1.

12. Human Rights Watch, *Toxic Justice: Human Rights and Toxic Waste in Cambodia* (New York: Human Rights Watch, 1999).

13. Ibid., "Summary and Recommendations," <www.hrw.org/hrwreports/1999 cambotox/>.

14. Margaret E. Keck and Kathryn Sikkink, "Environmental Advocacy Networks," *Activists Beyond Borders: Advocacy Networks in International Politics* (Ithaca, N.Y.: Cornell University Press, 1998), 121–63.

15. Sierra Club Legal Defense Fund, reorganized in 1996 as Earthjustice, accessible at <www.earthjustice.org>.

16. Adriana Fabra Aguilar and Neil A. F. Popovic, "Lawmaking in the United Nations: The UN Study on Human Rights and the Environment," *Review of European Community and International Environmental Law* 3 (1994): 197–205. See also Popovic, "In Pursuit of Environmental Human Rights: Commentary on the Draft Declaration of Principles on Human Rights and the Environment," *Columbia Human Rights Law Review* 27, 3 (Spring 1996): 487–603.

17. To keep up with recent events in this area, see the website of the University of Minnesota Human Rights Library, "Global Business Responsibility Resource Center: Codes of Conduct," <www1.umn.edu/numanrts/links/gbrcodes. html>.

18. Craig Scott, "Multinational Enterprises and Emergent Jurisprudence on Violations of Economic, Social and Cultural Rights," in Asbørn Eide et al., *Economic, Social, and Cultural Rights: A Textbook*, 2nd ed. (Boston: Kluwer International Law, 2001).

19. *Doe I v. Unocal*, 963 F. Supp.880 (Cent. Dist. Cal., 1997); and 27 F. Supp. 2d 1174 (Cent. Dist. Cal., 1998). See also International Labour Organization, "Resolution on the Widespread Use of Forced Labour in Myanmar," Res. 17.06.1999 *International Legal Materials* 38 (1999): 1215.

20. "Unocal Shareholders Reject Myanmar Resolutions," Brea, California, Reuters, 21 May, 2001.

21. Francis Bacon, *Essays, Advancement of Learning, New Atlantis, and Other Pieces* (New York: Library Classics, 2000).

22. Amnesty International, *Chile* (London: Amnesty International, 1974), 63.

23. "Médicos piden termino de apremios ilegítimos," *Mercurio*, 25 November 1983, p. 1.

24. Matthew Lippman, "The Protection of Universal Human Rights: The Problem of Torture," *Universal Human Rights* (subsequently *Human Rights Quarterly*) 1, 4 (October-December 1979): 25–56 at 48. See also Medical Association, *The Medical Profession and Human Rights* (New York: Zed Books, 2001), chap. 4, "Torture, Cruel and Degrading Treatment."

25. Rosemary Chalk, Mark S. Frankel, and Sallie B. Chafer, *Professional Ethics Activities in the Scientific and Engineering Societies* (Washington, D.C.: American Association for the Advancement of Science, 1980), "Conclusions," 101–2.

26. Panel on Scientific Responsibility and the Conduct of Research, Committee on Science, Engineering, and Public Policy, National Academy of Sciences, National Academy of Engineering, and the Institute of Medicine, *Responsible Science: Ensuring the Integrity of the Research Process* (Washington, D.C.: National Academy Press, 1992), 147.

27. Toronto Resolution, Eric Fawcett, "Working Group on Ethical Considerations in Science and Scholarship," *Accountability in Research* 3 (1993): 69–72, <www.scienceforpeace.sa.utoronto.ca/ FrontPageFiles/TorResScien.html>.

28. Dortmund, Germany, The International Congresses of Engineers and Scientists publishes at <www.inesglobal.org>.

29. John Peet, "Science, Engineering and Ethics for a Finite World: The Code of Ethics of the Institution of Professional Engineers New Zealand," <www.ipenz. org.nz>.

30. Joseph R. Herkerts, "Future Directions in Engineering Ethics and the Role of Professional Societies," *Science and Engineering Ethics* 7, 3 (2001): 403–14.

31. Michael Edwards, "Civil Society and a Global Norm," *UN Chronicle* 28, 4 (2000): 26–27.

32. Oren Lyons, "Ethics and Spiritual Values and the Norms of Environmentally Sustainable Development," *Akwesasne Notes* (Winter 1996), excerpts at <www.ratical.org/co-globalize/OLexcerpts.html>.

Bibliography

Abrambulo, K. *Strengthening the Supervision of the International Covenant on Economic, Social and Cultural Rights, Theoretical and Procedural Aspects.* Utrecht: School of Human Rights Research, 1999.

Addo, Michael K. *Human Rights Standards and the Responsibility of Transnational Corporations.* Boston: Kluwer Law International, 1999.

Alston, Philip, ed. *The United Nations: A Critical Appraisal.* Oxford: Clarendon Press, 1992.

Alston, Philip, and James Crawford, eds. *The Future of UN Human Rights Treaty Monitoring.* New York: Cambridge University Press, 2000.

Amnesty International. *Chile.* London: Amnesty International, 1974.

———. *Prescription for Change: Health Professionals and the Exposure of Human Rights Violations.* London: Amnesty International, 1996

Anaya, S. James, and James E. Rogers. *Indigenous Peoples in International Law.* New York: Oxford University Press, 1996.

Andreopoulos, George J., and Richard P. Claude, eds. *Human Rights Education for the Twenty-First Century.* Philadelphia: University of Pennsylvania Press, 1997.

Annas, George J., and Michael. A. Grodin, eds. *The Nazi Doctors and the Nuremberg Code: Human Rights in Human Experimentation.* New York: Oxford University Press, 1992.

Arditti, Rita. *Searching for Life: The Grandmothers of the Plaza de Mayo and the Disappeared Children of Argentina.* Berkeley: University of California Press, 2000.

Arup, Christopher, *The New World Trade Organization Agreements: Globalizing Law through Services and Intellectual Property.* New York: Cambridge University Press, 2000.

Association of Major Religious Superiors in the Philippines. *Political Detainees in the Philippines.* Manila: Task Force Detainees—Philippines, 1977.

Bacon, Francis. *Essays, Advancement of Learning, New Atlantis, and Other Pieces.* New York: Library Classics, 2000.

Badash, Lawrence. *Scientists and the Development of Nuclear Weapons, from Fission to the Limited Test Ban Treaty, 1939–1963.* Atlantic Highlands, N.J.: Humanities Press, 1995.

Baldwin-Ragaven, L., and Grouchy J. de London. *An Ambulance of the Wrong Colour: Health Professions, Human Rights and Ethics in South Africa.* Rondebosch, South Africa: University of Cape Town Press, 1999.

Ball, Patrick, Herbert F. Spirer, and Louise Spirer, eds. *Making the Case: Investigating Large Scale Human Rights Violations Using Information Systems and Data*

Analysis. Washington, D.C.: American Association for the Advancement of Science, 2000.

Ball, Patrick. *Who Did What to Whom? Planning and Implementing a Large Scale Human Rights Data Project.* Washington, D.C.: American Association for the Advancement of Science. 1996.

Ball, Patrick, Paul Kobrak, and Herbert F. Spirer. *State Violence in Guatemala, 1960–1996: A Quantitative Reflection.* Washington, D.C.: American Association for the Advancement of Science, 1999.

Banisar, David, and Susan Davies. *Privacy and Human Rights, 1998: An International Survey of Privacy Laws and Developments.* Washington, D.C.: Electronic Privacy Information Center, 1998.

Bauman, Zygmunt. *Globalization: The Human Consequence.* New York: Columbia University Press, 2000.

Baxi, Upendra. *The Future of Human Rights.* New York: Oxford University Press, 2000.

Bayefsky, Anne F. *The UN Human Rights Treaty System: Universality at the Crossroads.* Ardsley, N.Y.: Transnational Publishers, 2001.

Bernal, J. D. *The Social Function of Science.* Cambridge, Mass.: MIT Press, 1967.

British Medical Association. *The Medical Profession and Human Rights: Handbook for a Changing Agenda.* New York: Zed Books, 2001.

Burgerman, Susan. *Moral Victories, How Activists Provoke Multilateral Action.* Ithaca, N.Y.: Cornell University Press, 2001.

Burton, John W. *Global Conflict: The Domestic Sources of International Conflict.* London: Wheatsheaf Books, 1984.

Cahn, Edmond Nathaniel. *Confronting Injustice: The Edmond Cahn Reader.* Ed. Lenore L. Cahn. Boston: Little, Brown, 1966.

Caplan, Arthur L., ed. *When Medicine Went Mad: Bioethics and the Holocaust.* Totowa, N.J.: Humana Press, 1992.

Cassin, René. *La Pensée et l'action.* Paris: Editions du Centre National de la Recherche Scientifique, 1981.

Chalk, Rosemary, Mark S. Frankel, and Sallie B. Chafer. *Professional Ethics Activities in the Scientific and Engineering Societies.* Washington, D.C.: American Association for the Advancement of Science, 1980.

Chapin, Mac, and William Threlkeld. *Indigenous Landscapes: A Study in Ethnocartography.* Arlington, Va.: Center for the Support of Native Lands, 2001.

Chapman, Audrey R. *Health Care Reform: A Human Rights Approach.* Washington, D.C.: Georgetown University Press, 1994.

Chapman, Gary, and Joel Yudken. *The 21st Century Project: Setting a New Course of Science and Technology Policy.* Palo Alto, Calif.: Computer Professionals for Social Responsibility, 1993.

Chouhan, T. R. et al. *Bhopal, the Inside Story: Carbide Workers Speak Out on the World's Worst Industrial Disaster.* New York: Apex Press, 1994.

Clair, Renée. *The Scientific Education of Girls: Education Beyond Reproach?* London: Jessica Kingsley Publishers-UNESCO Publishing, 1995.

Clark, Ann Marie. *Diplomacy of Conscience: Amnesty International and Changing International Norms.* Princeton, N.J.: Princeton University Press, 2001

Cook, Rebecca, J., ed. *Human Rights of Women: National and International Perspectives.* Philadelphia: University of Pennsylvania Press, 1994.

———. *Women's Health and Human Rights: The Promotion and Protection of Women's Health Through International Human Rights Law.* Geneva: World Health Organization. 1994. co-published with the American Public Health Association. 1997.

Curd, Martin, and Larry May. *Professional Responsibilities for Harmful Actions.* Module Series in Applied Ethics. Chicago: Center for the Study of Ethics in the Professions, 1984.

Delissen, Astrid J. M., and Gerard J. Tanja, eds. *Humanitarian Law of Armed Conflict: Challenges Ahead, Essays in Honour of Frits Kalshaven.* Dordrecht: Martinus Nijhoff, 1991.

Dembo, David, Clarence J. Dias, Ayesha Kadwani, and Ward Morehouse, eds. *Nothing to Lose But Our Lives: Empowerment to Oppose Industrial Hazards in a Transnational World.* New York: New Horizons Press, 1988.

di Padirac, Bruno, ed. *The International Dimensions of Cyberspace Law.* Paris: UNESCO Publishing, 2000.

Dobson, Andrew. *Justice and the Environment: Conceptions of Environmental Sustainability and Theories of Distributive Justice.* New York: Oxford University Press, 1999.

Donnelly, Jack. *Universal Human Rights in Theory and Practice.* Ithaca, N.Y.: Cornell University Press, 1989.

Donnelly, Jack, and Rhoda Howard, eds. *International Human Rights Handbook.* Boulder, Colo.: Westview Press, 1987.

Dreyfuss, Rochelle, and Diane L. Zimmerman. *Expanding the Boundaries of Intellectual Property.* New York: Oxford University, 2001.

Drinan, Robert. *The Cry of the Oppressed.* San Francisco: Harper and Row, 1987.

Drinan, Robert. *The Mobilization of Shame: A World View of Human Rights.* New Haven, Conn.: Yale University Press. 2001.

Edwards, Michael. *Future Positive: International Co-operation in the 21st Century.* London: Earthscan Publications, 1999.

Eide, Asbørn, Helge Ole Bergesen, and Pia Rudolfson Goyer, eds. *Human Rights and the Oil Industry.* Utrecht: School of Human Rights Research, 2000.

Eide, Asbørn, Catarina Krause, and Allan Rosas. *Economic, Social, and Cultural Rights: A Textbook.* 2nd ed. Boston: Kluwer International Law, 2000.

Eide, Asbørn et al., eds. *The Universal Declaration of Human Rights: A Commentary.* Oslo: Scandinavian University Press, 1992.

Elbers, Frank. *Human Rights Education Resourcebook,* Cambridge, Mass.: Human Rights Education Associates, 2000.

Ellsberg, Mary Carroll, Lori Heise, and Elizabeth Shrader. *Researching Violence Against Women, A Practical Guide for Researchers and Advocates.* Geneva: Center for Health and Gender Equity and World Health Organization. 2001.

Evans, Tony. *The Politics of Human Rights.* London: Pluto Press, 2001.

Falk, Richard. *Human Rights Horizons: The Pursuit of Justice in a Globalizing World.* London: Routledge. 2000.

———. *On Humane Governance: Toward a New Global Politics.* University Park: Pennsylvania State University Press, 1995.

Fals-Borda, Orlando, and Muhammad Anisur Rahman, eds. *Action and Knowledge: Breaking the Monopoly with Participatory Action-Research.* New York: Apex Press, 1991.

Fidler, David P., ed. *International Law and Public Health: Materials and Analysis of Global Health Jurisprudence.* New York: Transnational Publishers, 2000.

Fijalkowski, Agata, ed. *The Right of the Child to a Clean Environment.* Brookfield, Vt.: Ashgate, 2000.

Finocchiaro, Maurice. *The Galileo Affair: A Documentary History.* Berkeley: University of California Press, 1989.

Florini, Ann M., ed. *The Third Force: The Rise of Transnational Civil Society.* Washington, D.C.: Brookings Institution and Carnegie Endowment for International Peace, 2000.

Flowers, Nancy. *The Human Rights Education Handbook: Effective Practices for Learning, Action, and Change.* Minneapolis: Human Rights Resource Center, University of Minnesota, 2000.

Ford, Paul. *AIDS and Accusation: Haiti and the Geography of Blame.* Berkeley: University of California Press, 1993.

Forsythe, David P. *Human Rights in International Relations.* Cambridge: Cambridge University Press, 2000.

Fox, Gregory H., and Brad R. Roth, eds. *Democratic Governance and International Law.* New York: Cambridge University Press, 2000.

Franck, Thomas M. *The Empowered Self: Law and Society in an Age of Individualism.* New York: Oxford University Press, 2000.

Freire, Paulo. *Pedagogy of the Oppressed.* Trans. Myra Bergman Ramos. New York: Cambridge University Press.

Fujimura-Fanselow, Kumiko, and Kameda Atsuko, eds. *Japanese Women.* New York: Feminist Press, 1995.

Gibbons, Maurice M. et al. *The New Production of Knowledge: The Dynamics of Science and Research in Contemporary Societies.* London: Sage, 1994.

Gillespie, Alexander. *International Environmental Law, Policy and Ethics.* New York: Oxford University Press, 1998.

Glendon, Mary Ann. *A World Made New: Eleanor Roosevelt and the Universal Declaration of Human Rights.* New York: Random House, 2001.

Goldhaber, Michael. *Reinventing Technology: Policies for Democratic Values.* New York: Routledge and Kegan Paul. 1986.

Grossman, Lewis A., Robert G. Vaughn, and Jonathan Harr, eds. *A Documentary Companion to A Civil Action.* New York: Foundation Press, 1999.

Guest, Iain. *Behind the Disappearances: Argentina's Dirty War Against Human Rights and the United Nations.* Philadelphia: University of Pennsylvania Press, 1990.

Gurr, Ted Robert. *Peoples Versus States: Minorities at Risk in the New Century.* Washington, D.C.: United States Institute of Peace, 2001.

Haller, William, ed. *The Leveller Tracts.* New York: Columbia University Press, 1944.

Hanna, Susan, Carl Folke, and Karl-Göran Möle, eds. *Rights to Nature: Ecological, Economic, Cultural, and Political Principles of Institutions for the Environment.* Washington, D.C.: Island Press for Beijer International Institute of Ecological Economics, Royal Swedish Academy of Sciences, 1996.

Hannum, Hurst. *Guide to International Human Rights Practice,* 3rd ed. Ardsley, N.Y.: Transnational Publishers, 1999.

Hannum, Hurst, and Dana D. Fischer, eds. *U.S. Ratification of the International Covenants on Human Rights.* Irvington-on-Hudson, N.Y.: Transnational Publishers, 1993.

Hansen, Stephen A. *Getting Online for Human Rights: Frequently Asked Questions and Answers About Using the Internet in Human Rights Work.* Washington, D.C.: American Association for the Advancement of Science, 1998.

———. *Thesaurus of Economic, Social, and Cultural Rights: Terminology and Potential Violations.* Washington, D.C.: American Association for the Advancement of Science, 2000.

Harr, Jonathan. *A Civil Action.* New York: Vintage Books, 1996.

Henkin, Louis. *The Age of Rights.* New York: Columbia University Press, 1990.

———. *The Rights of Man Today.* Boulder, Colo.: Westview Press, 1980.

Hick, Steven, Edward F. Halpin, and Eric Hoskins, eds. *Human Rights and the Internet.* New York: St. Martin's Press, 2000.

Homer-Dixon, Thomas. *The Ingenuity Gap: How Can We Solve the Problems of the Future?* New York: Knopf, 2000

Horgan, John. *The End of Science, Facing the Limits of Knowledge in the Twilight of the Scientific Age.* New York: Broadway Books, 1996.

Howse, Robert, and Makau Mutua. *Protecting Human Rights in a Global Economy: Challenges for the World Trade Organization.* Montreal: Rights and Democracy/ International Centre for Human Rights and Democratic Development, 2000.

Hufton, Olwen, ed. *Historical Change and Human Rights: The Oxford Amnesty Lectures, 1994.* New York: Basic Books, 1995.

Human Rights Internet. *For the Record: The UN Human Rights System* in printed, web-based and CD-ROM versions <www.hri.ca>. Ottawa: Human Rights Internet, 1999.

Human Rights Watch. *Toxic Justice: Human Rights and Toxic Waste in Cambodia.* New York: Human Rights Watch, 1999.

Humphrey, John P. *Human Rights and the United Nations: A Great Adventure.* Dobbs Ferry, N.Y.: Transnational Publications, 1984.

Hunt, Paul. *Reclaiming Social Rights: International and Comparative Perspectives.* Aldershot: Dartmouth Publishing, 1996.

Huxley, Julian. *Freedom and Culture.* Freeport, N.Y.: United Nations Educational, Scientific and Cultural Organization Books for Libraries, 1971.

Iles, Alastair T., and Morton H. Sklar. *The Right to Travel: An Essential Freedom for Scientists and Academics.* Washington, D.C.: American Association for the Advancement of Science, 1996.

Innes, Brian. *The History of Torture.* New York: St. Martin's Press, 1998

International Human Rights Internship Program. *Ripple in Still Water: Reflections by Activists on Local- and National-Level Work on Economic, Social and Cultural Rights.* Washington, D.C.: Institute of International Education, 1997.

Jabine, Thomas B., and Richard P. Claude. *Human Rights and Statistics, Getting the Record Straight.* Philadelphia: University of Pennsylvania Press, 1992.

Josephson, Paul R. *Totalitarian Science and Technology.* Atlantic Highlands, N.J.: Humanities Press, 1996.

Joyce, Christopher, and Eric Stover. *Witnesses from the Grave: The Stories Bones Tell.* Boston: Little, Brown and Company, 1991.

Keck, Margaret E., and Kathryn Sikkink. *Activists Beyond Borders: Advocacy Networks in International Politics.* Ithaca, N.Y.: Cornell University Press, 1998.

Kendall, Henry. *A Distant Light: Scientists in the Policy Process.* New York: Springer-Verlag, 1999.

Kennedy, Paul. *Preparing for the Twenty-first Century.* New York: Random House. 1993.

Kim, Jim Yong, Joyce V. Millen, Alec Irwin, and John Gershman. *Dying for Growth, Global Inequality and the Health of the Poor.* Monroe, Me.: Common Courage Press. 2000.

Kohn, Stephen M. *Concepts and Procedures in Whistleblower Law.* Westport, Conn.: Quorum Books, 2000.

Korey, William. *NGOs and the Universal Declaration of Human Rights: "A Curious Grapevine".* New York: St. Martin's Press, 1998.

Krimsky, Sheldon, and Alonzo Plough. *Environmental Hazards: Communicating Risks as a Social Process.* Dover, Mass.: Auburn House, 1988.

Kuznick, Peter J. *Beyond the Laboratory: Scientists as Political Activists in 1930s America.* Chicago: University of Chicago Press, 1987.

Lauren, Paul Gordon. *The Evolution of International Human Rights: Visions Seen.* Philadelphia: University of Pennsylvania Press, 1998.

Lauterpacht, Hersch. *An International Bill of Rights of Man.* New York: Columbia University Press, 1945.

Levy, Barry S., and Victor W. Sidel. 1997. *War and Public Health.* New York: Oxford University Press,

Livezey, Lowell. *Nongovernmental Organizations and the Ideas of Human Rights.* Princeton, N.J.: Center of International Studies, 1988.

Mack, Timothy, and Kenneth Hunter, eds. *Human Rights and Responsibilities for the 21st Century.* Westport, Conn.: Greenwood Publishing Group, 1996.

Mann, Jonathan M., Sofia Gruskin, Michael A. Grodin, and George J. Annas, eds. *Health and Human Rights.* New York: Routledge, 1998.

Maresca, Louis, and Stuart Maslen, eds. *The Banning of Anti-Personnel Landmines. The Legal Contribution of the International Committee of the Red Cross, 1955–1999.* New York: Cambridge University Press, 2000.

Masters, Dexter, and Katherine Way, eds. *One World or None: A Report to the Public on the Full Meaning of the Atomic Bomb.* New York: McGraw-Hill, 1946.

McChesney, Allan. *Promoting and Defending Human Rights: A Handbook.* Washington, D.C.: American Association for the Advancement of Science, 2000.

McConnel, Terrance. *Inalienable Rights: The Limits of Consent in Medicine and the Law.* New York: Oxford University Press, 2000.

McGucken, William. *Scientists, Society and State: The Social Relations of Science Movement in Great Britain 1931–1947.* Columbus: Ohio State University Press, 1984.

Mendlovitz, Saul H., and R. B. J. Walker. *Towards a Just World Peace: Perspectives from Social Movements.* London: Butterworths, 1987.

Miller, Kelly, *Our War for Human Rights.* 1919. Reprint as *Kelly Miller's History of the World War for Human Rights.* New York: Negro Universities Press, 1969.

Morsink, Johannes. *The Universal Declaration of Human Rights: Origins, Drafting, and Intent.* Philadelphia: University of Pennsylvania Press, 1999.

Northrop, F. S. C. *The Logic of the Sciences and the Humanities.* New York: Macmillan, 1947. Reprint Cleveland: Meridian Books, 1959.

Muñoz, Elisa, ed. *Directory of Persecuted Sciences, Engineers, and Health Professionals.* Washington, D.C.: American Association for the Advancement of Science, 1996.

Newbold, Heather, ed. *Life Stories: World Renowned Scientists Reflect on Their Lives and the Future of Life on Earth.* Berkeley: University of California Press, 2000.

Newman, James R. *The World of Mathematics.* 4 vols. New York: Simon and Schuster, 1956.

Olson, Mancur. *The Logic of Collective Action: Public Goods and the Theory of Groups.* Cambridge, Mass.: Harvard University Press, 1971.

Panel on Scientific Responsibility and the Conduct of Research, Committee on Science, Engineering, and Public Policy, National Academy of Sciences, National Academy of Engineering, and Institute of Medicine. *Responsible Science: Ensuring the Integrity of the Research Process.* Washington, D.C.: National Academy Press, 1992.

Peterson, James C., ed. *Citizen Participation in Science Policy.* Amherst, Mass.: University of Massachusetts Press, 1984.

Physicians for Human Rights. *El Salvador, Health Care Under Siege, Violations of Medi-*

cal Neutrality During the Civil Conflict. Boston: Physicians for Human Rights, 1999.

Physicians for Human Rights (USA). *Health Care Held Hostage: Human Rights Violations of Medical Neutrality in Chiapas, Mexico.* Boston: Physicians for Human Rights, 1999.

Polanyi, Michael. *Knowing and Being, Essays.* Ed. Marjorie Grene. Chicago: University of Chicago Press, 1969.

Revesz, Richard L, Philippe Sands, and Richard B. Stewart, eds. *Environmental Law, the Economy and Sustainable Development.* New York: Cambridge University Press, 2000.

Rifkin, Jeremy. *The Biotech Century: Harnessing the Gene and Remaking the World.* New York: Jeremy P. Tarcher/Putnam, 1998.

Risse, Thomas, Stephen C. Ropp, and Kathryn Sikkink, eds. *The Power of Human Rights: International Norms and Domestic Change.* New York: Cambridge University Press. 2000.

Roosevelt, Eleanor. *On My Own.* New York: Harper, 1958.

Rosenau, James N. *Turbulence in World Politics: A Theory of Change and Continuity.* Princeton, N.J.: Princeton University Press, 1990.

Rosenau, James N., and Ernst-Otto Czempiel, eds. *Governance without Government: Order and Change in World Politics.* Cambridge: Cambridge University Press, 1992.

Rosenbaum, Alan, ed. *The Philosophy of Human Rights, International Perspectives.* Westport, Conn.: Greenwood Press, 1980.

Rotblat, Joseph, ed. *World Citizenship: Allegiance to Humanity.* Cambridge, Mass.: Palgrave, 1997.

Sakharov, Andrei. *Memoirs, Andrei Sakharov.* Trans. Richard Lourie. New York: Knopf, 1990.

———. *Moscow and Beyond, 1986–1989.* Trans. Antonina Bouis. New York: Knopf, 1991.

Salomon, Jean-Jacques, Francisco R. Sagasti, and Céline Sachs-Jeanet, eds. *The Uncertain Quest: Science, Technology, and Development.* Tokyo: United Nations University Press, 2000.

Schachter, Oscar, and Christopher C. Joyner. *United Nations Legal Order.* 2 vols. Cambridge: Cambridge University Press, 1991.

Schoenberger, Karl. *Levi's Children: Coming to Terms with Human Rights in the Global Marketplace.* New York: Atlantic Monthly Press, 2000.

Sclove, Richard E. *Democracy and Technology.* New York: Guilford Press, 1995.

Sclove, Richard E., Madeleine L. Scammell, and Breena Holland. *Community-Based Research in the United States: An Introductory Reconnaissance, Including Twelve Organizational Case Studies and Comparison with the Dutch Science Shops and the Mainstream American Research System—Executive Summary.* Amherst, Mass.: Loka Institute, 1998.

Scott, Craig, ed. *Torture as Tort: Comparative Perspectives on the Development of Transnational Litigation.* Portland, Ore.: Frank Cass, 2001

Shelton, Dinah. *Commitment and Compliance: The Role of Non-Binding Norms in the International Legal System.* New York: Oxford University Press, 2000.

———. *Remedies in International Human Rights Law.* New York: Oxford University Press, 1999.

Shiva, Vanda. *Biopiracy: The Plunder of Nature and Knowledge.* Boston: South End Press, 1997.

Shuman, Michael, and Julia Sweig. *Technology for the Common Good.* Washington, D.C.: Institute for Policy Studies. 1993.

Smith, George P., II. *Human Rights and Biomedicine.* The Hague: Kluwer Law International, 2000.

Soroos, Marvin S. *Beyond Sovereignty: The Challenge of Global Policy.* Columbia: University of South Carolina Press, 1986.

Spirer, Herbert F., and Louise Spirer. *Data Analysis for Monitoring Human Rights.* Washington, D.C.: American Association for the Advancement of Science, 1997.

Stauber, John, and Sheldon Rampton. *Trust Us, We're Experts: How Industry Manipulates Science and Gambles with Your Future.* New York: Jeremy P. Tarcher/Putnam, 2001.

Stevis, Dimitris, and Valerie J. Asseto, eds. *The International Political Economy of the Environment: Critical Perspectives.* Boulder, Colo.: Lynne Reinner, 2001.

Stover, Eric, and Richard Pierre Claude. *Medicine Under Siege in the Former Yugoslavia, 1991–1995: A Report.* Boston: Physicians for Human Rights, 1996.

Strategy One. *Institutional Trust: A Five Country Survey.* New York: Edelman Publications Worldwide, 2001.

Street, John. *Politics and Technology.* New York: Guilford Press, 1992.

Swann, Brenda, and Francis Abrahamian. *J. D. Bernal: A Life in Science and Politics.* London: Verso, 1999.

Teich, Albert H., and Mark S. Frankel. *Good Science and Responsible Scientists.* Washington, D.C.: American Association for the Advancement of Science, 1992.

Teitel, Ruti G. *Transitional Justice.* New York: Oxford University Press, 2000.

Threlkeld, Bill. *Indigenous Landscapes: A Study in Ethnocartography.* Arlington, Va.: Center for the Support of Native Lands, 2001.

Timerman, Jacobo. *Prisoner Without a Name, Cell Without a Number.* New York: Knopf, 1981.

UNESCO. *Human Rights, Comments and Interpretations.* Westport, Conn.: Greenwood Press, 1949.

UNESCO. *World Science Report 2000.* Paris: United Nations Educational, Scientific and Cultural Organization, 2000.

United Nations. *HIV/AIDS and Human Rights: International Guidelines.* New York: United Nations Publications, 2000.

———. *The Role of the World Trade Organization in Global Governance.* New York: United Nations Publications. 2001.

United Nations Development Program. *Human Development Report 2000: Human Rights and Human Development.* New York: United Nations Publications. 2001.

Vasak, Karel, and Philip Alston, eds. *The International Dimensions of Human Rights.* 2 vols. Westport, Conn.: Greenwood Press, 1982.

Verdoodt, A. *Naissance et signification de la Déclaration universelle des droits de l'homme.* Louvain: Editions Nauwelaerlts, 1963.

Vincent, R. J. *Human Rights and International Relations.* Cambridge: Cambridge University Press, 1986.

Wackers, G. L., and C. T. M. Wennekes, eds. *Violations of Medical Neutrality.* Amsterdam: Thesis Publishers, 1992.

Weeramantry, C. G., ed. *Human Rights and Scientific and Technological Development.* Tokyo: United Nations University Press, 1990.

———. ed. *The Impact of Technology on Human Rights.* Tokyo: United Nations University Press, 2000.

————. *Justice Without Frontiers: Protection of Human Rights in the Age of Technology.* 2 vols. The Hague: Kluwer Law International, 1998.

Weiss, Edith Brown, ed. *Environmental Change and International Law.* Tokyo: United Nations University Press, 2000.

Weiss, Thomas G., and Leon Gordenker, eds. *NGOs, the UN, and Global Governance.* Boulder, Colo.: Lynne Reinner, 1996.

Welch, Claude, Jr., ed. *NGOs and Human Rights: Promise and Performance.* Philadelphia: University of Pennsylvania Press, 2001.

Wells, H. G. *The Rights of Man or What Are We Fighting For?* Harmondsworth: Penguin, 1940.

Willetts, Peter, ed. *"The Conscience of the World": The Influence of Non-Governmental Organizations in the UN System.* Washington, D.C.: Brookings Institution, 1996.

Wronka, Joseph. *Human Rights and Social Policy in the 21st Century.* Lanham, Md.: University Press of America, 1992.

Young, Oran R. *Governance in World Affairs.* Ithaca, N.Y.: Cornell University Press, 1999.

Ziman, John M. *Of One Mind: The Collectivization of Science.* New York: American Institute of Physics, 1995.

————. *Real Science: What It Is and What It Means.* Cambridge: Cambridge University Press, 2002.

Index

Acknowledgments

Ideas set out here have benefited greatly from critical discussion in various fora, most importantly in my experimental undergraduate course, "Science and Human Rights," sponsored by the Princeton University Council on Science and Technology in 1996. Without the students' enthusiasm for the topic and the encouragement for that endeavor by Professor Shirley Tilghman, this book would not have materialized. I am especially indebted to Dr. Audrey Chapman, Director of the Science and Human Rights Program of the American Association for the Advancement of Science (AAAS). She originally commissioned me to undertake the research reflected in Chapters 3 and 4, and she and Sage Russell contributed substantially to my thinking on science and human rights. Parts of those chapters appear in a different format in my essay, "Scientists' Rights and the Human Right to the Benefits of Science," in *Building a Framework for Economic, Social and Cultural Rights,* ed. Audrey Chapman and Sage Russell (Brussels: Intersentia Uitgevers, 2002).

Research reflected in Chapter 5 (with Bernardo Issel) was invited by the François-Xavier Bagnoud Center for Health and Human Rights (Harvard University) and appeared under the title "Health, Medicine, and Science in the UDHR," *Health and Human Rights* 3, 2 (Harvard School of Public Health, 1998).

Many people to whom I am indebted read early drafts of parts of the book critically and generously offered comments and suggestions, proposals for alterations, and recommendations about how to clarify my presentation for the general reading public. They include Clarence Dias (Center for International Law in Development), Stephanie Grant (United Nations Office of the High Commissioner for Human Rights), Dr. Maja Naur (Danish International Development Agency), Professor Emeritus Herbert Spirer (University of Connecticut) and Louise Spirer (human rights consultant), Thomas B. Jabine (Fellow of the American Statistical Association), Patrick Ball and Stephen Hansen (Science and Human

Rights Program, AAAS), Elisa Muñoz (Crimes of War), Richard Garfield (Columbia University), and A. M. Mayer (Hebrew University, Jerusalem).

I eagerly acknowledge the substantial influence of three people on the formation of this project. Historian Richard Alan White read and critically commented on the entire project in its several incarnations, ensuring that I labored for coherence and spared my readers academic pretense and jargon. David Forsythe jolted me into reorganizing parts of the volume so as to make it more accessible to the general reader. Eric Stover, Director of the Human Rights Center at the University of California, Berkeley, deserves my grateful acknowledgment as the historic facilitator behind many of the projects described here under the heading of science in the service of human rights. For that reason, I consider him my mentor on this topic.

Like Stover, physics Professor John Ziman, Bristol University, was also a pioneer in analyzing the mix of science and human rights issues, and his encouragement was important to me at an early stage of developing this project. Perhaps for a longer time than anyone else, Justice C. G. Weeramantry formerly of the World Court has written about and followed developments relating to science, technology, and human rights. I feel privileged to enjoy his encouragement.

I am indebted to Professor Edy Kaufman, Director of the Harry Truman International Institute for Peace, Jerusalem, for providing me with several fora at Hebrew University to present some of the research reflected in this book. My presentation on science and human rights to the Life Sciences Faculty of Hebrew University Jerusalem in 1998 elicited critical perspectives I tried to take into account here. The role of gracious host was also played by Professors George Andreopoulos, Peter Juviler, and Stephen Marks, who arranged for airing some of these topics at a Columbia University Faculty Seminar in 1999.

Several people set me straight on issues associated with health and human rights: Vincent Iacopino, MD (University of California School of Public Health, Berkeley), Allen Keller, MD (Bellevue Clinic for Torture Survivors), John Salzberg (Center for Torture Victims), Susannah Sirkin (Physicians for Human Rights USA), and Bernard Hamilton (Physicians for Human Rights UK). On health and human rights issues in Asia, I learned much from June P. Lopez, MD (Manila), Aurora Parong, MD (Manila), Kek Galabru, MD (Phnom Penh), and Irene Fernandez (Kuala Lumpur). On indigenous peoples' issues in Central and South America, I was fortunate to receive guidance from Bill Threlkeld and Mac Chapin (Center for the Support of Native Lands). Dr. Harry Skinner provided the peaceful setting of his Deer Lake, Wisconsin, home, a memorably good place for fishing and editing.

My research assistant Bernardo Issel undertook countless tasks without complaint and, heretofore, with insufficient thanks. Help on locating photos came from Amy Crumpton (American Association for the Advancement of Science), Anita Spies (Union of Concerned Scientists), Nathaniel Raymond and Tim Moriarty (Physicians for Human Rights USA), Gilles Peress (Gilles Peress Studio, New York), and Jeanne Dixon (United Nations Library). Finally, I want to thank the ever diligent Alison A. Anderson for working her editing magic on this manuscript and Anne Venzon for her indexing skills.

Of course, my debts to others stop where my responsibility begins, and that includes owning up to any shortcomings in this volume.